AF328819

Disrupting the Patrón

Disrupting the Patrón

*Indigenous Land Rights and the Fight
for Environmental Justice in Paraguay's Chaco*

Joel E. Correia

UNIVERSITY OF CALIFORNIA PRESS

University of California Press
Oakland, California

Suggested citation: Correia, J. E. *Disrupting the Patrón: Indigenous Land Rights and the Fight for Environmental Justice in Paraguay's Chaco.* Oakland: University of California Press, 2023. DOI: https://doi.org/10.1525/luminos.151

Cataloging-in-Publication Data is on file at the Library of Congress.

ISBN 978-0-520-39310-3 (pbk.)
ISBN 978-0-520-39311-0 (ebook)

32 31 30 29 28 27 26 25 24 23
10 9 8 7 6 5 4 3 2 1

To the Indigenous peoples of the Chaco and their allies fighting for more just futures.

CONTENTS

TABLES

Disrupting the Patrón would not have been possible without the contribution of many people who have shared their time, thoughts, and lives with me. Fieldwork for this project began in 2013, though its rough outlines were forged in 2012. Over the course of so many years, I have incurred many debts and benefited from much help along the way. Knowledge creation is a work in progress and always embedded in an ecology of relations that is ever changing. Although I figure as the author of this book, the work derives from many deep relations. I have tried to map some of those relations here and in the pages of this book and its citations. Invariably, I have missed some people. Any oversights are not intentional, and all errors are mine alone.

A book that grapples with settler colonialism and colonial power relations in Paraguay must begin by acknowledging the many settler geographies from where the pages of this work have been written. Over the course of this project, I have lived on Ute and Arapaho lands in Colorado; Tohono-O'odham lands in Arizona; Timucua, Seminole, and Miccosukee lands in Florida; and Enxet and Sanapaná lands in Paraguay. The histories of dispossession and continuing settler occupation of Indigenous lands across the Americas inform my thinking about research in Paraguay. But they also make clear the responsibilities that non-Indigenous peoples, of which I am one, living on unceded lands and benefiting from them, have to understand those histories, their ramifications in the present, and the work necessary to unsettle colonial geographies and foster better relations. I hope that this book contributes in some small way to such ends.

I am eternally grateful to friends, colleagues, and interlocutors in Paraguay without whom this book would not exist. Thanks to the Yakye Axa, Sawhoyamaxa, Xákmok Kásek, and Kelyenmagategma communities for welcoming me and trusting me. Many community members shared their time, energy, thoughts, and feelings but also supported this work in intangible ways. To Clemente and Nelsi; Mario, Desiderio, and Cristian; Milciades, Ignacia, Eulalio, Luciano, Tomás, Felix, Charlie, Maxi, Gerardo, Elijio, Serafín and Ramona, Bascilio and Mirta, Leonardo, Nancy, Anibal, Anivel, Celso, Eriberto, Mariana, Gladys, Amancio, Belén, Carlos, Cabara, Kyja, Ramón, Felipe, and all of your families, thank you for inviting me to your homes, for sharing tereré, and for your solidarity. *Topehasa porã mbaite! Tapeime mbar'ete. Tase! Tasik!* Folks from Tierraviva a los Pueblos Indígenas del Chaco helped me establish connections with each community, introduced me to key actors in the government, shared hours of conversations explaining complex legal processes, and took me on trips to the Chaco from time to time. Thank you for trusting me and for sharing your time and energy to help with this project. To Óscar Ayala, Julia Cabello, Ireneo Telléz, Santiago Bobadilla, Lidia Ruíz Cuevas, Ricardo Morínigo, and Adriana Agüero, thank you! I am especially grateful to the late José Paniagua for his dedication to Indigenous rights, friendship, and enduring positivity; as he often said, "No, ha oiporã!"

The University of Colorado Boulder Department of Geography was my intellectual home when the first contours of this work began to take shape. Joe Bryan was instrumental in my early work on this project. His generous, critical insights and scholarship have left an indelible mark on my thinking and approach to this work. Emily Yeh and Tim Oakes provided sharp insights that helped me work through some of the early (quite rough) framings that this work builds from. Together, these three people helped me better understand the potential of critical geography and the responsibilities that we have when embarking on research and writing. Kregg Hetherington and Mario Blaser also read early versions of this work and provided keen insights to help me hone my ethnography. Many friends in Boulder also read early drafts of work that eventually made its way into the pages of this book. Thanks for conversations and critical feedback from Galen Murton, Eric Lovell, Kaitlin Fertaly, Max Counter, Daniela Marini, Aaron Malone, Caitlin Ryan, Yang Yang, Meredith Deboom, and Lauren Gifford. Colleagues and friends from the University of Arizona deeply shaped my thinking on the ethics of field research and public scholarship. For that, I am especially grateful to Marcela Vásquez-León, Tracey Osborne, Diane Austin, the Public Political Ecology Lab, the Bureau of Applied Research in Anthropology, and the Center for Latin American Studies. At the University of Florida, I benefited from an outstanding cohort of colleagues and students who have provided feedback on different facets of this work—from discussing ideas to reading drafts. Special thanks to Carmen Martínez-Novo, Susan Paulson, Cynthia Simmons, Bob Walker, Richard Kernaghan, Simone Athayde, Neha Kohli, Marcelo Santos Rocha da Silva, Britany Green, Nashia Graneau, and members of the MALAS Indigenous Studies specialization.

There are many others who have also shaped this project. Rodrigo Villagra-Carrón has been a friend and colleague with whom I have learned much about

Indigenous rights in Paraguay and the Inter-American System. Marco Castillo, Alejandra Estigarribia, Carolina Castillo, and Tomas Jönsson have been good friends whose insights inspired me and whose care helped me through the process of field research. This is especially true of Noni Florencio; thank you for your solidarity, for taking care of me when I had dengue, and for welcoming me into your life *como un hijo más*. Paola Canova, Lorna Quiroga, Valentina Bonifacio, Marcos Glauser, Ana Estigarribia, Jorge Estigarribia, Gustavo Setrini, Adelina Pusineri, Jennifer Tucker, Cari Tusing, Sofía Espíndola, and Marilin Rehnfeldt have also been wonderful interlocutors to think about Indigenous rights, land, and struggles for justice in Paraguay. I am also grateful for the many state functionaries and officials who trusted me with their time and thoughts; their insights helped me better understand the workings of the Paraguayan state, its bureaucracy, and the many challenges to human rights in the country. Special thanks to the late Andrés Ramiréz, whose role in the Yakye Axa case before the Inter-American Court and deep knowledge of Indigenous rights law in Paraguay were formative.

Several funders have generously supported different facets of the research and writing that made this book possible. At the University of Colorado Boulder, the Beverly Sears Graduate Research Grant, Graduate School Travel Fellowship, Latin American Studies Center, Center to Advance Research and Teaching in the Social Sciences, Jennifer Dianburg Memorial Fellowship, and Graduate School Dissertation Completion Fellowship supported my early research and writing. Fellowships and grants from the Department of Education (a Foreign Language and Area Studies Grant as well as a Fulbright Hays Doctoral Research Abroad) and National Science Foundation Doctoral Research Improvement Grant (#1459366) supported field research in 2013 and during thirteen months in 2015–16. Many thanks are due to Christian Lund's "Rule and Rupture" research group at the University of Copenhagen and especially to Penelope Anthias and Kasper Hoffman, who invited me to workshop a paper from which chapter 5 draws. Funding from the University of Florida Global Fellows Program provided support for field research in 2019. With support from the Margaret and Robert Rothman Endowment, the University of Florida Center for the Humanities and Public Sphere sponsored a book review workshop where Kyle Whyte and Carmen Martínez-Novo each reviewed full drafts of this project before submission to the University of California Press. Their generous critiques and thorough comments helped me refine this work in meaningful ways. I am grateful for their time and support. With support from a 2021 American Council of Learned Societies (ACLS) Fellowship, I was able to dedicate time to complete this project. Here I would also like to recognize the University of Florida Center for Latin American Studies (the Center) and Carlos de la Torre for support of this project and my dedication to it during my time as an ACLS Fellow. Open access publication was made possible through funding from the Center.

I am grateful for the advocacy, encouragement, and excitement of my editors at the University of California Press, Stacy Eisenstark and Emily Park. Your belief in this project and insights throughout the process were invaluable. Sheila Berg provided copy editing, Naja Collins steered me through the many technical aspects of the publication process, and Enrique Ochoa-Kaup provided insights in the final stages; thank you. Two anonymous peer reviewers also provided excellent feedback with constructive critique that helped me refine my argumentation and analysis. Thank you for finding time to support this work during the height of the pandemic. Anitra Grisales provided crucial editorial guidance to help me find my authorial voice while I was developing this project. Thank you for all that you do! Cynthia Landeen provided expert indexing. Several other interlocutors during academic conferences and presentations also provided helpful insights on different aspects of this work, particularly Nancy Postero, Tom Perreault, Penelope Anthias, Kiran Asher, Sharlene Mollett, Gastón Gordillo, Michael Levien, Silvia Hirsch, Mercedes Biocca, Hannes Kalisch, Sarah Kelly, Laurel Bellante de Escalante, Farhana Sultana, Gary Martin, Carolyn Finney, Marcus Taylor, Teo Ballvé, Amalia Leguizamon, Elizabeth Oglesby, Margaret Wilder, Sapana Doshi, Antonio Bacelar da Silva, Jennifer Cyr, Anthony Bebbington, Denise Humphreys-Bebbington, Jennifer Devine, and Bret Gustafson, to name a few.

The support of my family has been vital throughout the years that I have worked on this project. Special thanks to my parents, Doug and Pat, and also to Dustin, Bridget, Claire, and Noah Correia. Though I am often far away for work, you are always close in my mind and heart. To Karen, your enduring belief in this work, encouragement, support, and inquiry have helped sustain me. There is no way that this project would have been completed without you. I am eternally grateful. Thank you for your friendship and love. Even though Leo is too young to know what this book is about, his entry into the world during its final phases continues to inspire me to work toward more just futures. I hope this book inspires him to do the same.

Introduction

Environmental Justice Otherwise

The encampment lined the city block in front of Paraguay's Institute for the Indigenous (INDI) where at least one hundred people had mobilized to demand the return of their lands. Black plastic tarps tied to an orange brick wall stretched across the sidewalk and were held down at the edge of Don Bosco Street with small wooden stakes. Woven between tree trunks, a web of ropes hung above the tarps on which clothes dried in the morning sun. Plastic buckets served as seats, sinks, and storage containers. Small fires sent smoke into the air, carrying the smell of fried tortillas. Many camp residents milled about in the shade of trees watching people enter and leave INDI directly across the street. "Hai hue," muttered Gerardo in exasperation as we walked toward the building's entrance, "que barbáro," how terrible. "Mby'a pea," they're Mby'a, noted Serafin with a nod. Clemente remained silent. Members of different Indigenous communities frequently come to Asunción to demand that INDI adjudicate their land claims. The tent encampments are a regular but ephemeral sight, often appearing in the night only to be razed days later once officials or local residents grow tired of the disruptions. The itinerant residents are loaded into military cargo trucks or put on buses and taken back to the lands that they seek but do not control. Before Asunción's mayors installed fences around the city's central plazas to police their use, they were regular sites for the landless who came to the capital seeking restitution.[1] Now the dispossessed camp on the steps of an institute responsible for their care but incapable of assuaging their plight.

INDI is always busy. This day was no different. We walked up the front steps, weaving through a small crowd of people who packed into the entryway as they waited to talk with the general receptionist team to request meetings or follow up on paperwork. Clemente led the way past the crowd, around the corner, and up the staircase to the second floor, where the executive, legal, and technical team offices were located. The landing at the top of the stairs opened to a small, windowless waiting room with an L-shaped couch lining two walls and a receptionist desk that Clemente approached. He presented his state identity card, saying, "We are here from Xákmok Kásek for an 11:00 meeting with President Saldivar about our land." The receptionist looked over his ID, then to a registry below the counter, then closed the window and made a call. Opening the window, she gestured toward the couch: "Please take a seat, the president is running late. It should not be too long." The room was quiet and calm. We were the only people there. Minutes passed to hours as we watched people come up the stairs. Some were INDI employees who greeted us with "mba'etekopiko" or "mba'e la porte," how's it going, as they passed through the room and disappeared behind closed office doors. Some of the people were Indigenous representatives from other communities who repeated the ritual of checking in with the receptionist for their scheduled appointments before joining us on the diminishing couch space; the rest took a seat on the stairs or stood against the wall. At one point, two middle-aged men dressed in blue jeans, boots, and button-down shirts, and with bellies that strained their belt lines, walked through the waiting room without greeting the small crowd. They were ushered into the executive wing of the building behind the receptionist's desk. "Ganaderos," ranchers, noted Serafin with a sneer. "Ha'e," that's right, Clemente responded. Another man leaning against the wall with his arms crossed plainly stated, "Patrón." Sitting and watching, it was clear Indigenous peoples had to wait while everyone else seemed to enter and exit with ease.

The hours passed. The day grew hotter. With no windows or fan, the room was stifling. Under the weight of the humid Paraguayan summer, sweat beads formed on our foreheads as the empty water cooler taunted us. The number of people waiting increased—they were all Indigenous. We waited, talked, and checked in with the receptionist. "It should not be too much longer," she reassured. Fortunately, two of us brought thermoses and *tereré*, Paraguay's ubiquitous yerba mate tea consumed cold and often shared. We drank thermos after thermos until the yerba mate lost its flavor and drinking was more a shared act of connection than done for the tea's energizing qualities. Eventually, the tereré got to me. Employees and special guests used locked restrooms. So I walked downstairs to the public restroom that INDI clients use. Pushing open the wooden door, I was hit with a tremendous smell. The pungent, stinging odor of ammonia, a sign of dehydration and urinary tract or kidney problems, dominated the small unventilated room, making my eyes water. Feces, urine, and a wet film covered the floor. Black mold crawled from the corners and along the grout around the sink. In stalls without doors, the porcelain toilet bowls were full to the brim and writhing with maggots, indicating that this was not a freak backup of the plumbing system but a systemic failure. This was not a latrine. It was a plumbed indoor restroom in a state institute, the only one for the constituents it is charged with caring for. There were no other options than to use the facilities.

"We always have to wait." Serafin shook his head, growing more frustrated by the time I returned. "They do not respect our time or the sacrifices we have made to be here." An older Avá Guaraní man dryly replied, "peicha che ra'a," that's the way it is, my friend. Meanwhile, Gerardo was at the receptionist desk again. "We have been here since 11:00 in the morning. We arrived on time for our appointment, and it has been over five hours. We haven't eaten. We came from very far away, kilometer 346 of the Trans-Chaco [Highway] for this meeting. When will we see the president?" Turning away from the desk, he looked at the group before sitting again, saying, "Incredible." Ten or fifteen minutes later, just after 5:00 p.m., a chipper young man in dark slacks with a tie and pressed white shirt opened the door to the meeting room and invited the group in. The meeting for which we had a private appointment now was shared with twelve other people from seven different Indigenous communities who had also been waiting. The president apparently wanted to make a group intervention. With high ceilings and a large map of Paraguay overlooking the room, three rows of tightly arranged chairs lined the wall facing a large oblong table. It was remarkably cold, with air-conditioning that brought goosebumps after hours in the sauna next door. The young functionary left us in the room, "The president will be here momentarily." We sat in relative silence for the next fifteen minutes, waiting.

A door swung open and the acting president of INDI burst into the room clad in a navy-blue suit and a fresh haircut. "I am sorry to keep you waiting! I did not know we had a meeting. Thank you for coming to talk. I hear there are many matters we need to discuss." As he sat at the table, Clemente, Serafin, and Gerardo moved to join him. "Mr. President, we are a delegation from Xákmok Kásek here to follow up on how our case is proceeding, to inquire about the return of our lands at Retiro Primero," Gerardo stated.[2] The INDI president had only recently replaced his predecessor, who was ousted after he kicked an Avá Guaraní woman in the stomach during a protest in front of the building.[3] "Yes, yes. I know your case," the INDI president reassured. He sat with no pen or assistant while the delegation reminded him about the intricacies of their case. In 2010, the Inter-American Court of Human Rights (IACHR) found Paraguay culpable of human rights violations against Xákmok Kásek and ruled the state should restitute their ancestral land. The company that owned the disputed lands was ready to sell. INDI is legally responsible for acquiring the land but failed to do so for months, despite having funds. Sixty-three families from Xákmok Kásek had reoccupied the land in February 2015 to force the state to act. "Everything is in order. Why hasn't INDI returned our land?" Clemente asked.

Instead of responding, he stood abruptly and looked around the room. "Does anyone know why I am wearing such fine clothing today, a nice suit, new shoes, and this fancy watch? I do not normally wear such nice clothes." After a moment of silence, a man sitting in the last row of chairs ventured, "Because you are the president of INDI?" Pointing to the man, the president replied, "No! I am wearing these clothes because you are presidents, presidents of your own communities!" He pointed his finger to the seated men to emphasize the point. "I am wearing these clothes out of respect because I knew that we were going to have this meeting. I put on my finest clothes to meet you the same as if I were meeting with the president of another country." His comments were met with silence. Sitting, he turned back to Gerardo, "I am doing everything in my power to see that the land is returned. But I ask you to be patient. I alone cannot make this decision because the President of the Republic must decide. *El patrón manda* [The patrón is in charge]." He suggested we go to the Ministry of Finance, in charge of state payments, or to the Office of the Vice President, responsible for the supervision of international human rights sentences against the state. Serafin added, with a notably frustrated tone, "We began with the vice president, who referred us to the Ministry of Finance that referred us to you. We know that Law 904 says INDI is responsible for completing this transaction." Pausing to consider this information, the president replied, "The issue is out of my hands. But I will personally speak with President Cartes to see what can be done." With that, he excused us.

• • •

Disrupting the Patrón investigates how Enxet and Sanapaná peoples of Paraguay navigate racialized land politics in pursuit of environmental justice. I tell a story of environmental justice by tracing the interwoven experiences of Indigenous activists, settler colonists, human rights lawyers, ranchers, and state officials from dusty cattle ranches built on Enxet and Sanapaná lands to IACHR hearings and back to the Paraguayan Chaco. Throughout, I examine a hallmark of settler power, *legal liminality*: spaces, situations, and subjects that simultaneously lie within and outside the juridical order. Legal liminality is a de facto mode of governance that the state uses to manage Indigenous dispossession of land and rights in the current conjuncture. In effect, state actors and agencies have used Indigenous rights as a facade of care that attempts to distract from the persistent forms of neglect that facilitate extractive development. However, this book is more than a critique of settler colonialism. I argue that my Enxet and Sanapaná interlocutors employ dialectics of disruption—strategically working with and against settler law—to unsettle racialized regimes of land control. Despite long-standing efforts to replace Indigenous lifeways with settler cattle ranching, Enxet and Sanapaná persist. This book shows how three communities—Yakye Axa, Sawhoyamaxa, and Xákmok Kásek— are rebuilding relations with their territories by disrupting state and settler power in an era of radical social-ecological change. Enxet and Sanapaná endurance is radical, future-oriented resistance that shows the pursuit of environmental justice is more than a juridical solution to harm but the ability to maintain collectives in the face of existential threats.

Paraguay is a country divided. The eponymous river that bisects Paraguayan territory not only splits the country's landmass along a north-south axis; it also marks a dialectic tension between the two primary political economic activities that define contemporary land politics, cattle ranching and soybean production. Currently the world's fourth largest exporter of soybeans and the sixth largest exporter of beef, the agro-export economy dominates domestic affairs and frames nearly all Indigenous land claims as antithetical to economic growth.[4] From the 1960s to the mid-2000s, the drive to establish the agrarian frontier southeast of the Paraguay River resulted in astronomical deforestation rates and violent dispossessions that reduced a region of rich biocultural diversity to a veritable tableau for monocultures—soybeans and settler colonists. Today, upwards of 85 percent of the Interior Atlantic Forest that once covered those lands has been razed, with much of that now covered in soybean fields.[5] The rapid and extensive land-use change has fueled contentious politics.[6]

The northwestern region of Paraguay called the Chaco had long been a peripheral site within the global economic order, though it is now emerging as a central node in agricultural commodities trading and transport. A multibillion-dollar road development campaign started in 2019 includes creating several new international highways and bridges to facilitate commodity exports that state officials promise will create a regional "logistics hub" for agro-capitalism.[7] Akin to the political ecologies of monoculture palm-oil plantations in Colombia or the veritable sea of soybeans that spans the Southern Cone, the Paraguayan Chaco is dominated by a land-extensive development model that reduces biocultural diversity to a singular commodity: beef.[8] As of this writing, nearly 95 percent of the land in the Paraguayan Chaco, more than 233,000 square kilometers, is held as private property, with the majority of those landholdings used for cattle ranching.[9] The advance of ranching made the Paraguayan Chaco a global deforestation hotspot where nearly eight million hectares of forestland was leveled between 1985 and 2020.[10] With falling trees and growing herds, Paraguay has risen higher in global rankings of beef exporters and is now on the cusp of breaking into the top five, having edged out its renowned neighbor Argentina for tons of beef shipped annually.[11]

Cattle ranching is thus the backbone of settler colonialism in Paraguay's Chaco, which is a region that covers more than half the country's territory but is home to only 3 percent of its total human population.[12] At the national scale, cows outnumber Paraguayans almost 2:1, but in the Chaco, the ratio nears 50:1.[13] The patchwork of private ranches has created Indigenous enclaves that often serve as de facto labor camps for the ranching industry.[14] Although the country's constitution guarantees Indigenous peoples' land rights, the realization of those rights has often been hampered by party politics, a labyrinthine state bureaucracy that ensures disenfranchisement, and violent dispossessions by non-Indigenous landowners seeking to expand agrarian commodity production.[15]

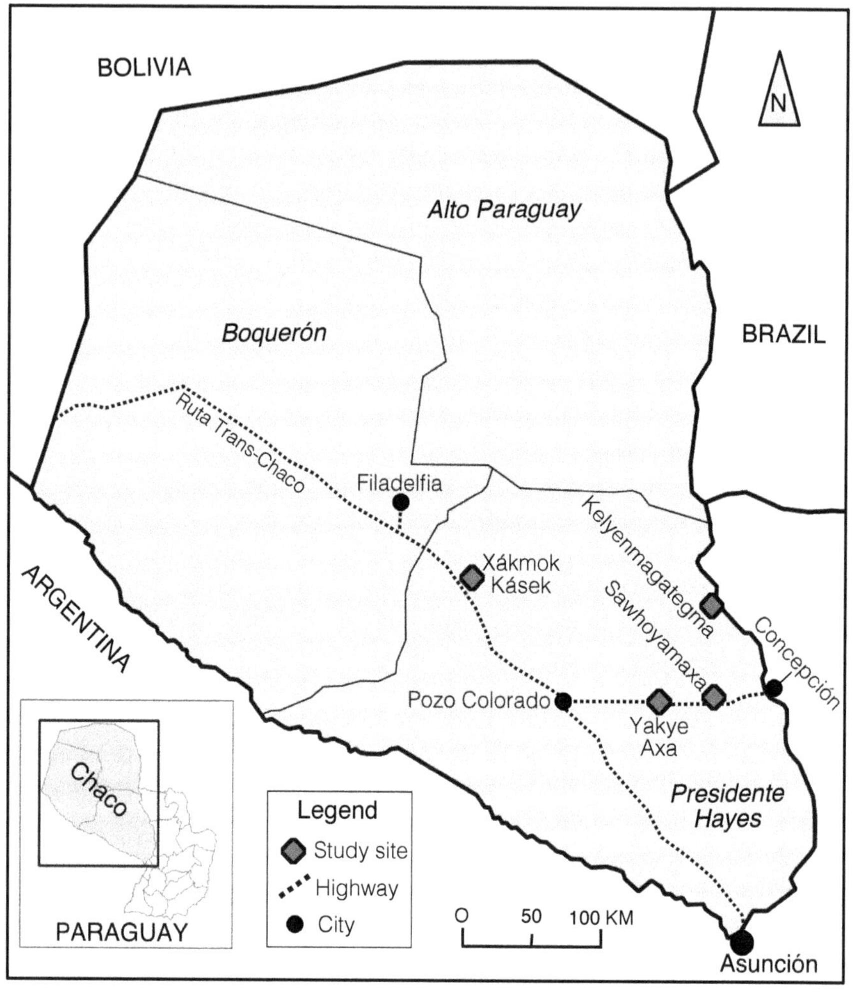

MAP 1. The Paraguayan Chaco and primary study sites. Elaborated by author.

RETHINKING ENVIRONMENTAL HAZARDS

This book centers on the particularities of land rights, environmental racism, and Indigenous struggles in Paraguay but speaks far beyond its borders. The theoretical framework weaves insights from scholarship and activism across the Americas, yet is grounded in Paraguay's Bajo Chaco. Indigenous land struggles across the Americas have often been framed in relation to debates about neoliberal multiculturalism. State-led efforts to recognize multicultural rights for Indigenous peoples in Latin America are often political struggles over the control of "the environment" and resource access when viewed through the lens of land rights. Some scholars analyze this dynamic through the lens of the "territorial turn," but here I shift attention to the environmental violence that land dispossession generates.[16] Enxet and Sanapaná territorial struggles cannot be divorced from the resource extractive economies of the Chaco founded on Indigenous land theft. The denial of Enxet and Sanapaná land rights is directly associated with state violations of human rights to life and dignity, among others, as evidenced by multiple IACHR rulings and everyday life conditions.[17] Such rights violations occur along racial lines and the ability, or not, to live free of exposure to environmental hazards.[18] Environmental justice research and activism in the United States began in response to the siting of hazardous industries and toxics in communities of color.[19] I employ a broader conceptualization of hazards exposure and environmental harms than those associated with emblematic cases like those of Warren County, Carver Terrace, or "Cancer Alley" that have shaped this field of study to date in the United States.[20] Thinking environmental justice otherwise requires not only rethinking notions of justice beyond Euro-modern epistemologies but also what constitutes hazards and harms.[21]

Environmental hazards often associated with environmental justice analyses include direct exposure to toxic wastes, construction and zoning practices that create greater risk of the adverse effects of extreme weather, and the siting of industrial polluters in marginalized communities. What about the forms of insecurity, harm, and trauma that result from land dispossession? Conceptualizing the environment beyond the nature/culture dualism that animates much thinking in Euro-modern ontologies shifts attention to social ecologies whereby "the environment" is not an external realm but one intimately related with human practice and belief systems.[22] These are issues that have long animated Indigenous and Native environmental justice struggles in what is now called North America.[23] In the Latin American context, Indigenous struggles against colonialism and environmental change are often described in US- and European-based scholarship as "popular environmentalism," read through the lens of human rights, or simply framed as "resistance" rather than viewed with explicit attention to environmental justice.[24] Such discursive framings are due, in part, to traditions of mobilizing against the distinct forms of colonial power manifest in Latin America and the region's recent legacy of authoritarian dictatorships, as well as the distinctly US origins of the environmental justice movement as so named.

The geographic, historical, and social specificity of environmental conflicts and the actions frontline communities use to protect themselves matter. In many parts of Latin America, land dispossession—a process at the root of colonial power and extractivism—creates complex environmental harms that should impel analysts to think with and beyond how environmental justice has long been defined and deployed in the United States. Working with the specificity of environmental hazards that the Yakye Axa, Sawhoyamaxa, and Xákmok Kásek communities confront, I center environmental racism in debates about development and the politics of recognition in Latin America.[25]

The history of US environmental justice activism and scholarship places the movement at the intersection of civil rights and exposure to environmental harms.[26] Yet given the global circulation of environmental justice discourse and activism in recent years, the US frame only tells part of the story.[27] I do not presume to tell "the whole story," though I want to highlight the role of Indigenous and Latin American histories of resistance to colonialism that bring texture, depth, and distinct understandings to environmental justice otherwise. Language from the first People of Color Environmental Leadership Summit in 1991 is informative. The summit drew together people from across the United States with several participants from Latin America to strengthen collaborative action for environmental justice. Among calls to invigorate an international movement focused on ensuring healthy and safe environments for historically marginalized and racialized peoples, the guiding document produced at the summit centers environmental justice in the lasting effects of colonization, seeking "to secure our political, economic and cultural liberation that has been denied for over 500 years of colonization and oppression, resulting in the poisoning of our communities and land and the genocide of our peoples."[28] Here I underscore that Indigenous efforts to recover stolen lands are environmental justice struggles where the capability to maintain self-determination, relations, and responsibilities is vital to collective well-being.[29] Environmental justice otherwise emerges through tensions between the impossibility of return and the everyday politics of resurgence that animate Enxet and Sanapaná refusal to relinquish the pursuit of more just futures.

INDIGENOUS ENVIRONMENTAL JUSTICE

Milciades and I sat outside the home he and his wife had built on the land that sixty-two families from Xákmok Kásek had recently reoccupied after more than thirty years of fighting for restitution. Some flowers grew in a plastic bottle made into a hanging planter that adorned the one-room home's exterior wall. I arrived in the early afternoon, bringing tereré to share. We sat and talked about life for several hours. Milciades grew up on Estancia Salazar, the ranch built on the ancestral lands of his community. His father, Eulalio, labored for much of his life as a peon on that ranch. Together, they lived with other members of Xákmok Kásek until they were forced to leave the ranch and occupy other lands. The reencounter with the lands where Milciades had built his home was generations in the making. As we talked, the sun transited the sky. Suli invited me to stay for a dinner of roasted armadillo that we ate with a serving of rice the state National Emergency Services delivered in the food rations that month. Xákmok Kásek has received the rations since the early 2000s, when the Inter-American Commission ordered Paraguay to provide emergency aid until it resolved the community's claim for land restitution. The aid was intended as a temporary measure. Yet, like being the subject of rights that are routinely denied, the decades-long assistance has become a part of daily life. We moved to hammocks as night fell, and darkness enveloped our conversation. Thinking about the prospect of land restitution, Milciades stated, "We will always be scarred from what they have made us live through. I don't think that land will bring justice, but it will help us find a sense of peace."

Milciades's words capture the aporetic nature of the law-justice relation—that the very structure of Indigenous land rights (re)produces legal geographies that limit what justice is and can be.[30] This aporetic relation is acute in Enxet and Sanapaná land struggles because settler law not only circumscribes "acceptable" Indigenous difference, but partitions Indigenous peoples from the territorial relations that sustain their lifeways.[31] Potawatomi scholar Kyle Whyte draws from Anishinaabe intellectual traditions to argue that settler colonialism is a form of environmental injustice because it severs the ability of Indigenous peoples to maintain "collective continuance," the interdependencies, systems of responsibilities, and mobilities that enable social resilience.[32] Anishinaabe practices and ontologies that inform collective continuance are distinct from Enxet and Sanapaná practices. However, Whyte's theorization provides a valuable lens through which to examine settler colonialism as environmental injustice across Indigenous geographies.[33] The dispossession of Enxet and Sanapaná peoples from their lands and simultaneous exploitation of their labor on those lands since the turn of the twentieth century has radically altered social-ecological relations, traditions, and the ability to maintain cultural practices over generations, including language transmission. Settler colonial dispossessions have thus disrupted, though not extinguished, Enxet and Sanapaná social collectives and relations with place. If there is one common theme that defines Indigenous environmental justice work across settler geographies, it is an unrelenting refusal to succumb to the enduring forms of colonialism that produce the uneven distribution of social-environmental harms.

Indigenous environmental justice studies of North America critically evaluate the legal relationship between Native Nations and the US or Canadian federal government to show that Indigenous rights must also ensure environmental self-determination.[34] Jarratt-Snider and Nielsen argue that environmental (in)justice experienced by Native and Indigenous peoples is distinct from "mainstream" environmental justice due to "the continuing effects of colonization."[35] Settler colonialism drives Indigenous environmental injustice because, as Whyte insists, "one society rob[s] another society of its capacities to experience the world as a place of collective life that its members feel responsible for maintaining into the future."[36] On the other hand, Voyles shows how settler extractivism converts Navajo lands *and* bodies into sites of toxic pollution by treating both as wastelands.[37] Native scholars, Nick Estes, Dina Gilio-Whitaker, and the contributors to the *Standing with Standing Rock* edited volume, have reframed environmental justice through their analyses of the #NoDAPL Movement and ways that state-sanctioned violence in defense of the Dakota Access Pipeline project draw attention to the tensions between settler colonialism and Indigenous resurgence.[38] The broader dynamics that underpin these issues are not confined to the United States and Canada but resonate broadly across the Americas through the persistence of "settler capitalism" and its effects on Indigenous lifeways.[39] Note, however, that this book does not purport to present a unitary theorization of Indigenous environmental justice that can be neatly applied to other contexts. The Yakye Axa, Sawhoyamaxa, and Xákmok Kásek struggles are singular to each community. However, the cases are not unique when placed into the context of Indigenous land struggles across the Americas where frontline communities continue to fight for the environment as freedom.[40]

The urgency to disrupt enduring forms of coloniality requires analysts and activists to think beyond the categories of race, gender, and indigeneity that have long facilitated, and been shaped through, extractive relations in Latin America.[41] Recent environmental justice scholarship from the region stresses the connection between environmental change, marginalization, and resistance while centering place-based conceptions of justice and social-environmental relations.[42] Throughout, scholars call for attention to the geographic specificities of environmental justice beyond the US frame by centering other epistemologies of justice that emerge through Indigenous struggles for well-being in the context of extractivism.[43] Environmental racism predicated on histories of land dispossession and resource control has long threatened Indigenous and Afro-descendant well-being across the region. From early colonization to the present, land, water, and resource grabs undermine preexisting social-environmental relations. Indeed, the very categories used to describe Indigenous peoples in many parts of Latin America are inextricably linked to the appropriation of land and life that derive from Euro-modern conceptions of who and what constitutes value. Thus, in thinking with recent provocations to decolonize environmental justice studies, this book attends to place-based struggles of Enxet and Sanapaná peoples while centering my interlocutors' theorizations of justice and visions for the future.[44] In so doing, I seek to advance a notion of environmental justice otherwise, enriched by hemispheric conversations about Indigenous politics in the Americas but always attentive to the lived experience of land struggles in Paraguay's Bajo Chaco.

While returning lands is a first step toward Indigenous environmental justice, Milciades's remarks remind us that land alone is insufficient. The scars of epistemic and physical violence that Enxet and Sanapaná have endured remain, even after community members recover their lands. Milciades's words also remind us that there is no simple solution. In this regard, justice is both an aporia and a utopia, a horizon to push toward but not often remedied only by procedure, distribution, or recognition. Despite these limits, the return of stolen lands does open the possibility for more just futures that enable collective well-being in a form that Enxet and Sanapaná determine for themselves. Thus the book does not dwell on settler colonial erasure but instead highlights forms of futurity that "invoke many other temporalities, other spaces, and yet-to-be possibilities" created through Enxet and Sanapaná efforts to reclaim lands and rebuild relations to their territories.[45] Enxet and Sanapaná strategies to envision a future beyond dispossession—even under the most oppressive circumstances—highlight possibilities that engender Milciades's invocation of "a sense of peace," where endurance and resurgence enact environmental justice otherwise.[46]

RACIAL GEOGRAPHIES

In January 2016, I sat under a grove of algarrobo trees drinking tereré with Eulalio, a spiritual leader of Xákmok Kásek. He recalled times living on Estancia Salazar and working as a peon on the ranch. During our conversation, Eulalio looked across a clearing before us until his eyes settled on an old building that he helped construct and that had been used to house non-Indigenous ranch laborers. "They [the ranchers] just used up the Indigenous," he said. He spoke slowly and deliberately, with a pause between each sentence. "They barely gave us any food . . . We'd work twelve, sixteen, sometimes eighteen hours putting up fences, riding horses, whatever. It was hard work . . . day after day. If you got sick, there was no doctor . . . If you died, you died . . . We were practically slaves until we learned we had rights."[47] As we sat, passing tereré, he explained how ranchers exploited Sanapaná and Enxet laborers through discriminatory practices that included less pay and worse working conditions than for non-Indigenous peons. Eulalio argued that the operation of cattle ranches denied Indigenous peoples control over their territories, instead forcing them to work their stolen lands as wage laborers or in conditions of debt peonage.

Eulalio's insights inform my analysis in two important ways. First, land-labor relations, particularly Indigenous dispossession and labor exploitation, are central to the enduring structures of settler colonialism in Latin America—structures predicated on patrón-Indigenous social relations.[48] The incipient cattle-ranching economy in Paraguay's Bajo Chaco required Indigenous labor. It effectively ensured that labor availability through land enclosures that limited economic opportunities outside of ranching. As with the establishment of cattle ranching in the Bajo Chaco to the present day, Indigenous peoples are often the ranch peons who clear forests, plant pasture, erect fences, run cattle, and build the houses used for ranch operations. Ranching, therefore, undergirds the racial geography of settler colonialism in the Paraguayan Chaco by structuring social-spatial relations vis-à-vis the ranch as a site of Indigenous dispossession and non-Indigenous capital accumulation.[49] Settler territorializations of Enxet and Sanapaná lands produced distinct racial geographies where people were spatially organized in specific ways based on a simple binary calculus: non-Indigenous folks owned land via private property, and Indigenous peoples often labored on the lands taken from them. This racial geography persists to the present. In effect, white male landholders are imagined to command economically productive industries. In contrast, Indigenous peoples are imagined as those justifiably dispossessed of land because they stand "in the way of" progress, simultaneously out of space and out of time with modernist notions of agrarian development.[50] The processes of colonizing the Bajo Chaco and the resulting spatial organization of land and bodies (both human and bovine) articulate with the nuanced dynamics of settler colonialism in Latin America.

There are rich debates about the valences of coloniality in Latin America, given the region's distinct relation with European expansionism and widespread campaigns to enslave or eliminate Indigenous peoples. I do not map the contours of those debates here but focus on two distinct yet intersecting colonial processes: settler and internal colonialism. Scholars in, of, and from Latin America have often used "postcolonial" as a historical marker to index the period that followed direct European colonization. As newly independent countries pursued different development pathways in the postcolonial era, many leaders sought to exert greater control over their territories and the Indigenous populations living within them. The Mexican sociologist Pablo Gonzalez Casanova's classic analysis is helpful: "The notion of 'internal colonialism' has its roots in the great independence movement of the old colonies." He continues, "With the disappearance of the direct domination of foreigners over natives . . . the substitution of domination of Spaniards by that of the 'creoles' [ensued]. Interestingly, the exploitation of the Indians continues, having *the same characteristics* it had before independence."[51] Casanova and his contemporaries were writing during a period when agrarian reforms incentivized the movement of citizens to the hinterlands of many Latin American countries through the promise of "land for those who work it."[52] Internal colonization through agrarian reforms often produced conflict when non-Indigenous settler campesinos and state actors dispossessed Indigenous peoples from their lands to promote agrarian development, as was the case in Paraguay and numerous countries. While internal colonization is evident in Paraguay's eastern frontier, in the Chaco the dynamic is different. It is a site of settler colonization.

Wolfe's oft-cited argument that colonialism is a "structure, not an event" helps explain the violence that conditions Enxet and Sanapaná struggles, not as *post*colonial but as wrought by the *ongoing* effects of settler colonialism.[53] Recent studies have evaluated settler colonialism as a transhistorical process of social, political, and economic change attendant to dispossession, the rule of law, environmental governance, and labor predicated on controlling Indigenous life.[54] Unlike externally imposed colonial efforts like those of Spain in pre-independence Latin America designed to extract resources, settler colonists come to stay and establish new societies. Settler colonialism in many parts of Latin America is distinct from internal colonization as framed by Casanova and from Wolfe's influential analysis in the US context, where he observes that Indigenous peoples were dispossessed of land and enslaved Africans were forced to work those lands for the accumulation of white settlers.[55] Enxet and Sanapaná were dispossessed *in place* and forced to labor on ranches built on lands often taken from them by foreign missionaries and investors. The resulting dynamic evokes the simultaneous inclusion and exclusion of "settler capitalism" that Speed argues has come to define the geographies of Indigenous dispossession in Latin America.[56]

SETTLER GOVERNANCE OF DISPOSSESSION

Before moving further, I return to my conversation with Eulalio to flag the second way that his insights inform this book. Eulalio's comments draw attention to distinct modalities of governance at play in Enxet and Sanapaná land struggles, from confronting racial capitalism to the different ways that the politics of recognition manifest across settler geographies in Latin America. Suggesting that Indigenous peoples "were basically slaves" until learning they had rights, Eulalio indexed the trans-scalar practice and evolution of Indigenous activism. Legal recognition from the Paraguayan state, and later from the IACHR, flagged vital shifts in Xákmok Kásek political subjectivity through the "emancipatory potential of human rights politics."[57] Consequently, Xákmok Kásek, like Yakye Axa and Sawhoyamaxa, used human rights law and discourse as a basis to shame the state and claim legal protections by condemning Paraguay for supporting cattle ranching instead of upholding Indigenous land rights. With the evolution of rights frameworks, from emergent labor rights to constitutional rights to the collective ownership of ancestral territory, Enxet and Sanapaná crafted new political strategies to advance their struggles for self-determination, changing from "indio" wards of missionaries and ranchers to Indigenous victims of state-led human rights abuse to a political force that is disrupting the legacies of settler governmentality.[58] Enxet and Sanapaná peoples thus forged new interethnic relations between non-Indigenous activist anthropologists and *indigenistas* (Indigenous rights advocates) to leverage rights-based claims that challenged settler land control, albeit with uneven outcomes.[59]

In the wake of Paraguay's nascent democratic transition in 1989 and the subsequent suite of Indigenous rights reforms, Enxet and Sanapaná peons demanded restitution of the ranches where they had lived and labored since the enclosure of the Chaco. During two decades, Yakye Axa, Sawhoyamaxa, and Xákmok Kásek leveraged all legal strategies possible within Paraguay to demand the state restitute their lands per the law. Exhausting all legal options in Paraguay, members of each community petitioned the Inter-American Commission on Human Rights to adjudicate an amenable solution. After failing to reach a resolution before the Commission, the IACHR arbitrated each case, issuing judgments in 2005, 2006, and 2010. In each ruling, the IACHR argued that denying land restitution violated the right to property, and thereby the state was directly responsible for a suite of human rights abuses against members of each community. Attentive to the limits of Paraguay's Indigenous rights framework, the IACHR subsequently ordered

Paraguay to follow measures I call *restitution as development*—coupling land restitution with economic redistribution to support Indigenous development initiatives.

Despite the IACHR judgments, Paraguay refused to resolve the Enxet and Sanapaná land claims, instead allowing each community to remain in precarious living conditions on the margins of cattle ranches and the side of a major highway. Here it is important to note that when I refer to "the margins," I do so in two senses: the literal geographic margins of ranches or highways where my interlocutors have long lived; and the metaphorical margins of citizenship, of being inside and outside the juridical and human order through liminality created by discretionary application of the law. The uncertainty of living with and without rights coupled with the routinized violence of living on the margins of cattle ranches for decades exacted grave tolls on the people of Yakye Axa, Sawhoyamaxa, and Xákmok Kásek. Many people died from preventable diseases and the denial of basic services necessary to ensure their well-being, while the cattle that live on Enxet and Sanapaná ancestral lands, mere feet from each community's respective encampments, receive extraordinary care to ensure they live. The prioritization of cattle life over Indigenous life that the Paraguayan state has repeatedly shown through several generations is a form of neglect where some populations are made to live and others let to die.[60] Together, neglect and legal liminality create a structure of social and spatial relations that have become a de facto mode of settler governance.

DIALECTICS OF DISRUPTION

My analysis of restitution as development shows that state officials treat Indigenous rights as discretionary, acts that reveal the aporia of justice within settler legal systems. In this regard, state officials often exercise their power by granting or withholding vital resources—a troubling pattern that resonates across every Indigenous land-rights case the IACHR has ruled on in the Americas.[61] Having long abided by the law yet endured repeated dispossessions, the Enxet and Sanapaná protagonists of this story increasingly began to take extralegal means to disrupt settler land control. Serafín López, a leader of Xákmok Kásek, often explains this to me by stating, "We refused to wait any longer with our arms crossed."

Enxet and Sanapaná struggles are founded on hope, but questions I heard throughout my research show these struggles are also conditioned by perpetual uncertainty. Political anthropologists have argued that states express authority through the politics of making people wait as they navigate bureaucracy, whereby time becomes a tool of governance that begets uncertainty.[62] Writing of Bolivian migrants working in Chile, Ryburn frames uncertainty as a constant state of flux experienced by "being here and not-here, of constantly 'going,' constantly 'becoming,' of the present as a means to the future."[63] Uncertainty works on temporal, affective, and material registers that manifest as legal liminality in Enxet and Sanapaná land struggles. Liminality is the condition of being a threshold, a transitional phase between two states of being, and is often used to describe subject-formation processes that accompany rituals.[64] The politics of recognition and the act of claiming land rights through state frameworks are conditioned by acts that can be read as ritual: they are repeated and practiced to promulgate the norms of a specific social-legal order. And like many other forms of ritual, the outcomes of legal procedure are bereft with uncertainty. In this context, the liminal is thus marked by hope for a particular outcome and uncertainty that will become—something many interlocutors expressed through the word *ikatu.*

The Guaraní word *ikatu* connotes both possibility and affirmation, meaning "it is possible" or "you may," depending on the context. The word thus carries an aspirational charge that indexes hope while also centering uncertainty. "Will ranchers react violently to land reoccupations? Ikatu." "Can I take a seat here? Ikatu." "Will state officials bring the monthly ration supply? Ikatu." "Will it rain today? Ikatu." "Will the ambulance arrive in time, or ever? Ikatu." Such are the utterances and contexts in which my interlocutors use the term, often in ways that speak to the liminal legal state that has ensnared many Enxet and Sanapaná communities for decades—simultaneously recognized and protected by the law but always excluded from its protections with the hope that one day the state will comply.

My interlocutors' strategies over the long arc of their struggles for land embody a *dialectics of disruption.* In its most basic formulation, a dialectic has two terms—the thesis and antithesis. One term of the dialectic the Enxet and Sanapaná mobilize can be defined by what the Aymara scholar Cusicanqui has called the "indio permitido"—the authorized Indian who acts within the limits of settler legal and social orders, doing little to disrupt the power structures that precede recognition and rights.[65] Enxet and Sanapaná peoples long comported themselves within the settler legal order's confines, following outlined procedures and navigating state bureaucracy to advance their claims. Yet the Paraguayan state neglected adjudicating their cases for decades, reproducing the "structured dispossession" of the politics of recognition.[66] If following the law is the dialectic's thesis in this context, breaking the law is the antithesis through which disruption takes a new form.

By following the struggles of Yakye Axa, Sawhoyamaxa, and Xákmok Kásek from their inception to the present, I trace how Enxet and Sanapaná people work with and against the law to erode settler control of their ancestral territories. Kahnawà:ke Mohawk anthropologist Audra Simpson's *Mohawk Interruptus* shows how refusal to accept the tenets of settler law interrupt the authority of the settler state and exert Native sovereignty.[67] On a related point, Dene scholar Glenn Coulthard argues that the politics of recognition operates on a dispossessive logic that recenters the settler state's authority instead of supporting Indigenous self-determination or mutual recognition.[68] Critical scholars of Latin American studies, such as Restrepo, Martínez-Novo, Paschel, and Hale, respectively assess the limits of multicultural recognition by highlighting lasting forms of racism and discrimination that result from such reforms.[69] A common thread weaves through this literature: resistance is often the only path by which Indigenous autonomies emerge due to state violence and the aporia of justice in colonial legal orders.

Enxet and Sanapaná of Yakye Axa, Sawhoyamaxa, and Xákmok Kásek have taken a tack that shifts between selectively following and breaking the law to force state officials and cattle ranchers to capitulate to their land claims. In other words, the dialectics of disruption encapsulate never fully refusing but never fully accepting the settler legal order, instead both refusing and engaging facets of the law to articulate territorial autonomies.[70] This is not a story that romanticizes resistance or portrays a homogeneous experience as each community transits an uneven terrain of struggle with variegated outcomes. Yet there are common power relations and patterns of dispossession that Enxet and Sanapaná efforts disrupt.

PATRÓN, A POWER RELATION AND PATTERN

Patrón is a commonly used Spanish word that means "boss."[71] The concept is ubiquitous in Paraguay. In colloquial use, the patrón commands laborers and controls resource access, is most often a man of white or mestizo descent, and holds greater power in relation to others who do not have the same resources or social status but who share a social relation with the patrón, often through labor.[72] Thus when people invoke the notion of the patrón, they simultaneously index a gendered, racialized, and class-based relation, something clearly demonstrated in the rupture that opens this introduction. Yet the asymmetrical power of the patrón in relation to the peon is marked by a tenuous form of reciprocity. To put it differently, the patrón depends on the peon's labor and the peon on the resources of the patrón, but the authority of the patrón is not total over the peon. Therefore, the patrón-peon relationship is based on unequal, *yet shifting*, forms of reciprocity that reveal relationships of mutual interdependence with asymmetrical access to resources.[73] In the Bajo Chaco, patrón-peon relations are conditioned by histories of ranching and agrarian rationalities.

Colonization and cattle ranching began in the Bajo Chaco—the southeastern, humid portion of the Paraguayan Chaco—when the Paraguayan state sold off nearly all its landholdings in the region to finance debts incurred in the devastating Triple Alliance War (1864–70). As a result of the sale, (mostly) foreign investors purchased tracts of land sold by the league with Indigenous communities inside the newly formed properties.[74] The region was devoid of an official state presence throughout the first thirty years of colonization, relying instead on Anglican missionaries, cattle ranchers, and loggers whose presence was the surrogate for state power. The imposition of private property rights and expansion of the ranching economy over Enxet and Sanapaná territories limited traditionally mobile lifeways where movement was necessary to live with the annual flood and drought cycle that defines the region's physical geography.[75] Indigenous relations with ranchers and state officials seen as *patrones* are also spatial relations because they are often mediated by struggles for land rights and unequal access regimes.[76] With the expansion of ranches and increased enforcement of private property, many Enxet and Sanapaná became the peons to the ranching patrones, a process I discuss in depth later.[77]

With attention to patrón-Indigenous relations, I show that power and political subjectivities are dynamic, constantly being reworked as actors vie to exert control over land and resources. In his work *Intimate Enemies*, Bobrow-Strain suggests the patrón-peon relation is an "implied contract of reciprocal responsibilities" that structure socio-spatial relations and resource access.[78] Within such relations of reciprocity lies a great deal of heterogeneity. Interdependence between patrones and peons creates dynamic relations of reciprocity and exchange that shift vis-à-vis one's ability to control resource access.[79] For example, a patrón can be a state official who offers bribes to communities for votes, or people can use the word jokingly to ask for something from a friend: "Give me a smoke, patrón." When I would arrive at the Xákmok Kásek reoccupation after going to a local town to purchase food to share with a family who hosted me, Ramona would jokingly announce, "My patrón has arrived!" On other occasions, people often recalled their work on ranches by referring to "good" or "bad" patrones based on how forthcoming a ranch owner was with pay or perks such as providing extra beef for meals at holidays. These examples demonstrate how the notion of the patrón as a keeper of resources permeates social imaginaries while indicating subtleties of unequal relations. Reciprocity and exchange permeate patrón-Indigenous relations and are informative for understanding how the Paraguayan state manages Indigenous dispossession to maintain the political economy of cattle ranching.

In addition to an asymmetrical social relation, the word *patrón* also means "pattern" in Spanish. Therefore, I use the dual meaning of patrón to flag the socioeconomic, racial, and gendered differences associated with Enxet and Sanapaná interlocutors' usage and draw attention to the patterns of behavior and spatial relations that emerge through Indigenous-settler and Indigenous-state interactions. State officials and local ranchers repeatedly deny Indigenous rights, creating a pattern of racialized inequities. In contrast, the patchwork of pastures marked by fences built with Indigenous labor inscribes a pattern of racialized land dispossession across the Chaco. Thus the book's title evokes the dual meaning of the Spanish word *patrón* to highlight predominant social relations and patterns while flagging the endurance of Enxet and Sanapaná efforts to disrupt long-standing settler-state-Indigenous relations by working with and against the law.

My use of the Spanish *patrón* should not be confused with the vast literature on patron-client relations. My concern lies with how patrón-Indigenous relations reveal nuances of settler colonialism in Latin America that also inform our understanding of how Indigenous peoples and their allies work to disrupt prevailing oppressive systems. Nevertheless, political patronage networks have deep roots in Paraguay and shape how the politics of recognition and environmental justice struggles intersect. The country is often cited for having high levels of corruption and opaque transparency, characteristics common throughout the Alfredo Stroessner dictatorship, from 1954 to 1989. Stroessner ruled Paraguay as if he were the country's patrón by using the military, political favors, and violence to maintain order.[80] Despite the democratic transition that followed Stroessner's ouster in 1989, much of the formal and informal governance structure his administration established has not significantly changed. Stroessner's Colorado political party has remained the dominant political force even in the wake of his ouster in 1989, mainly because the state bureaucratic apparatus has long functioned along with a durable structure of patron-client relations.

The legacy of Stroessner's patronage networks is borne in the enduring influence of agrarian elites whose political lobbies have a direct influence on state policies, from the minimal taxation of export soybeans to the adjudication of Indigenous land claims.[81] The latifundias that Stroessner's policies and political favors created continue to define land inequality issues and the concentration of political power in the country.[82] Indeed, two recent Paraguayan presidents have directly benefited from Stroessner. Horacio Cartes established his cigarette smuggling empire in the waning years of the dictatorship; Mario Abdo Benitez's father was Stroessner's primary adviser.[83] Stroessner's rule thus established popular imaginaries of the Paraguayan state as an authoritarian patrón who controls resources, an imaginary with material consequences.

ON METHODS:
RESEARCH AS/IS RELATIONAL PRACTICE

The multisited ethnography that animates this book is a relational story, not a comparative analysis. The chapters never focus solely on one community or case but draw insights from actors and processes across multiple sites to reveal a broader array of social-spatial patterns and practices of co-resistance that are neither merely disparate cases nor a uniform movement but efforts interwoven across time and space.[84] The book follows a roughly chronological order to chart how settler colonialism emerged not only as a structure, but as a process of recurrent dispossession that simultaneously incited recurrent and ever-changing forms of resistance on the part of Enxet and Sanapaná peoples. Over the chapters and ethnographic interludes—ruptures—that appear between chapters, I map how Enxet and Sanapaná struggles emerge and change over time while highlighting their dynamism and contradictions.[85] I draw on an eclectic body of information, from Anglican missionary accounts and IACHR documents to interviews with cattle ranchers, state officials, human rights lawyers, and Indigenous activists. The basis of my ethnography is participant observation in activities that range from everyday life in Yakye Axa, Sawhoyamaxa, and Xákmok Kásek to countermapping, protests, and meetings with state officials from the vice president to clerical staff.

Ethnography is a relational practice. Since 2013, I have traveled to Paraguay seven times to conduct research that informs this book.[86] Trips lasted between two weeks and thirteen months, totaling over twenty months. The study's long-term quality has allowed me to build lasting and deeply meaningful relationships with many people whose stories animate this book. Indeed, those stories and relationships find their root in embodied experience and conversation. In practice, my research adapted to, and adopted, practices of storytelling and conversation common among Indigenous communities in the Paraguayan Chaco.[87] Within many Indigenous knowledge systems, storytelling plays a vital role, as both a form of pedagogy and how people build relations to one another and other-than-human relations.[88] Rather than rely on a rigid, structured question-answer interview format, my research with Enxet and Sanapaná peoples revolved around what the Nêhiyaw and Saulteaux scholar Margaret Kovach calls conversation as method: "a dialogic approach to gathering knowledge that is built upon an Indigenous relational tradition" utilizing open-ended questions "to prompt conversation where participant and research co-create knowledge."[89] More often than not, such conversations often took place while drinking tereré.

More than a beverage, tereré is a cornerstone of Paraguayan national identity built on a ritual of sharing and conversation. *Tereré jere* is a Guaraní phrase for the tereré circle, where one person with a pitcher or thermos filled with water serves tereré to all in attendance by pouring water over yerba mate in a cup, then passing that cup sequentially to each person in the circle. The recipient drinks from a straw that filters the tea, and generally takes their time, in the process talking with everyone in attendance. When one person finishes drinking their cup of tereré, they pass the empty cup back to the server, who refills and passes it to the next person. And so it goes, from person to server to person, round and round. No matter where you go in Paraguay, from the Supreme Court to a packed bus to a tent encampment at the edge of disputed lands, you will likely find tereré and someone who will invite you to sit, drink, and talk. The ritual draws people together to slow down, share, and be in space with one another. In this way, tereré jere became a method of storytelling and relationality that informs this book. The everyday practice of drinking tereré in community helped build relationships that were vital to my understanding of Enxet and Sanapaná land struggles.

Although the three communities that I focus on have distinct histories, struggles, and cases before the IACHR, they are also all intimately related along colonial, juridical, political, and familial lines. Colonization and its settler legacies on Enxet and Sanapaná territories have been driven by a conjoined effort to spread the Anglican faith and establish cattle ranching in the wake. The three communities' legal struggles are related through jurisprudence established by the IACHR decisions. Findings from the Yakye Axa case were used to argue for the Sawhoyamaxa community's rights, just as the Xákmok Kásek case directly builds from the jurisprudence established in *Sawhoyamaxa v. Paraguay* (2006). Legal jurisprudence used to support Indigenous territorial claims is another example of how lines of legal inquiry connect place-based struggles through counter-topographies that form a relation across distinct geographies.[90]

The communities share a relationship with the same legal counsel, the human rights nongovernmental organization (NGO) Tierraviva a los Pueblos Indígenas del Chaco (Tierraviva). People from Yakye Axa, Sawhoyamaxa, and Xákmok Kásek have worked with Tierraviva's staff since the early 1990s, collaborating to strategize how to advance their land claims and the rights of Enxet and Sanapaná peoples. Their work has forged lasting interpersonal relationships between many people who share deep affection for one another. When traveling to Asunción for meetings with state officials or Tierraviva staff, many Enxet and Sanapaná stay at the Tierraviva offices in housing provided free of charge. The space is a dynamic site of interchange where people from across the Bajo Chaco convene, often talking late into the night long after office doors have closed for the day. Moreover, the three communities often coordinate with one another about how to pressure the state to comply with the IACHR, sending delegations from one community to the other when the opportunity to do so arises. It is no surprise, then, that over the years of collective struggles and exchange, some members of Yakye Axa, Sawhoyamaxa, and Xákmok Kásek have intermarried to form new kin relations among the communities. Consequently, I tell a story of relations, not of comparison.

The research for this book grew in part from my interest in human rights and Indigenous land struggles and in part from Enxet and Sanapaná interests in using research to increase the visibility of their cases. Over the years this study has unfolded, I have worked closely with leaders in Xákmok Kásek, Sawhoyamaxa, and Yakye Axa, conferring and collaborating with them on research design and discussing the research process during meetings where community members provided feedback. I also met frequently with colleagues at Tierraviva, who helped me better understand the political-juridical realities of adjudicating Indigenous land-rights cases in Paraguay and its labyrinthine state bureaucracy.[91] I accompanied their lawyers and staff on various tasks related to the implementation process, giving me a clearer view on the murky bureaucratic and legal procedures involved in each case while also showing me what solidarity research looks like in everyday practice. Tierraviva staff and lawyers entertained hours of my curiosity and gave me access to vital archival data and information about each of the cases. These documents include communications with the Paraguayan state, historical accounts by colonizers, anthropological studies, media reports, property titles, maps, and communications with the Inter-American System—a wealth of historical and contemporary documents that would have taken months of dedicated work to find on my own. In addition, I attended high-level meetings with state officials, participated in political actions led by community members, and assessed negotiations over compliance with the IACHR judgments. Throughout those activities, I conducted more than 170 semistructured and informal interviews.[92] The quotations and ethnographic details derive from a mix of audio or video recordings, handwritten and transcribed field notes, and photographs I have taken. I conducted all interviews in Guaraní or Spanish and translated them into English with feedback from interviewees where possible.[93] While most interviewees wanted to have their names used in the text, some did not, in which case I use pseudonyms or a general title to protect their privacy.

ETHICS, REPRESENTATION, LIMITS

Conducting research on human rights violations and environmental injustice is delicate and difficult. Questions, conversations, and topics transit painful sites, even when they focus on future visions of what could be (but by extension is not yet). In this context, aspirational politics, hope, and resistance conjure new possibilities but do so in reference to ongoing and past harms. At the close of an interview with Serafín López, I asked, "Who else should I speak with about these matters, about your community's case before the court [IACHR]?" Serafín, who had just spent the previous hour and a half vividly recalling decades of struggle through moments of laughter, gravity, and defiance, went silent. His eyes welled with tears and turned bloodshot as he looked beyond me before turning to say, "Ña Antonia Ramirez. She was a great fighter for the community. She traveled all the way to Lima to testify to the court. She died not long after the trip and was never able to return to this land here. She knew the *lucha* [fight]." Moments like this make clear the stakes of research and limits of representational practices. There are no innocuous questions. The writing of the findings matters immensely.

Through the research process, many Enxet and Sanapaná interlocutors sought to denounce wrongs they had experienced and continue to live with. Given the high-level profile of the Yakye Axa, Sawhoyamaxa, and Xákmok Kásek cases, community members have long engaged NGOs, state officials, and international human rights advocates to recount their experiences to advance their land claims. By granting permission and inviting me to conduct the research that informs this book, community members saw an opportunity to share their experience with other audiences and charged me to share their accounts. The charge is a heavy one that intersects with politics of research and representation. How do researchers maintain fidelity to their interlocutors while articulating the insights they share with broader conversations (e.g., academic theory and debate)? How can academic writing meet the charge of ethically sharing traumatic experiences in ways that do not romanticize oppression, abstract lived experience through theories derived in other places, or flatten the heterogeneity of complex social processes and actors to fit a uniform explanation? Research and writing are always political because they pertain to uneven power, representation, and the coloniality of academic knowledge production.

Throughout the book, I endeavor to center Enxet and Sanapaná narratives and experiences in ways that drive the analysis. My use of academic theory, citations, and storytelling intends to draw connections between schools of thought—academic and otherwise. My aim is not to read Enxet and Sanapaná experiences through theory derived from scholars (both Indigenous and non-Indigenous) based in North America, Europe, or provincial sites in Latin America but to think with insights shared by interlocutors in this research and bring them to bear on established theory to provide another way of understanding environmental justice, human rights, and Indigenous land restitution in the current conjuncture. Bringing Enxet and Sanapaná storytelling practices into conversation with academic storytelling (i.e., citationality) does not eschew the coloniality of representational politics. The political economy of academic writing—not only the word limits authors work with, but the intellectual currency of advancing debate—and push to abstract theorization from everyday life create limits and challenges to solidarity research that involves publication. I do not intend to "speak for" or "give voice to" any of the people who participated in this research. Members of Yakye Axa, Sawhoyamaxa, and Xákmok Kásek have voices and speak for themselves in their ongoing struggles, advocacy, and everyday life. One of my goals, however, is to amplify my interlocutors' insights, and thus this book is written as a form of reciprocity made in a spirit of using research as resistance to honor Enxet and Sanapaná struggles for self-determination.[94]

Despite those intentions, I am aware that ethnography has long been a colonial tool, forged as a practice to codify cultural differences, distinguish "others," define notions of superiority, and reaffirm white supremacy.[95] Critical scholars have trenchantly, and rightly, critiqued the forms of ventriloquism that academic writing often produces, underscoring that the inequities inherent to this form of knowledge production and circulation speak for subaltern actors.[96] Linda Tuhiwai Smith eloquently states, "Academic writing is a form of selecting, arranging and presenting knowledge. It privileges sets of texts, views about the history of an idea, what issues count as significant; and, by engaging in the same process uncritically, we too can render indigenous writers invisible or unimportant while reinforcing the validity of other writers. If we write without thinking critically about our writing, it can be dangerous."[97] Despite my efforts to center self-reflexive critical analysis and Enxet and Sanapaná perspectives, this book invariably produces its own silences through the process of weaving together distinct grounded experiences and diverse academic theories.

Yet through accessible language and upon eventual translation, I hope the book will serve meaningfully for the Enxet and Sanapaná communities with whom I have worked on this project for many years. I also hope the analysis is useful to students, scholars, and activists who read the work. In this way, the writing itself intends to disrupt staid academic convention and speak to a broad readership of critical scholars, activists, and those who participated in the research. This book is the product of thinking, conversing, and living *with* Enxet and Sanapaná collaborators; however, it does not provide a holistic account of Enxet and Sanapaná struggles, indigenista organizing, the Paraguayan state, or settler experiences. *Disrupting the Patrón* is but one story of environmental justice among many that can be told about Indigenous rights and land in Paraguay's Bajo Chaco.

BOOK OUTLINE

I begin by laying the groundwork for understanding the stakes of the legal struggles Enxet and Sanapaná wage to regain their lands. To do this, I examine the establishment and structures of settler colonialism in the Bajo Chaco by attending to Anglican missionization and the early years of cattle ranching. Anglican missionary accounts and settler rancher testimonies show that Enxet and Sanapaná peoples have long occupied a central yet peripheral position within Paraguayan state formation. The erasure of Indigenous lifeways was more than religious conversion or dispossession. It operated through efforts to produce a labor force that would build the infrastructures on which ranching has expanded and ultimately persisted. Drawing missionary, settler, and Indigenous narratives into conversation, I chart the emergence of the social and spatial relations of power that persist through contemporary patrón-Indigenous relations.

Not entirely unlike the evangelical Christians who led the colonization of the Chaco, activist anthropologists and indigenistas sought to evangelize Enxet and Sanapaná peoples in a new way of being—through the knowledge and language of rights. The mid-1970s project, called Marandú ("News" or "Information" in Guaraní), sought to spread information about rights to empower Indigenous peoples who had been exploited on ranches across the country. For many, interactions with these actors represent a critical historical conjuncture when the knowledge of rights—first for better working conditions, then eventually for land, and, finally, as humans—changed their political outlook. Thus chapter 2 traces relationships between labor, law, rights, and Indigenous political mobilizations.[98] By drawing attention to racial capitalism and its effects on the politics of recognition, I suggest that Enxet and Sanapaná land struggles cannot be reduced to neoliberal multiculturalism. Instead of facilitating state governance or enabling the state to co-opt Indigenous struggles, new multicultural rights frameworks opened a field of struggle conditioned by the *longue durée* of patrón-Indigenous land and labor relations.

As Yakye Axa, Sawhoyamaxa, and Xákmok Kásek waged legal struggles to reclaim land from the ranches where they lived and labored, each community was eventually forced to leave those ranches. Two communities occupied the margin of a highway in front of the lands they claimed, and the third moved onto lands of a sympathetic Indigenous community. Life is hard on the ranches as it is on the margins. Drinking water and firewood are scarce. There is no land to garden, let alone hunt or fish. Ceding to pressure from local NGOs during the 1990s, two presidents of Paraguay declared a state of emergency in each community, authorizing the delivery of food rations and drinking water. Eventually, the IACHR ordered Paraguay to maintain the emergency services until the government resolved the stalled land claims. More than a generation later, the states of emergency remain, and the claims have not been fully resolved. With everyday emergencies in mind, chapter 3 argues that the Paraguayan state governs Indigenous dispossession through a biopolitics of neglect.[99] Here I draw attention to stark disparities in how cattle raised on stolen Indigenous lands are valued more than Enxet and Sanapaná life on the margins of cattle ranches. I show that neglect emanates from legal abandonment, creating a life condition where the only predictable thing is unpredictability.

After exhausting all legal avenues within Paraguay, Yakye Axa, Sawhoyamaxa, and Xákmok Kásek scaled up their struggles by petitioning the Inter-American System of Justice to arbitrate. In three judgments, the IACHR ordered Paraguay to recognize its human rights violations, return ancestral lands to each community, and provide funds for development projects as restitution. Whereas the development of the Chaco drove Enxet and Sanapaná dispossession, the IACHR strategy frames ethno-development as a form of restitution. The IACHR issued its judgments in 2005, 2006, and 2010, with a clear mandate that the state implement the orders within three years of each decision. Nevertheless, the responsible state institutions have only complied with the IACHR in uneven, discretionary ways that intensify legal liminality rather than resolve it. Chapter 4 investigates the IACHR strategy of restitution as development and focuses on the politics and practice of implementing that strategy in Yakye Axa and Sawhoyamaxa.[100] In theory, restitution as development is a vehicle to support Indigenous self-determination and decenter the state's authority by placing decision making with affected communities. In practice, a more complicated terrain of struggle followed after "winning" the case in court. Implementation politics expose the depth of Paraguay's biopolitics of neglect and motivate Enxet and Sanapaná activists to use more radical forms of resistance.

The final chapter focuses on extralegal practices that complete the dialectics of disruption. Rather than everyday forms of resistance, the dialectics of disruption revolve around strategically breaking select laws through public acts that compel a state response while simultaneously using those situations to draw attention to how the state violates Indigenous human rights. Doing so reworks the terms of recognition by making the state negotiate directly with Enxet and Sanapaná leaders, simultaneously recognizing their authority and self-determination and delineating an emerging Indigenous environmental justice. My interlocutors show Enxet and Sanapaná renewal is neither abject rejection nor total acceptance of the politics of recognition but always negotiated and somewhere between. The chapter brings nuance to analyses of the evolving strategies of resistance and renewal used to disrupt settler colonial power.

Disrupting the Patrón concludes by drawing experiences from Yakye Axa, Sawhoyamaxa, and Xákmok Kásek into conversation with one another vis-à-vis scholarship on decolonial politics in the Americas. I resist fetishizing Indigenous struggle by highlighting the lasting ambiguities and newfound challenges that come after land restitution. The goal of recovering land has animated the Yakye Axa, Sawhoyamaxa, and Xákmok Kásek struggles for decades. Yet life after land restitution has been highly uneven in each community. Whereas time and the uncertainty of legal liminality have been undeniably oppressive, Enxet and Sanapaná leverage endurance as a radical act of resistance in efforts to restore their relations with land in pursuit of environmental justice.

Open/Closed

Waiting at the gate, we heard the tin sputter of a motor scooter approaching and soon saw Marcelino weaving to follow the smoothest path along the rough dirt road as he approached us. After brief pleasantries, he unlocked the gate, and we entered the ranch, following him to the small house where he and his wife lived when they are looking after things. Marcelino is now *capataz* of the ranch, responsible for watching over the herd, coordinating work parties when they are needed, and keeping an eye on things while the patrón is away. He is also one of the four leaders of Xákmok Kásek and had long played a central role in the community's land struggles. We came to visit so he, Clemente, and Serafin could discuss new developments in their case. But we also came to fish.

The ranch Marcelino works for is located on land with a storied history. International Products Company purchased this land, the traditional territory of Sanapaná peoples, in the late 1800s, then transferred ownership to a trio of English and US ranchers who started the Eaton & Cía. cattle ranch. Eventually, a Mennonite settler purchased the parcel, and he is now Marcelino's patrón. The process of purchase, sale, and subdivision came with an ordered but unruly expansion of fences to delineate cattle pastures in a landscape defined by seasonal variations in flood and drought, where meandering streams challenge quadrilinear Cartesian logics. Working with the landscape and against the caprices of the region's climate, ranchers construct *tajamares* (stock ponds) that fill with floodwaters and sustain cattle during times of drought. The tajamares also fill with fish and have become reliable food sources for Indigenous peoples who used to move freely over these lands but are now bound by ranching's enclosures. After talking business over tereré, Marcelino grabbed his fishing gear and took us to his favorite tajamar on the ranch.

The sun was low in the sky, temperatures were dropping, and the mosquitos were swarming. "Okaru la pira," promised Marcelino. The fish would eat. Eat they did. The five of us spread out to different parts of the pond with a handful of raw beef chunks and a simple fishing setup—about ten meters of fishing line wrapped around a small square of wood with a lead weight and a hook. A piece of meat on the hook, a couple turns of the wrist, and a cast out into the water. They made it look easy. For me, it was less so, but I eventually got the hang of things as dusk turned to dark, and we continued to fish with the steel blue–gray light of the moon reflecting on the tajamar. With each fish landed came a yelp of excitement from one side of the pond to the next, "nde!" With each fish lost, a new cast onto the water. After a couple hours, we regrouped at Ireneo's truck to take stock of the haul. Marcelino had about twenty-five, Clemente and Serafin each brought in around twenty, Ireneo had twelve, and I had seven. We let Marcelino choose from our fish as a tribute to his inviting us to the tajamar and then set off to return to Retiro Primero, where sixty-three families from Xákmok Kásek had recently reoccupied the ranch in an effort to take back their ancestral territory.

The next morning, I sat with a group of men by the gate at the entrance to Retiro Primero. The anticipation that something would happen was palpable. Would the police come? Would the ranchers react violently? Would the state finally restitute these lands? Ikatu. But like many before it, this day passed without any resolution. For a land reoccupation some thirty years in the making, most days were surprisingly dull. So most people hung around and talked when they were not doing chores around their tents or off hunting or fishing. Felipe knew that we had gone to see Marcelino and had heard about the tajamar. "Okaru la pira," he asked. "Heê. Okaru." Yes. They ate, I replied. With that, Felipe recounted a story.

> The land used to be open. When my father was a boy in this area, the land was open. He said that we could go anywhere we wanted, to go fishing or hunting, to gather algarrobo seeds. We could go anywhere. Then the land changed. One day they found a fence [*alambre*]. It was *campo* [farmland]. The land was closed, and we stayed inside because they [the ranchers] would get very angry if we crossed [the fences]. They closed the land. We started living on the ranches and working there. Others came for work because all the land was closed, and the Indigenous people could no longer live like they used to. We had to stay and work.[1]

Over the course of my research for this project, several people, mostly elders, from Xákmok Kásek, Sawhoyamaxa, and Yakye Axa would all share an iteration of this story. While some of the details changed, the person who recounted this story always used the same two words to describe the dynamic: "open" (*abierto*) and "closed" (*omboty*). The expansion of the cattle-ranching industry and its impacts on social-spatial relations is vivid in the collective memory of Enxet and Sanapaná peoples, who have lived through the process of enclosure and still navigate its effects. Many elders and the parents or grandparents of middle-aged Enxet and Sanapaná lived through a time of radical change when cattle ranching spread and intensified in the region.

CHAPTER 1

"A Land in the Making"

The Paraguayan Chaco lay outside the path of colonization much longer than other parts of South America due to Indigenous resistance and settler ideas that the region was devoid of resources. Things changed in the late nineteenth century, after Paraguay entered the Triple Alliance War against Brazil, Argentina, and Uruguay. The ramifications were catastrophic. At the close of the war in 1870, nearly 90 percent of all Paraguayan males were dead, half the country's territory was ceded to the victors, and financial solvency gave way to crushing debt.[1] Though that war was not waged in the Chaco, nearly all of the land in that region at the time, which was *tierra fiscal*—owned by the state—was sold to pay the postwar debt. Between 1885 and 1887, the Paraguayan state subdivided and offered for sale more than 186,000 square kilometers of the Chaco—two-thirds of the territory—to financial speculators on the London Stock Exchange, the majority of which were British and Argentine.[2] The Paraguayan state had previously claimed all lands in the Chaco via the 1825 Government Act, thereby codifying the exclusion of Indigenous peoples from land rights, though the Chaco land sale was the first material action to appropriate Indigenous lands.[3] Upon arriving in the region, British Anglican missionaries described the process of propertizing the Chaco in the following terms:

> This they succeeded in doing by marking off the bank of the River Paraguay into sections a league wide, and drawing imaginary lines due west to the frontier. In a very short time the Government has sold the entire country, even the few reserves they had at first determined to maintain. The early missionaries were therefore confronted with the anomaly of a country as large as Great Britain practically unexplored, its inhabitants heathen barbarians, no centre of government or representative authority in the whole of the vast interior, and yet the whole land, although unsurveyed, sold by the Government and bought by speculators.[4]

Aside from a handful of riverine settlements used as lumber camps for logging and tannin extraction, no settler colonies or state officials were present in Paraguay's

Chaco before the land sale.[5] The 1825 Government Act provided the legal means to facilitate colonization of the Chaco by actors who were not Paraguayan but primarily foreign investors. The process illuminates differences in the dynamics of internal colonization as described by Casanova and promoted by agrarian reforms from those of settler colonization where the state's intent was to entice foreign investors to establish permanent settlements and extractive industries to facilitate state territorialization.[6]

This chapter focuses on how Anglican missionaries helped establish settler political economy in the Bajo Chaco that created a racial geography defined by land-labor relations and cattle ranching. I assess early Anglican missionary accounts to trace the inception of settler colonialism in the Bajo Chaco to its roots in cattle ranching. The Anglican Mission in Paraguay played a pivotal role in establishing the discursive, political economic, and material structures through which settler colonialism has expanded and operated across the Chaco. The enclosure of Enxet and Sanapaná territories by ranchers and private land investors required dispossessing Indigenous peoples *in place*, then creating a new racialized class of laborers to work on the ranches built on stolen lands. Such dynamics are central elements in the geographies of settler colonialism that spur my interlocutors' ongoing struggles to reclaim their lands and lifeways. To understand contemporary Enxet and Sanapaná resistance, one must grapple with the historical role of missionization and cattle ranching and their intimate relations with settler colonialism in this region.

Private property in land is imperative to the production of racial geographies. It mediates relationships between people, often in ways that spatially inscribe and reinforce racialized difference.[7] But making private property in land did more than create a racialized regime of ownership in the Bajo Chaco; it also ensured that cattle would come to have greater occupancy rights than Enxet and Sanapaná peoples on whose traditional territories they graze. The Right Reverend Edward Every, the highest Anglican official directly responsible for overseeing the church's South American mission in Paraguay at the turn of the nineteenth century, provided prescient remarks in his 1915 writings:

> *The Chaco is still a land in the making*, consisting of vast dreary plains covered with anthills, palm trees, and low scrubby forest, and broken up by numerous swamps. Hence, as no white man coveted it, it formed for centuries a natural indian reserve. The conditions, however, are now rapidly changing, as the land has been found valuable for running cattle, and the indian no longer has the country to himself.[8]

If the Paraguayan Chaco was a "land in the making" in the early 1900s, when Every wrote these words, cattle ranching has since "made" the Chaco. Nothing has had a more significant impact on ecology and social relations in the region than ranching, a practice that has radically reconfigured the dynamics of land control through new racial geographies.

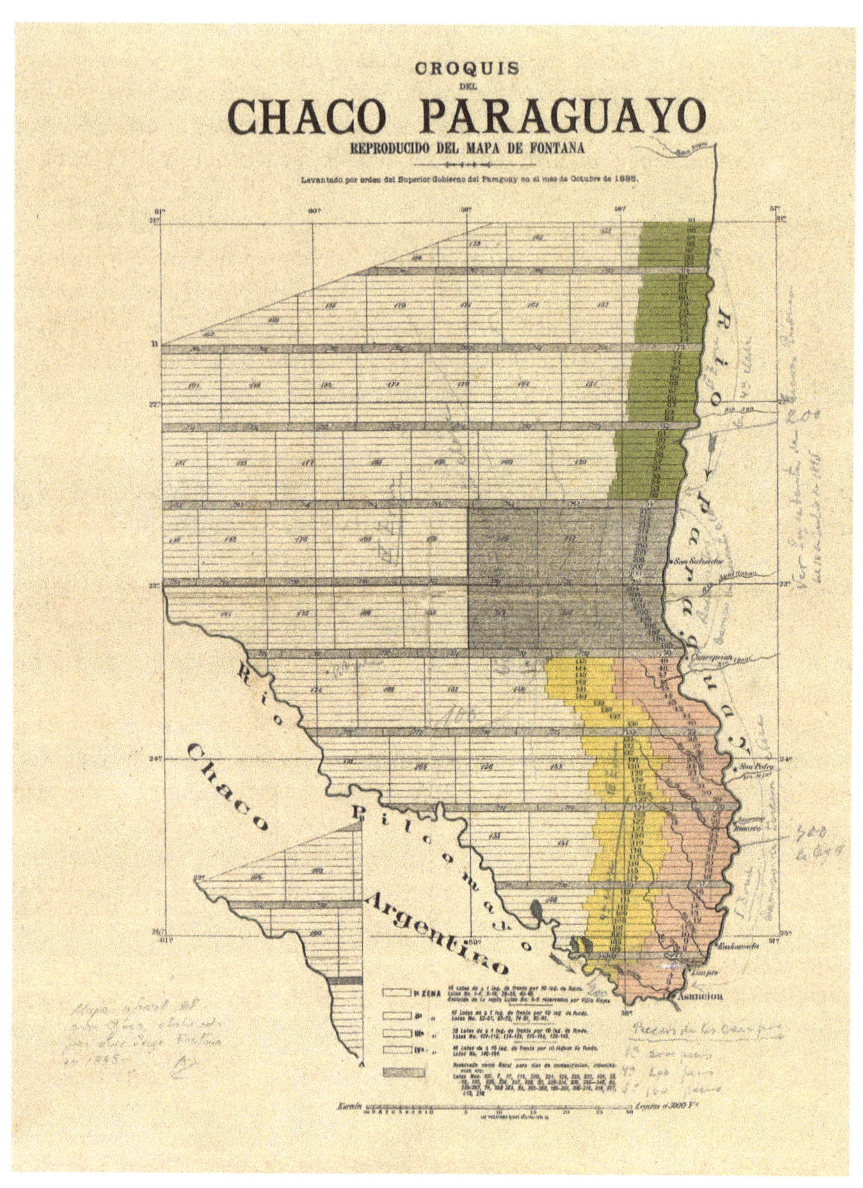

FIGURE 1. An 1885 map by Fontana depicts how the Paraguayan Chaco was divided for sale; varying prices correspond to the different colors. Enxet and Sanapaná territories lie in zones of the highest value (red and yellow). The original map title reads, "Croquis del Chaco Paraguayo Reproducido del mapa del Fontana. Levantado por orden del Superior Gobierno del Paraguay en el mes de Octubre de 1885."

Popular accounts of development in Paraguay's Chaco erase the role of Indigenous peoples by centering settlers as protagonists of progress, while Indigenous peoples are framed as victims of development, confined to radical alterity, or omitted entirely from the narrative.[9] However, I argue that Indigenous labor has been vital to making the Chaco; it has always been central to that process, though rendered invisible.[10] Yet the actual labor used in Chaco cattle ranching was, and in large part still is, Indigenous. The "making" of the Chaco has always been a project whereby the production of new spaces for cattle capitalism is intimately tied to efforts to create new Indigenous subjects whose labor is necessary to the settler political economy. The racial geographies that my interlocutors work to unsettle are thus conditioned by class relations of an Indigenous peonage working for non-Indigenous landowning patrones. In this regard, we should think of racial geographies as less like "the effects of imposed unitary structures of colonial or neocolonial power—of pillaging, extermination, and dispossession . . . and more as social processes that unfolded and enfolded over time."[11] Through a critical reading of Anglican missionary documents and reflection on Enxet and Sanapaná memories of life on cattle ranches, this chapter foregrounds the role Enxet and Sanapaná labor played in "making" the Bajo Chaco. I follow the nascence of settler colonialism in the Bajo Chaco to show how racial geographies produced through Indigenous peon and settler patrón labor relations endure in the present, playing out as processes of oppression, resistance, ambivalence, and resurgence that I trace throughout the book.

The chapter proceeds as follows. First, I briefly discuss the roots of cattle ranching in Paraguay, then link that to the role Anglican missionaries played in establishing the practice in the Chaco. Next I engage Anglican missionary accounts to trace the inception of settler colonialism in the Bajo Chaco to show how social-spatial relations between non-Indigenous patrones and Indigenous peons persist to the present and continue to influence Enxet and Sanapaná land struggles. My aim, however, is not to detail a history of Anglican missionization but to consider how the Mission and its ranches were instrumental in creating a racial geography in the Bajo Chaco, an ordering of people, political economy, and space that reveals how settler colonialism works as a structure *and* a process.[12] Second, I suggest that investigating settler colonialism through the lens of patrón-peon labor dynamics brings nuance to understandings of how the structures of settler colonialism operate as transhistorical, racial, and gendered processes distinct from internal colonization.[13] State-led agrarian reforms incentivized mestizo campesinos to occupy lands east of the Paraguay River in what was the country's most significant effort to spur internal colonization.[14] However, early colonization of the Chaco almost exclusively relied on non-Paraguayan actors—from the foreign investors who capitalized on the land sale to Anglican missionaries used to establish a presence in the region and, later, to Mennonites who founded large agricultural settlements in the central Chaco. The process of colonizing the Paraguayan Chaco was distinct within the country and exhibits a clear dynamic of Indigenous land dispossession and large-scale enclosures to support non-Indigenous settler life that persists to the present through the region's demography and distribution of land control. Third, I frame how Enxet and Sanapaná labor functions as a form of infrastructure alongside the fences and ranches built with that labor. Viewing labor as infrastructure, I show how the Anglican Mission recast Enxet and Sanapaná from "heathen barbarians" to peons, a process with social and spatial ramifications for how settler colonialism has unfolded in Paraguay's Chaco.

THE LEGEND OF SEVEN COWS AND ONE BULL

In an extensive presentation on the history and evolution of cattle ranching in Paraguay, the country's oldest and most influential rural producer organization, the Asociación Rural del Paraguay (ARP; Rural Association of Paraguay), contends that the country's relation with cattle started with the introduction of seven cows and one bull in 1545.[15] Arguing that "the first bovines in Paraguay saw that the country was a paradise [where] they found the best and most beautiful pasturelands and watering holes in the world," the document frames the country as a fecund territory populated only by animals and well suited for the introduction of settler colonialism's ultimate companion species.[16] The ARP presentation follows the evolution of ranching from the introduction of eight bovines through many waves of colonization and state expansion by which the "troop" expanded through varied means: the expulsion of unwanted settlers (i.e., the Jesuits in 1768) and confiscation of their herds; incorporation of new colonizing genetics like Hereford, Angus, and Brahman; technological innovation from the establishment of canned, conserved meatpacking to the first refrigerator ship to export fresh meats to international markets; and widespread biosecurity campaigns to regularly vaccinate all cattle against foot and mouth disease, among other bovine plagues. Throughout, state officials and ranchers celebrate the growth and expansion of cattle capitalism as a "miracle" produced not through divine intervention, but the hard work and labor of visionary patrones whose investments have transformed Paraguay's so-called green hell into productive spaces through which the national character is founded.[17]

It bears noting that the ARP was founded in the years immediately following the Triple Alliance War, an era when land rights were radically reconfigured by the privatization push used to fund war debts and empower a class of large-scale landholders that still wields considerable political influence in Paraguay.[18] Kleinpenning's encyclopedic economic geography of rural development in Paraguay underscores the importance of the postwar period to the enduring land tenure inequality, of which cattle ranching was one of the principal economic sectors that most benefited.[19] Drawing from a broad compendium of government documents and secondary analyses written from 1870 to 1963, he shows that cattle have been necessary to smallholder livelihoods and long complemented a diversified farming strategy. On the other hand, Kleinpenning notes, commercial ranching in Paraguay has always been land-extensive, with herds greater than five hundred head, and commercial operations dominate ranching practices; this trend persists.

The three departments that comprise the Paraguayan Chaco simultaneously have the largest cattle herds and, not surprisingly, some of the highest levels of land-tenure inequality in the country measured by the GINI coefficient.[20] Miguel Lovera and Inés Franceschelli of the Paraguayan research organization Heñoi argue that the structure and politics of cattle ranching are "oriented to enrich an oligarchic group of society that is fundamentally feudal, tracing their establishment from the close of the Triple Alliance War to our current time and that their subsistence derives from cattle capitalism [*capitalismo ganadero*]."[21] With the help of Anglican missionaries, Anglo settlers first established cattle ranching on Enxet and Sanapaná territories of the Bajo Chaco, then gradually pushed their practice north and west toward the borders with Bolivia and Argentina.[22] Cattle ranching now defines settler political economy and conditions Enxet and Sanapaná land struggles.

My analysis begins with a critical reading of Anglican accounts because the Mission fomented cattle capitalism while simultaneously making new racial subjects—an Indigenous peonage. Ranching in Paraguay's Chaco has relied on Indigenous labor from its inception to the present. If racial capitalism is at its most basic "a theory of the inseparability of race and capitalism," as Pasternak suggests, then it is impossible to extricate the Anglican Mission from how it actively racialized Enxet and Sanapaná "others" as the disposable labor force from which ranching advanced.[23] Thus the history of Indigenous labor exploitation flags the co-joined nature of settler colonialism and the specific form of racial capitalism present in Paraguay's Chaco. In the Chaqueño context, ranching has long been framed as the path to modernity by making the region a space for Christian beliefs, private property, and state territory via agrarian development.[24] These are the hallmarks of the region's enduring racial geography forged through settler colonialism.

RACIAL ORDERS AND THE RIGHT DISPOSITION

The Anglican Church was intimately connected to Britain's efforts to expand its reach through the eighteenth and nineteenth centuries, with missionary efforts present on six continents by the late 1800s.[25] The South American Missionary Society (SAMS) funded the Anglican Mission there. With robust efforts afoot in Argentina, SAMS began planning the Paraguay mission in 1887, on the heels of the great land sale.[26] The Anglican movement into the Bajo Chaco was influenced by British investors who had purchased land in the area. For example, the British consul in Asunción shared a direct relationship with a consortium of British investors who purchased nearly 250,000 hectares in the Bajo Chaco and core members of the SAMS decision-making committee who had also purchased land in Paraguay.[27] Throughout its hundred-year history working in the Bajo Chaco, SAMS missionaries established twelve mission-stations beginning at Carayá Vuelta on the Paraguay River and moving west some 200 kilometers.

Arriving in Paraguay from a short stint in Tierra del Fuego, Wilfred Barbrooke Grubb led the Anglican Mission in Paraguay's Chaco from 1889 to 1919. With support from SAMS, Grubb and his team worked for decades to "pacify" the Enxet and Sanapaná peoples of the Bajo Chaco so that British-backed ranching interests could expand in the region. This point is made clear in several historical accounts, such as those popularized in travelogues by the British Anglican Margarette Daniels.

> When one thinks that but ten years ago it was dangerous to one's life to venture into the Chaco, while now there are numerous *estancias* [ranches] on the border, and one can now go for a hundred and more miles into the interior with comparative safety, it shows that the missionaries have got the "thin edge of the wedge" well thrust in. These men and women are making savages into reasonable, peace-abiding people, and—what touches the commercial world more—they are making what was once considered a piece of waste land, the size of England and Scotland, of real commercial value. Landowners in the Paraguayan Chaco owe all this to the English Mission, and especially to Mr. W.B. Grubb, the pioneer and backbone of the whole undertaking.[28]

Daniels's account, from her book *The Makers of South America*, foregrounds the role of the non-Indigenous pioneer as the protagonist of change. This trope resonates with a narrative that centers the labor of settlers while marginalizing the role Indigenous labor played in the Mission's "success" and expansion of ranching. I have heard many versions of productive pioneer narratives while living, working, and researching in Paraguay, retold in different forms by ranchers, cab drivers, campesinos, and state officials across the country. It goes something like this: "The Indigenous don't want to work. When they get land, they don't produce anything and look to the state for handouts. The [insert settler archetype: *pioneers, Mennonites, ranchers, etc.*] are the ones who have made something out of the Chaco." The productive pioneer narrative works discursively to place Indigenous peoples spatially, as those outside the property system but whose labor is necessary to convert "waste lands" into sites of agrarian accumulation. The narrative simultaneously occludes the fact that the "productivity" of the pioneer is predicated on the alienation of labor through which the production of space, like "making" the Chaco, is achieved. Thus the pioneer—a racialized white/non-Indigenous male-gendered subject—is exalted while racialized Indigenous laborers are rendered "savage," invisible, and/or outside the productive system.

Grubb embodied the pioneer archetype through his missionary work and travelogs. Indeed, he played the definitive role in expanding the Anglican Mission in the Bajo Chaco and forging a new geography based on racial and class difference. An avid writer and later lecturer for Oxford University, his cataloged missionary

FIGURE 2. Enxet children playing in front of the church at Makxawáya circa 1938. The Paraguayan flag flies atop the steeple. Photographer unknown. Photograph courtesy of the Anglican Church of Paraguay.

efforts provide some of the most detailed written accounts of the initial colonization process. In his writings, Grubb makes clear the rationale for the Bajo Chaco mission: "The South American Missionary Society gave instructions to their men, not only to enter into and dwell in their [i.e., Enxet] land, whatever the risk, but to attempt no less a task than that of opening up this unknown land, of revolutionizing the native customs, habits, modes of life, and laws."[29] By "opening up" the Bajo Chaco, Grubb's missionary work also served as a surrogate for state territoriality. Pictures from the era show that Anglican churches built in the Bajo Chaco provided a space to worship and pledge allegiance to Paraguay, where the nation's dual images—the Christian cross and Paraguayan flag—were often displayed side by side. Given that the Paraguayan state had no presence in the Chaco before the arrival of the Anglicans, the Mission helped establish a new order of social and spatial relations along the country's western frontier.[30] As a result, Paraguayan officals named Grubb Comisario General del Chaco y Pacificador de los Indios—the Chaco's Justice of the Peace and Pacifier of the Indians.

Grubb's work with the Mission produced racial geographies as social-spatial governmentality based on indoctrinating Enxet and Sanapaná in the "right" modes of conduct and proper disposition of things.[31] SAMS magazines circulated in Britain in the early 1900s make clear this vision. One article read, "Those who have an interest in Chaco lands can surely not fail to see the benefit of a numerous, trained and willing population of workers with whom to develop the lands in which they have placed their capital. The question of suitable labour will always be an important one in this world. . . . We are practical enough to not neglect such training as will fit these people to take their *proper place* in the world."[32] Narratives from early missionary work show that the "proper place" for Enxet and Sanapaná peoples was as a central yet always marginal(ized) facet of broader imperatives to territorialize the Chaco as a site for the expansion of settler interests, whether through ranching or state territoriality. Enxet and Sanapaná peoples were thus first interpellated as part of the Paraguayan state through their relationship with the Anglican Mission. On this point, I return to Grubb, who stated, "[SAMS] sought to form not only a Christian Church among these savage and nomadic tribes, but also industrial communities, and was entrusted by the Paraguayan Government, who claimed that the region was their territory, with the task of binding the tribes together in unity, and of *instructing them in government*. The policy of the Mission was to endeavor to *make the people rule themselves*."[33] Grubb's accounts detail not only the governance of Indigenous life, but the settler governmentality of the Mission that hinged on establishing a particular social-spatial order.

Such accounts also assume that Enxet and Sanapaná lived in a state without rule or order before the Anglican arrival. "Our task was," Grubb argued, "to give them a system of government; to raise them to the level of property-holders; to induce them to adopt an industrious, settled, and regular life[;] . . . to awaken a desire for culture and progress; to fit them to receive the offer of the Paraguayan Government and citizenship in that Republic; to make them useful members of a society."[34] Grubb's words presuppose that order derives from a Euro-modern ontology and its concomitant social-spatial relations, the co-joined processes of colonizing to spread Christianity and the reach of capitalism. An implicit racial logic is also evident in Grubb's words when he equates Anglican interventions as devised to raise Indigenous peoples to the "level of property-holders," simultaneously inferring a hierarchical stratification based on property and indexing liberal ideals of humanity with property rights. Actively working to disrupt existing Indigenous norms and spatial relations, Grubb argued that Enxet and Sanapaná lifeways were morally reprehensible and ontologically impossible.[35] The goal was thus to supplant Indigenous lifeways with two interwoven orders: the divine order of Christianity and capitalism's political economic order.

OF PROPERTY AND LABOR

The floodplains of the Bajo Chaco, where Grubb focused his work, are the territories of the Chanawatsan Enxet, Sanapaná, Angaité, and Maskoy peoples, whose lifeways were fluid like the braided streams that reach east to the Paraguay River, moving across the open floodplains with the interannual flood and drought cycle.[36] The new property-rights regime inscribed throughout the Chaco required a spatial order that limited Indigenous mobility so new landowners could run cattle and harvest timber. One Anglican missionary working in the area where the present-day Xákmok Kásek community is located wrote the following in the SAMS magazine in 1944: "The indian's hunting grounds are cut across by fences; the stealthy tread of the camouflaged ostrich hunter has given place to the galloping cowboy and bellowing cattle; the ring of the lumberman's axe is heard in the forest instead of the hunter's calls. . . . [T]he indians have had to give way to cattle."[37] This account, like that of Hunt's framing of the Chaco as a land in the making, shows that settler territorialization of the Chaco has been predicated on creating spaces for cattle life and demanding that Indigenous peoples abide by that political economic order.

Although the enclosure of the Chaco predated most of my interlocutors' lives, many elders recounted stories of how "closing" the land affected Enxet and Sanapaná lifeways. Sitting with Teofilo, an Enxet elder from Sawhoyamaxa whose eyes shine but reveal the cloudy spread of cataracts, once recounted to me, "They closed it with wire. Before that, the land used to be open. The Indigenous used to be free to go where they wanted before the estancias. When I was a boy people talked about how we would move here and there. We had different areas. But all of that changed." Like Teofilo, several of my interlocutors referenced times when the land used to be "open" and would often equate those times with greater freedom. "We used to live in the forest. All of this was forest. Nice forest!," Gladys explained, as we sat in front of the small home she had recently built on an old cattle pasture that members of Sawhoyamaxa had reoccupied. "But they grabbed up all our land, cut the trees, and put up fences. Now it's just cows, and the Indigenous have no place but by the highway." Teofilo's and Gladys's accounts resonate with Felipe's story in Rupture One. These stories collectively recount how enclosure limits Indigenous lifeways. The fences that closed the Chaco perform private property in land by ordering relations between Indigenous peoples, missionaries, and non-Indigenous landowners.

Such orderings and their performance are not inherent but must be learned, or coerced. To settle Enxet and Sanapaná life and create a labor force that would work on the privately owned cattle ranches of the Bajo Chaco, missionaries had to compel Indigenous peoples to abandon collective, mobile life. Imparting the ownership model of private property—that with "a unitary, solitary owner, appropriately engaged in self-regarding actions that concern him or herself alone and the things owned"—was imperative to achieving this end.[38] In his homage to Grubb, the Anglican reverend Hunt described the Mission's strategies to coerce Enxet and Sanapaná to adopt this sedentary life, namely, through the ownership of private property: "A more permanent type of house was to take the place of the grass huts so easily built and even more quickly demolished. The possession of tables and chairs, beds and kitchen utensils, together with cattle, was to be an offset against their old ways, causing them to settle down more quietly and to check their wandering instincts."[39] Notably, the ownership model the Anglican missionaries promoted was one based on goods, not land. Indigenous peoples were excluded from the ownership model in land, though they had to abide by its dictates or risk violent retaliation. Therefore, as Nichols suggests, "'making' property refers not to the creation of a new material object but to a new juridical and conceptual object—an abstraction—that serves to anchor relations, rights, and ultimately, power."[40] The new regime of property ownership spurred by the Chaco land sale and reinforced by material enclosures through fencing sought to anchor Enxet and Sanapaná peoples in place. Such dispossession in place operated alongside the education received at Anglican mission-stations to reinforce social relations based on thwarting Indigenous mobilities and instilling notions of private ownership predicated on sedentary life. Performing the ownership model of property in land is thus an act of writing the world, a geo-graphing that helped codify racial difference vis-à-vis unequal access regimes and the production of clear social hierarchies.[41]

The (re)ordering of life through the imposition of settler law and normative discourses equates private property with civilized life in ways that translate to racial hierarchies where landholders are viewed as superior to the dispossessed.[42] Here it is important to note that such hierarchies resonate with different forms of patronage. Historical accounts show that Christian missionaries were discursively framed as superior to indio "barbarians" without religion.[43] The missionaries controlled access to purported spiritual salvation through conversion to Christianity. Similarly, property-owning ranchers were framed as superior to the newly formed landless Indigenous peonage because they were seen to bring value to the Paraguayan state through agrarian production. The first Anglican missionaries thus sought to create an Indigenous peonage that was "civilized" enough but not so much that it would organize resistance. In this way, the racial hierarchy between settler patrón and Indigenous peon allowed a certain degree of alterity while demanding an embrace of select "modern" principles, namely, language, religion, and a new work ethic. In spatial and political economic terms, such hierarchies manifest as highly unequal land-tenure relations. Limited access to income outside of ranching created a structure of social, economic, and ecological relations that maintain Indigenous dispossession as a de facto source of labor for ranches. For decades, landholding elites across the Americas and in Paraguay's Chaco bought and sold land, with Indigenous peoples considered part of those sales, consequently establishing varied forms of exploitative labor relations from debt peonage to slavery. As lawyer and member of the Standing Rock Sioux Tribe Vine Deloria Jr. argues with regard to the United States, "Discovery negated the rights of the Indian tribes to sovereignty and equality among the nations of the world. It took away their title to their land and gave them the right only to sell."[44] The right to sell labor is predicated on the assumption that landholders and patrones pay for that labor. In the Latin American context, scholars have shown processes similar to those discussed by Deloria, but they also underscore the prevalence of debt peonage, slavery, and dispossession/alienation dynamics that fuel settler capitalism.[45]

FIGURE 3. Sanapaná men and their Anglican supervisor taking a break while digging a well near Campo Flores, circa 1939. Photographer unknown. Photograph courtesy of the Anglican Church of Paraguay.

DISPOSSESSION AS THE DISPOSITION

As the Anglican Mission in Paraguay grew, so did the cost of operating it, which required a concerted effort to generate local revenues. Grubb established the Paraguayan Chaco Indian Association in 1901 that operated an industrial school and ranch at Maroma that they called El Paso. Started with an initial investment from SAMS, El Paso grew to become a sizable ranch with 3,500 head of cattle by 1907 and later converted to a private company that British investors acquired. Stephen Kidd, an Anglican missionary turned anthropologist, argues, "The major significance of the venture [El Paso] was that it was the first cattle ranch to be established in the interior of the Chaco and served as an example to the other landowners of the economic possibilities."[46] Operations like El Paso also played an important role in Anglican efforts to teach Enxet the ways of property and labor in the settler economy. Grubb stated that his goal with this mission-station was to "enable the [Indigenous] people to obtain profitable work and industrial training, and thus to localize them at the mission-stations, where they could be more efficiently dealt with."[47]

I read Grubb's notion of relocating Indigenous peoples to missions with an eye toward efficiency through Michele Foucault's vision of government as "the right disposition of things, so as to lead to a convenient end."[48] Mobile populations without private property or interest in wage labor posed a challenge to the stable spatiality of property in land and ranchers' need for laborers.[49] Thus creating a way to efficiently organize Indigenous peoples on ranches and bring them into the settler political economy would lead to a convenient end for missionaries seeking souls to save, ranchers seeking laborers, and state officials seeking to territorialize the Chaco. Achieving this end thus required teaching Enxet and Sanapaná peoples Spanish or Guaraní, acculturating them to Paraguayan social norms, and creating a disciplined workforce. Consequently, the Anglicans created industrial schools at their ranches that they used to educate Enxet and Sanapaná in skills like logging, fence building, and running cattle, all of which supplied labor to the mission-stations and local ranches. Apparently, becoming a good Christian also meant adopting the cultural norms of the Paraguayan nation and capitalist class relations. For Grubb, the right disposition of things was both spatial and social. By creating a space for the Anglican Church, the Mission's actions reinforced the Chaco's newly formed private property rights regime that placed the Chaco within the Paraguayan state while simultaneously replacing Enxet and Sanapaná lifeways with a burgeoning settler society.

Here I want to note that the mission-stations had an impact on Enxet and Sanapaná territories in general but are directly related to the labor and land histories of the Yakye Axa, Sawhoyamaxa, and Xákmok Kásek communities. The El Paso ranch is significant because it was built on the site of *yakye axa*, the eponym of the Yakye Axa community. The Enxet who labored at El Paso for Anglican missionaries continued to live on the ranch after it was transferred to private ownership; many now live just outside its gates, where they continue to demand land restitution, which I explain in depth later. Missionaries also established "substations," smaller temporary outposts from which they expanded their influence. In 1939, missionaries established a substation at "Tlhagma Kasic" on land owned by the International Products Corporation (IPC), a site now known as Xákmok Kásek.[50] In accordance with agrarian reforms of 1940, IPC subdivided its landholdings and sold over 100,000 hectares to three former employees, who started Eaton & Cía, the company that built Estancia Salazar on the site of the Tlhagma Kasic Mission substation, where members of Xákmok Kásek would live and labor from the 1940s until 2008.[51] In addition to operating Mission ranches, SAMS missionaries often represented British financial interests in the region. Missionaries living near Loma Porã helped ranch operations by policing Indigenous peoples who did not abide by established property limits and also representing the company's interests in relation to other ranches in the region.[52] Loma Porã is the core ranch constructed on Sawhoyamaxa's traditional territories where many community members lived and labored since the Anglican arrival until the late 1990s, when they demanded the lands be returned to the community. To be clear, each of the mission-stations had a central living area and a church but "were essentially cattle ranches run for profit."[53] By 1949, the Anglican Mission in the Bajo Chaco derived the majority of its income from cattle ranching.[54]

The Anglican mission-stations' reliance on ranching for subsistence and income generation ultimately facilitated the spread of commercial cattle ranching by preparing a workforce and establishing the infrastructure to transport cattle from interior ranchlands east to the Paraguay River. To support their mission-stations, Anglicans developed the first road networks in the region, which settlers used to scout potential ranchlands and eventually run cattle to the Paraguay River for transport.[55] With the expansion of ranching, non-Indigenous settlers enclosed more lands, and more Indigenous peoples were drawn into the ranching economy as laborers on those ranches, often with close connections to the Anglican Church. In 1930, the missionary Andrew Pride reflected on the Mission's impact: "The Mission does not take credit for the present area of the Chaco now occupied, but for the lands occupied on the main road from the Riacho Negro to Nanawa and for lands occupied on either side of that road to an extent of at least ten leagues [i.e., the Anglican Zone] it can claim credit for their occupation. Years ago, the own-ers of the various estancias admitted that they were established in their positions owing to the presence of the Mission in the Chaco before them."[56] Such historical accounts demonstrate the importance of the Anglican Mission to the establish-ment of non-Mission ranches in the Bajo Chaco "Anglican Zone" from which they expanded farther into the Chaco.[57]

THE COLONIALITY OF SETTLER INFRASTRUCTURES

During its first forty years of work in the Bajo Chaco, the Anglican Mission in Paraguay created an infrastructure from which settler colonization of the region would follow, beginning with direct state territorialization. Although the Para-guayan state had laid legal claim to a vast territory in the Chaco following its inde-pendence from Spain in 1811 and sold much of those lands later that century, the border with Bolivia had never been formally established; each country claimed overlapping parts of the Chaco. With rumors of vast petroleum deposits spurred by competing oil companies, Standard Oil working in Bolivia and Royal Dutch Shell in Paraguay, both countries began building forts deep in the Chaco to estab-lish their land borders and claim the resources therein.[58] A brutal war ensued, lasting from 1932 to 1935. Paraguay's victory was due in large part to the exten-sive infrastructure built by Anglican missionaries, the expanding tannin industry established farther north on the Paraguay River, and the role of Indigenous scouts whose deep knowledge of the region aided Paraguayan troops.[59] By the start of the Chaco War, Anglicans had built over 700 kilometers of cart tracks and the north-ern tannin industry over 500 kilometers of small-gauge railroads that the military relied on for troop movements and resupply lines during the fighting.[60] The roads and buildings constructed to facilitate the spread of Christianity and cattle capi-talism thus laid the groundwork for the Paraguayan state to mobilize troops and assert a direct physical presence in the region. Although the war was fought north of Enxet and Sanapaná territories, the supply lines carrying goods and soldiers to the front lines traversed their territories and several mission-stations were used as field hospitals.[61]

One prominent cattle rancher whose family operated the largest ranch in the Bajo Chaco from the 1930s through the 1960s, Estancia Salazar, shared with me some accounts about helping Paraguayan soldiers during the war.

> During the Chaco War there was a place called Nanawa that was established next to an English [Anglican] mission.... And the road from Nanawa [that] goes toward the English mission was a road that my grandfather had established. During the battle of Nanawa, the Bolivians had cut the road. So they [the Paraguayan troops] discovered my grandfather's trail that brought them from Nanawa to Fortín Río Verde and there from Salazar to Isla Po'i. [Paraguayan] Coronel Estigarribia ordered that they found a *fortin* [fort] halfway between Salazar and Isla Po'i and another fortin at Salazar because if Nanawa fell they were aware that the aim of the Bolivians was to cut off communications at Isla Po'i.... They established a hospital in Salazar and a communications center in Salazar. My grandfather turned in his house to the fort and moved to where the center for Salazar is now.[62]

He continued to explain how his grandfather and father led convoys of Paraguayan troops to key sites near the front lines. At the close of the war, Paraguay withdrew most of its troops and again relied on the missionaries and settler colonists who remained to act as state surrogates whose actions served to advance new state policies of assimilation.[63]

The enduring influence of the Anglican Mission on patrón-Indigenous labor relations is evident in its more recent efforts to incorporate Enxet and Sanapaná within the ranching economy. Paraguay's 1944 Agrarian Statute was intended to break up large-scale "unproductive" landholdings in the Chaco by forcing landowners to either convert their properties to direct production or subdivide and sell them. The move further incentivized enclosing the Chaco by spurring a wave of smaller ranching operations that arrived in the wake of the Anglican Mission. With increasing land enclosure, the prospects for life outside of what became a near-total ranching system diminished, effectively forcing more Enxet and Sanapaná onto ranches for subsistence.[64] Kidd recorded the impacts of the land enclosures: "By the 1950s the landowners' control of Enxet territory was total, and the Enxet themselves had been almost entirely deprived of their freedom. They could only reside where they were given permission to by the owner of the land and were therefore restricted to villages next door to the Paraguayan ranch settlements. Economically, they were completely dependent on the will of the landowners who severely restricted their freedom of movement and frequently denied them permission to hunt, gather, fish, garden, or keep livestock."[65] In other cases, according to expert witness testimony in the IACHR judgment on the Xákmok Kásek land claim, English and US ranch owners "ordered the Indigenous into different

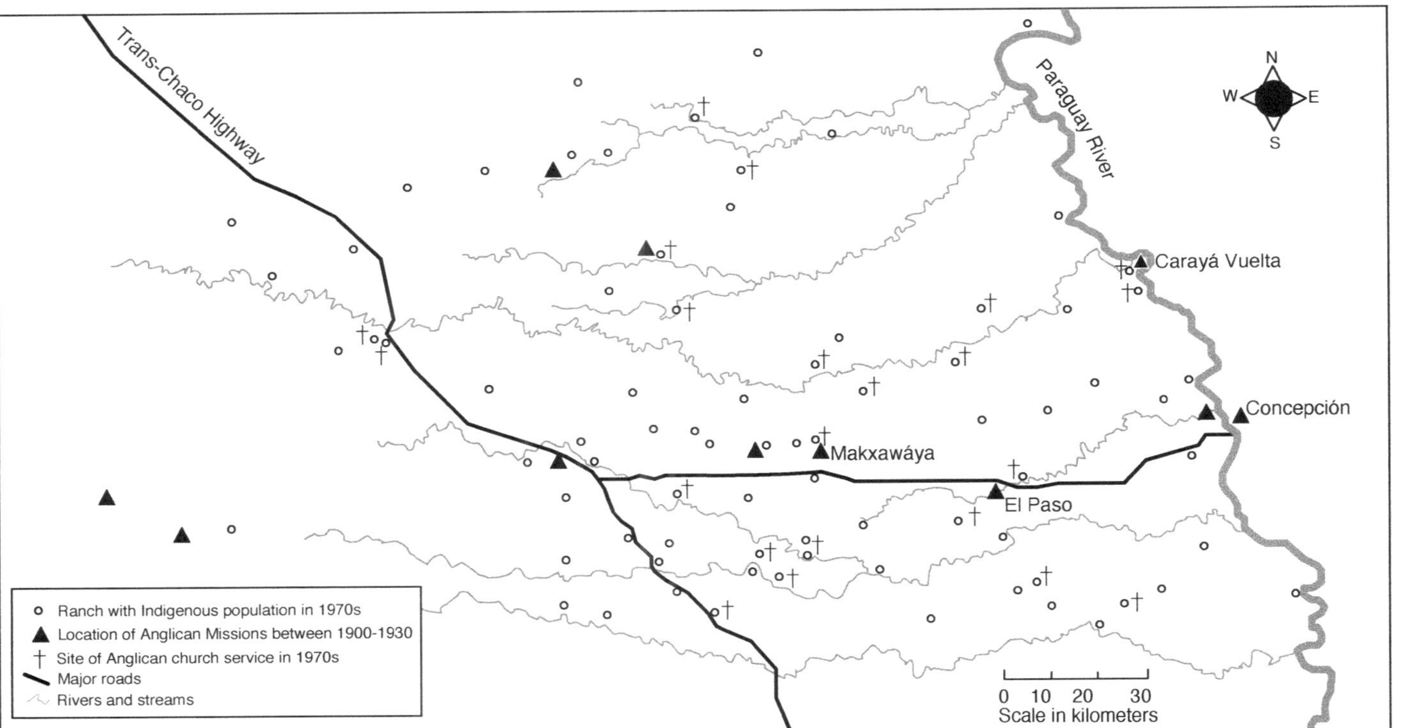

MAP 2. The approximate location of all Anglican missions in Bajo Chaco, 1900–1930, and ranches with Indigenous populations, 1978. Information based on an NGO census documenting 3,616 Indigenous peoples living on seventy-six cattle ranches. The 1981 national census recorded 5,048 Indigenous people in the same area. Map adapted from Powell 2007.

villages in the area to integrate and go live near the core of the ranch in order to have more control" over the population.[66]

Such orders recall the "efficient" disposition of Enxet and Sanapaná peoples onto the Anglican industrial schools and ranching mission-stations like El Paso that played a central role in facilitating this geography of dispossession. Written in celebration of the hundredth anniversary of the Anglican Mission in Paraguay, the historian David R. Powell's homage to the Mission's work clearly shows the indelible mark it left on ranching. Some twenty-three ranches either housed Anglican pastors or held formal church services through the 1970s, all of which also enclosed Indigenous communities that served as the ranch's labor force.[67] By the mid-twentieth century, the Mission's "thin edge of the wedge" strategy had made the Bajo Chaco a space of settler cattle ranching reliant on Indigenous labor. In 1991, over 93 percent of Enxet lands were enclosed by private ranches of more than 1,000 hectares in size.[68] Today, the President Hayes administrative department, where the Anglican missionaries worked, is home to the largest concentration of cattle in all of Paraguay and the longest continuing ranching operations in the Chaco.

THE INHERITANCE

The Mission adopted a new approach in the 1980s that attempted to reconcile the adverse effects of land dispossession and labor exploitation on Indigenous well-being produced by the cattle economy. State and mission policy at the time promoted assimilation, and the church sought to achieve this by enabling Enxet and Sanapaná to become landholding agriculturalists. La Herencia (The Inheritance) resettlement initiative marked the culminating Anglican assimilation project. The Mission purchased nearly 45,000 hectares of land through La Herencia to establish three communities of "Indigenous colonists" who would adopt the agrarian production systems of Paraguayan campesinos and the protestant morals of Anglican missionaries.[69] Two primary goals listed in the original La Herencia project proposal are to ensure that the Indigenous colonists first "form settled, ordered and fully functioning village communities" and to ensure that they "understand the values of [their] country."[70] The project proposal is testimony to the assimilationist legacies of the church that helped shape social relations of Indigenous peonage. La Herencia did succeed in securing the few titled Indigenous lands at the time that became important spaces for Enxet, Sanapaná, and Angaité peoples to establish independent communities. However, the vision of creating self-sufficient agrarian communities of Indigenous colonists never came to fruition. For one, farming in the Bajo Chaco is hard. The region is a large alluvial floodplain highly influenced by seasonal rainfall that results in a cycle of flood and drought that accentuates the effects of the clayey soil's high salinity content. When summer rains arrive, much of the area quickly floods, turning into a vast swampland. For these reasons, large-scale agriculture has never taken root in the Bajo Chaco, yet cattle production has.[71] The three Indigenous communities created by La Herencia served less as self-sufficient agricultural settlements and more as de facto labor camps for local ranches.[72]

Several Enxet and Sanapaná interlocutors recounted to me memories of living and laboring on ranches, often evoking the sentiment that ranchers valued their lives less than those of settlers. Ignacia, a Sanapaná woman from Xákmok Kásek whose family had lived for decades on Estancia Salazar, minced no words when she spoke of times on the ranch:[73] "We had to hunt because there was no money. They did not give us money. They made the people work but didn't pay. They would give very little, rice, dried corn, toasted mandioca flour, corn meal, and bad cooking fat." Recalling each item, she frowned. "That is what they [ranch owners and staff] gave then. One old peach can full per person. That's it. In a little bag. That's what you got for eight days. And for those eight days you did not go to the ranch store. No! You had to use the food well for eight days. You had to go and look for fish to feed your family. That was the only way." Looking across her yard toward one of her sons who was listening to music on a small radio, she commented, "Now people have more options to work and get money. Back then, no. The Indigenous struggled there. There was no money. You would exchange anything you could to get money. The Indigenous suffered. They gave so little food, so little meat. They gave more to the [non-Indigenous] Paraguayans who worked there. But the Indigenous, no." Pointing to her small house, she said, "There was no tin roof, only houses with grass roofs. It was cold, cold. There were bugs. That's how we lived. The Paraguayans lived well in nice houses. But the Indigenous, no. We were, I don't know, forty maybe sixty families, all crammed into four hectares." Ignacia evokes common themes that many of my interlocutors revisited in their stories of life on ranches. Indigenous peoples could live on ranches but were paid almost nothing for labor provided, instead given insufficient food staples that required reliance on hunting and fishing—two practices that were later prohibited by the owners of Estancia Salazar and the other ranches where members of Yakye Axa and Sawhoyamaxa lived. Moreover, the few non-Indigenous Paraguayans who worked on the ranches were always reported to have better living conditions, from houses and pay to food.

Serafin López recalled the following story one afternoon as he, his wife, Ramona, and I drank tereré while his daughters listened from the shade of their home. "Many people who worked did not earn what they deserved," he stated, referring to the times working for the ranch built on his community's ancestral territory. "In terms of food, very little. I worked all the time. In the morning, at six, you were at the office waiting for orders." Holding up his pointer finger, "If you were late they would forgive you one time. If you did it again, you would no longer have work. They'd give it to someone else. They never paid what you deserved." Gesturing as if to put something in his mouth: "Only that," Ramona chuckled. "They only gave workers a little food. You know the old cans for conserved meat? They filled that with yerba, sugar, and toasted yucca flower. That was all they got for one day. That was their food." Serafin jumped back in. "You would go out to cut down *karanda'y* [palm trees], three and a half meters long with an ax," he said. "You'd go far, really far. Then you'd load it onto a trailer. There were two trailers. Sixty-five [palms] fit on a trailer so you had to load 130. Sometimes you'd go in a group of four, each one cutting twenty-five to thirty karanda'y. Cut, measure, cut, then load by hand." With that he shook his head. "The Paraguayans didn't do anything. They would sit, drink tereré, or look around, but do nothing. We would do the work and load the trailers. They just drove. You'd return around 2:30 and unload. If you were lucky there'd be food. If not, the ranch store. We'd get a little can of meat or maybe some buns and sugar. If not, there was nothing. It was hard."

Ranching patrones needed Indigenous labor. They still do. In this regard, Indigenous peoples have become a central component in the (re)production of settler colonialism vis-à-vis infrastructure. If settler colonialism is a structure of social, spatial, and political economic relations, not merely an event that has passed, as Wolfe's influential formulation suggests, I argue that it is imperative to also query the infrastructures that allow such oppressive systems to persist.[74] Infrastructure can be understood empirically as the "things" that enable system function but so can the labor and life taken from peoples coerced to build the material things so often considered infrastructure—like the fences, corrals, stock ponds, pastures, roads, and buildings that enable ranching to work. Thus, through decades of resettlement and reeducation projects, Anglican missionaries created both the material infrastructures from which settler colonialism has expanded in the Chaco and the labor force that has always been central to that project but rendered invisible by it.[75] The doubling of Enxet and Sanapaná life, as both the target of salvation and a necessary labor force, reveals how extractive relationships shape everyday life in ways through which "Indigenous bodies (violated, neglected, annihilated) become the raw material for the making of the settler subject and the settler state," as Razack powerfully argues.[76] Eulalio, a spiritual leader from Xákmok Kásek, once described this process to me in plain terms: "The ranchers just used up the Indigenous. They worked us hard. . . . If you died, you died." I revisit conversations with Eulalio in detail in the next chapter but highlight his thoughts here because it is important to flag that I am not using infrastructure metaphorically. The violence of assimilation initiated by the missionary efforts, replicated on many ranches and later adopted as state policy, is a hallmark of the eliminatory logics that animate structures of settlement.

The inheritance left to Enxet and Sanapaná peoples by the Anglicans' missionary work, its relationship to the expansion of ranching, and its role in Indigenous dispossession shapes but does not determine the arc of Enxet and Sanapaná land struggles. Resettlement of Indigenous peoples and exploitation of their labor on mission-stations was a targeted project that resulted in what the Mission and the state saw as the "right" disposition of people in place. By all means, the project intended to assimilate by creating a self-governing labor force that would meet the needs of the burgeoning ranching economy. In this context, "making" the Chaco as a site for ranching was always a racial project, one mediated by private property in land coded as white space. Indigenous peoples were long excluded from that system of ownership only to be included as laborers who could not own land. Although assimilationist policies intended to change the issue of landownership, the dialectic relation of simultaneous inclusion and exclusion resonates with conditions of social, geographic, and legal liminality that permeate Enxet and Sanapaná relations with settlers to the present.

SETTLER FRONTIERS AS RACIAL GEOGRAPHIES

Bringing Indigenous labor to the fore of analysis instead of dwelling solely on the way land was taken focuses attention on how racial capitalism is woven into the social fabric of settler colonialism and its spatial expression. Such geographies are inextricably tied to the production of new racial orders mediated through the distribution of private property that upholds settler colonial regimes and their concomitant violence. Though this is not a story of their choosing, Enxet and Sanapaná have been active agents whose role has long been overshadowed. It is a role that many of my Enxet and Sanapaná interlocutors view in dramatically different ways, from a source of oppression to one of pride. Charting a history of violent dispossessions that began with the Anglican Mission helps reveal the processes and patterns of social-spatial relations that produced the racial geographies from which my Enxet and Sanapaná interlocutors have endured and mobilized their resistance.[77]

There are important distinctions that shape the structure and effects of settler colonialism in different geographies. Indigenous peoples in Paraguay, Argentina, and Bolivia were frequently dispossessed of land *and* forced to work that land for white settlers through the auspices of Christian missionary efforts.[78] Indeed, Speed argues that "labor regimes (*encomienda, repartamiento, hacienda*) were often the very mechanisms that dispossessed Indigenous peoples of their lands, forcing them to labor in extractive undertakings on the land that had been taken from them."[79] On the other hand, King argues for a focus on conquest instead of settler colonialism in Latin America, suggesting that white settler colonial studies rely too much on land, thereby decentering Indigenous genocide and erasing the violence of settler colonialism.[80] Keeping violence central is imperative. I employ settler colonialism as an analytic here due to the specific dynamics at play in the Bajo Chaco, a region that was not conquered through early Spanish or Portuguese efforts but one that was slowly colonized by settler ranchers, a process Indigenous peoples of the region have always resisted.

Chaqueño ranchers need(ed) laborers, and many prefer(red) cheap, readily replicable labor, not unlike Maya peons working for ladino patrones on Guatemalan coffee plantations or *jornaleros* picking cotton in Peruvian fields.[81] Indigeneity, in Paraguay's Chaco, and beyond, is thus often inextricably linked to histories of emplaced and embodied labor relations.[82] Those relations are embodied in the settler patrón–Indigenous peon dynamic that has reordered life and land in the Bajo Chaco. The Anglican missionary presence in the Bajo Chaco is minimal today, but the social and spatial relations that the Anglican assimilation strategies produced are the norm in a region where cattle ranching dominates land and economy. It is imperative to understand how labor regimes imbricated with, and created by, settler territoriality in the service of (re)producing racial geographies shape the present and future politics of Enxet and Sanapaná struggles, to which I now turn.

Boundaries

It is some 300 meters to the western shore where the Chaco "begins" from where we stood on the Paraguay River's eastern bank. I surveyed the river's expanse as rafts of plants the size of small barges drifted by, carrying with them egrets whose white feathers popped from the background of greens and browns. Concepción has long been a primary port for travelers of all sorts to stock up and depart on trips to northern Paraguay. The small ramp where we put our fifteen-foot aluminum outboard boat in the water lies in the shadow of the decaying, abandoned Picis resort, just barely a kilometer from the city's humble Anglican church, San Pablo. Celso, Juan, and I waited with the boat by the river's edge as Diego and Santiago went to park their truck before we departed on the trip north to Kelyenmagategma.[1] Looking north to the main port a couple hundred meters upriver, I watched men scurrying over a wooden plank perilously balanced 5 meters over the water between the boat and the shore. It bounced as they carried bags and boxes of cargo onto the Aquidaban riverboat freighter, which is also the primary water taxi for all destinations north. The port of Concepción is where the first Anglican missionaries embarked on the 45-kilometer trip upstream to Carayá Vuelta, where they first established a presence in the Chaco. Our trip would trace their route, though with different outcomes in mind.

Kelyenmagategma is a place of many names and many stories. Located where the Paraguay River makes a seemingly impossible turn that wraps more than ninety degrees around a resistant peninsula of low-lying earth, river travelers have long called the site Carayá Vuelta, howler monkey bend. When Anglicans arrived in the waning years of the nineteenth century, Carayá Vuelta was home to the small riverside ranching outpost of Puerto Colón. The fact that British Anglicans helped spur settler colonization of Paraguay's Bajo Chaco from a place that bears the Spanish surname of the most infamous colonizer in the Americas, Christopher Columbus, illuminates contrapuntal temporalities of colonialism that continue to shape the present. While our boat plied the sediment-laden waters and struggled against the current, Celso told me, "In our language, Kelyenmagategma means 'the place where the roofs shine.'" As with many Enxet community names, this is not a metaphor but a literal geo-graphing whereby place-names are born from descriptions of relations: Yakye Axa is the site of a palm island; Sawhoyamaxa is a particular grove of palms; and Xákmok Kásek is the place of many small parrots. Unlike toponyms that reference human-environment relations, Kelyenmagategma bears the traces of racial geographies forged through colonization. The name of the community derives from the site where the original Puerto Colón staff used tin roofs to adorn their buildings, roofs that shine in the sun. Celso described how he had learned that his people came to know the location by that name and had not used another for generations.

The histories that Enxet and Sanapaná peoples recount are not buried under the geological strata of time passed or erased by the limited spaces afforded Indigenous peoples through the politics of recognition. Instead, such histories are exposed in place-names like Kelyenmagategma, as if the seasonal floods that drive the constant rise and fall of the Paraguay River and inundate the Bajo Chaco carry away the possibility of burying the past. As I would learn on our trip to "walk the line" in the place where the roofs shine, the past is present in the lives of those who maintain their connections with the land and in the stories that they tell.[2] Indeed, historical violence that gives places new meaning shapes but does not determine the present struggles of Indigenous peoples who have recovered lands, yet confront the complex terrain of dispossession woven into the fabric of settler colonialism.

The trip to Kelyenmagategma was four years in the making. Unlike the other Enxet and Sanapaná communities where I conducted research for this book, Kelyenmagategma's case did not advance to the IACHR but reached a friendly settlement in 2011 mediated by the Inter-American Commission of Human Rights. Akin to Yakye Axa, Sawhoyamaxa, and Xákmok Kásek, the Kelyenmagategma community endured land dispossession by ranchers and was employed to work the ranches that enclosed their lands. They were also denied due process by the Paraguayan state to effectively resolve a long-standing demand for land restitution in accordance with state law. The Inter-American Commission determined such issues amounted to human rights violations but mediated a settlement whereby the owners of El Algarrobal company who had purchased Puerto Colón sold 8,748 hectares to INDI to satisfy the community's demand for restitution of its ancestral territories. Yet state officials had not conducted an in situ survey to establish the physical location of the property lines. The interceding years brought tense relations between two neighbors who disputed where Colón ends and Kelyenmagategma begins. Our trip was intended to remedy the situation by verifying the new property line.

After two hours on the water, Santiago steered our boat left, toward the western bank of the river. Excised into the land, the river often flows more than a meter below its surface. As we approached the shore, a handful of small, gray, palmwood homes with tin roofs came into sight, along with a herd of some twenty burros that grazed a grass expanse between the houses and an old retiro adorned with a large wraparound porch and a tarnished, rust-spotted tin roof. Constructed under the terms of the Inter-American Commission settlement, a large health post encircled by a short cyclone fence stood near the retiro with a sign at the peak of the roof that announced we had arrived at Carayá Vuelta, but it notably failed to name Kelyenmagategma. The boat slid onto the short, muddy bank, and we offloaded our things, then walked to the large retiro where Celso and his family now live. Sitting on the veranda of the old building, we planned the trip to the southern property line on the following day, as Celso's young son served us tereré.[3]

Early the next morning, we awoke to the sound of burros stomping the ground as they protested the saddles being put on them. As the floodwaters had not fully receded this year, Celso assured us the burros would make the trip easier. After a breakfast of *cocido, coquitos,* and tortillas, we divvied up the burros, loaded our gear, and set forth. Though just about 7 kilometers, the trip took hours. Straining under our weight as they navigated knee-high water and deep mud, the burros labored along a tight trail woven through the forest thicket. Eventually, the forest opened from the thorny undergrowth to a sparse palm forest and grass landscape that has come to define much of the Bajo Chaco ranching region. We made our way to a small clearing near a creek where we set up our camp. Though it was still before noon, Diego wanted to rest and eat lunch before beginning work. The seven members of Kelyenmagategma who guided Diego and Juan to the disputed boundary line were disappointed. After waiting so long for a surveyor to arrive, the last thing anyone wanted was to wait longer. Nevertheless, we all sat and ate.

It was already afternoon when Diego pulled out his reference map and GPS to begin verifying the location of the southern property line. Diego and Juan consulted with Mario to ascertain his understanding of the property limits, then used the GPS to verify the state-recognized limits, which they then marked by cutting blazes into trees. The rest of the crew and I followed with machetes, axes, a chainsaw, and shovels to clear brush and then cut and place fence posts. Despite the hard work, stifling heat, and pouring sweat, people laughed as each new post was placed and the line we geo-graphed inscribed a new story onto the land. After three hours, we had marked about 250 meters of the property line. But the work slowed when we noticed Diego, Juan, and Mario talking in a group with looks of frustration on their faces. One by one, crew members stopped working and walked over to see what the problem was. Our trajectory intersected a small but significant creek that meanders along the length of the southern property line and was swollen by seasonal rains. "We're done. The water in the creek is deep, and there is no way to cross without getting wet," Diego proclaimed. With a silent look of exhaustion and exasperation, Mario surveyed the waters and one of our crew members started to walk down the steep bank to investigate. But to no avail. Juan protested, "I only have one pair of shoes. If we go in, they will be wet for the rest of the days we are here. I think we should wait until it is dry to finish." Clearly displeased but not willing to push a confrontation with the INDI officials too far, a few men walked back to continue working on the last post they had set, muttering

FIGURE 4. Diego (right) and part of the Kelyenmagategma work crew talking after work was halted for the day. Note that the man second from the left is leaning against one of the newly crafted property line markers.

under their breath as they went. But Diego had made up his mind. We went back and sat around camp for the rest of the day.

As night fell, we lit several small fires to keep the clouds of mosquitoes and horseflies away from the burros. Although alcohol is prohibited in Kelyenmagategma, Diego and Juan had a small bottle of caña that they nursed by their own fire, talking loudly through the dark night. Mario and I stood by another fire. He was curious to know about Indigenous rights in the United States and how I had come to learn Guaraní. We talked for a long time, as he stared into the fire, his eyes surveying the flames. At one point, Mario changed topics and began to share stories of life at Puerto Colón, when the community was enclosed on the ranch property. The land known as Puerto Colón had changed hands several times since the Anglican arrival. In 2002, El Algarrobal took control. "The Enxet have almost always lived on the ranch and worked for the patrones. We lived on the ranch for a very long time until it got too bad with Algarrobal," Mario explained. He described the systematic ways that El Algarrobal administrators, staff, and police terrorized the community over several years. They burned the school to the ground. They regularly stole the community's burros. They armed themselves and stalked community members when they went to hunt or fish. They falsely accused community members of stealing cattle and had them arrested. Kelyenmagategma leaders denounced these violent acts by filing formal legal complaints with the aid of Tierraviva. At every turn, state officials neglected to adjudicate the claims or hold El Algarrobo staff accountable.

The violence took a new form when ranch administrators attacked the community under the supervision of Paraguayan police in 2003 and 2004, in an attempt to force the Kelyenmagategma community to abandon its claim for land restitution, initially filed in 2000. The Inter-American Commission describes the following key events.

> There were two critical moments in the pattern of violence against members of the Community in less than one year. The first took place on August 30, 2003, the date the indigenous people were expelled from their settlement by police, armed civilians, and two prosecutors, without a judicial order for eviction or search. The second was recorded on August 29, 2004, when employees of the El Algarrobal S.A. company assaulted Community members. They threw petards at dwellings and fired gunshots to again evict them violently from their settlement, forcing them to disperse and take refuge in the mountains.[4]

Still looking at the fire, Mario described these events in great detail. No one was given much time to evacuate their homes, and they were not allowed to return to gather their belongings before the ranch staff set fire to their houses. The ranchers shot into the air and at the houses to scare people. Community members scattered, hiding in the forest for fear that the ranchers would turn the guns on them. The event happened one year after police, accompanied by the ranchers, illegally evicted the community from their homes on the ranch. During that event, people fled eight kilometers to a site near the retiro where Celso now lives, where they hid on the banks of the Paraguay River for several days. An elderly woman died, and many children fell ill. Mario lamented, "They destroyed everything we had. We are poor people. There is no work out here. It takes a long time to get the money to buy things. It was a long time ago, but most of us have not been able to replace the things that we lost." Even though Kelyenmagategma now has land rights, it remains a neighbor of Puerto Colón. Mario said, "Many of us are still afraid to go out in the forest alone. The people from Colón have no shame. They could do anything. We want this property line, so they know where our land begins." We did not map the boundary the following day. Instead, on Diego's instructions, we split into two teams to investigate other parts of the property line, but we were foiled again by the floodwaters.

The boundaries between Kelyenmagategma and Puerto Colón surpass any cartographic or juridical imaginary of property in land. They are boundaries inherent to the fraught politics of recognition, defined not by fences but by juridical delays that harken to the legal liminality and geographies of power that result from patrón-Indigenous relations. Such boundaries reveal how patronage operates through the subtle but powerful outcomes of bureaucratic procedures, whereas state officials and institutions hold power over other citizens by either withholding or granting access to vital services or resources. Diego, Juan, Santiago, and I left early the next day. Kelyenmagategma would have to wait for the waters to recede before we could attempt to resolve any further questions about the boundaries that lie between their lands and those of Puerto Colón.

CHAPTER 2

Not-Quite-Neoliberal Multiculturalism

Mario's stories about Kelyenmagategma underscore the co-joined forces of Indigenous labor appropriation, land dispossession, and state recalcitrance that Enxet and Sanapaná struggles work to unsettle. His memories at Puerto Colón are one layer in a sedimented history of environmental violence that is not buried in the past but evident in the present.[1] The violence is both spectacular and mundane, though common to Indigenous land struggles across the country.[2] It is a violence conditioned by long histories of land enclosure, the political economy of agrarian production, and their relation to contemporary politics of recognition. That Kelyenmagategma community members have waited years for a state surveyor to officiate the boundary is a persistent form of neglect that defines state-Indigenous relations. Neglect reproduces social hierarchies wrought during generations of racial capitalism that expose the durable logics of settler colonial dispossession and control over access to resources. On Enxet and Sanapaná territories, such hierarchies were established through long-standing patrón-peon relations and reiterated through forms of political patronage that continually concentrated wealth and power among landed elites. Instead of rectifying past wrongs or even merely setting the stage for a more equitable future, the politics of recognition is tacitly used to ensure Indigenous dispossession by ensnaring Indigenous peoples in bureaucratic processes that produce new forms of violence.

Building from a history of settler colonization on Enxet and Sanapaná territories charted in chapter 1, here I pivot to tell a story about the politics of multicultural recognition in Paraguay by examining entwined labor and land rights struggles. I use the term "multiculturalism" to discuss state-led initiatives consisting of specific laws and policies intended to govern Indigenous and Afro-descendant populations through rights based on the recognition of ethnic or cultural difference from the non-Indigenous settler society.[3] My trip to Kelyenmagategma occurred well after the community's struggle for legal recognition and land restitution had commenced. I chose to begin with that episode because it highlights a common thread that weaves through the disparate struggles that this book grapples with: recognition comes without guarantees. Despite a legal framework that guarantees specific rights for Indigenous peoples, state recognition, and favorable rulings from the IACHR that bolster Indigenous rights, the Kelyenmagategma, Yakye Axa, Sawhoyamaxa, and Xákmok Kásek communities have struggled for decades to ensure those rights in practice. Whereas recognition promised to bring resolution to generations of struggle, it has created spaces and situations that exacerbate environmental violence against Enxet and Sanapaná peoples. This is a violence that values the lives of animals raised for slaughter that roam on Enxet and Sanapaná territories more than the peoples removed from those territories to whom the Paraguayan constitution and complementary multicultural policy guarantee rights. While the chapter grapples with the emergence of rights-based claims, it also challenges framing such dynamics as inherently neoliberal.

Given the particular confluence of Latin America's multicultural turn, the broad rollout of neoliberal reforms across the region, and the limited political opening that conjuncture created for Indigenous and Afro-descendant peoples, scholars such as Charles Hale have advanced "neoliberal multiculturalism" as a central analytical framework to evaluate contemporary Indigenous-state relations in Latin America.[4] Yet I fear that too tight a focus on the contemporary conjuncture occludes other forms of power with deeper historical roots that continue to shape systemic inequality. What of the spaces, situations, and struggles that are not-quite-neoliberal? The contours of Enxet and Sanapaná struggles impel me to shift focus from neoliberalism to reiterated forms of discrimination that emanate from older forms of racial capitalism. The effects of the politics of recognition that Enxet and Sanapaná navigate cannot be reduced to neoliberalism.

Much scholarship on neoliberal multiculturalism argues that states recognize Indigenous rights to co-opt Indigenous struggles and thereby advance the aims of the state. In such a calculus, recognition is largely symbolic and does not change colonial relations or resource redistribution but does extend new regimes of governance over previously "unruly" populations or "empty spaces."[5] However, in the context of the Bajo Chaco, state policies often associated with multicultural recognition, particularly regarding Indigenous land rights, exhibit a different character. The Paraguayan state is not co-opting Enxet and Sanapaná struggles through recognition but recasting dispossession in a different light by creating an edifice of care and inclusion.[6] Without doubt, neoliberal reforms and practices always intersect with and are conditioned by the geographic specificities of colonial power relations and existing forms of racial capitalism where reforms are implemented. Therefore, I am not suggesting that analysts should privilege attention to coloniality and racial capitalism over neoliberalism per se. But the shortcomings of multicultural policy here are due more to the *longue durée* of the racial capitalism that conditions Indigenous-settler relations than to recent neoliberal policy. Neoliberalism amplifies existing forms of racialization discrimination but does not supplant them.[7]

Attending to the politics of recognition in authoritarian and post-democratic contexts like those of Paraguay invites a rethinking of long-standing academic debates about the confluence of neoliberal political economic reforms and Indigenous political mobilization. Instead of being predominantly conditioned by neoliberalism, the politics of recognition in Paraguay stem from long histories of exploiting Indigenous labor. Such politics cannot be extricated from everyday or extraordinary forms of violence that maintain Indigenous dispossessions or the enduring promise of multicultural rights, even in light of the vast limitations of rights-based claims. For several Enxet and Sanapaná community leaders, building alliances with non-Indigenous indigenistas represented a critical conjuncture when the knowledge of rights—first for better working conditions, then eventually for land, and finally as humans—changed the politics of the possible and incited a new field of struggle that continues to the present.

"WE WORKED HARD"

In the wake of Anglican missionary work, many Bajo Chaco ranchers granted Indigenous peoples who lived on their ranches the right to hunt, fish, gather firewood, and tend subsistence gardens, suggesting that was compensation for their labor or ability to live within the private properties. One rancher with English and US heritage whose family has lived in the Bajo Chaco since the early 1900s, described the situation to me: "We let the indians live on our land. We had no problem with them. My father made the arrangement very clear. You could hunt and fish and set up your little home in a defined area. If you worked for us, you could still do those things but you would also earn a little food and some clothes. But back then there was no need for money. The indians didn't want money. So, we just let them be."[8] Some older Enxet men, like Venancio Flores, recalled their relations with ranching patrones differently: "When I lived on the estancia, I did all kinds of work. I did everything. The patrón never paid me what corresponded. We all lived on the estancia. My complete family. They treated us badly when we lived there back then. There was very little food and we were all very hungry. Then when we claimed land and we still wanted to hunt and go fish, that is when they made us leave."[9]

In practice, the ability to hunt or fish on ranchlands was contingent on the predilections of a particular patrón, though many ranches operated small stores that sold basic provisions, often locking people into de facto forms of debt peonage. The specific labor arrangements often involved employing Indigenous peoples without a fixed contractual arrangement, paying less than minimum wage per day of labor, and keeping payment until the end of the year, at which time patrones would first deduct the cost of a year's worth of food and clothing from the total amount.[10] Reporting from indigenista NGOs in the 1990s suggests that such labor arrangements signified that "they did not receive more than a 'salary' that could even reach eight dollars per year."[11] Renshaw's longitudinal study of Indigenous peoples and social-economic relations in the Paraguayan Chaco provides a comprehensive analysis of general trends in labor relations on cattle ranches of the region. Attentive to the extent of settler land control and cattle capitalism, he observed, "Where the Indians lack any rights to land, they are completely dependent on the landowner. The dependence is further intensified through other mechanisms, such as payment in kind or credit, which oblige the Indians to purchase all necessities from their employer."[12] Chase-Sardi, Brun, and Enciso provide a window into common patrón-Indigenous labor relations on Chaco ranches through the early 1990s.

> We confirm that groups of four or five indian peons were assigned to one lot of forests, around nine hectares, with the job to cut it all down. The land is bad and forest thorny. They gave them food but no pay [during the work]. This was given at the end, when the patrón or capataz accepted the deforestation, with land that was totally cleaned. This [the pay] consisted of one pair of pants, one shirt, one pair of socks, and one pair of basic shoes to each person. This was all the payment the four or five indians would receive for their hard work, with only food given during eight or nine months. And this is a good example of what happened in all the ranches of the region.[13]

Enxet and Sanapaná interlocutors I interviewed across many communities in the Bajo Chaco regularly reported similar experiences. Felipe Inter of Xákmok Kásek would often tell me about the payment scheme on Estancia Salazar. He once chuckled, as if almost in disbelief, "Early in the morning you went to see the capataz at one of the main buildings." He looked at his hands and made the shape of a small square with his forefingers and thumbs as if to hold something. "One can of *vaka'i* [ground beef, like spam]." He then looked at me with his aged right hand extended palm up, yet closed gently in the shape of a ball. "One handful of dusty yerba. Bad and bitter." With his left hand, he then formed another ball. "One handful of yucca flour." Dropping his hands to his lap, his gaze turned westward as if looking toward the old ranch. "That was all they gave us for the day. We would put it in a bag and leave to go do our work. We worked hard. . . . There was no other work because it was all ranches."[14] In addition to commenting on their material compensation, many of my interlocutors underscored the physical toll that years of hard labor exacted on the body. Anuncio Gómez, one of the few elders still living in Yakye Axa, shared memories with me as we sat on the side of a highway. His warm voice was frail with age and resonated in the unique tone of someone talking with no teeth. "When I was young, I didn't stay still. I came here from way over there in the hinterlands of [Estancia] Alegria. Over there," he said, waving his arm to the northeast. "Then I grew. Then I became a young man. And then I started to work. Horseback, horseback." He turned his head to the side and raised his eyebrows before grimacing and rubbing the small of his back. "That's the reason why I feel this. I feel everything. I feel everything. I am old. I lived in many places

FIGURE 5. Enxet laborers working on Estancia Loma Porã circa 1990, setting fence posts and preparing to string wire fencing. Photographer unknown. Photo courtesy of Mirta Ayala.

working: horseback, fences, cleaning land. There wasn't anything I couldn't do. And now, I can't do much of anything. That is how I lived."[15]

"MARANDÚ CHANGED EVERYTHING"

The prevalence of Indigenous labor exploitation in Paraguay incited an insurgent activist community that sought to advance a new rights framework amid the country's brutal Stroessner dictatorship. Started in 1973 by the anthropologists Miguel Chase-Sardi and Bartomeu Meliá at the Catholic University of Asunción, the Marandú Project had the express goal of training Indigenous leaders about their legal rights.[16] Chase-Sardi's activism and advocacy transcended the borders of Paraguay, as he played a central role in the then-burgeoning international movement for Indigenous rights exemplified by his participation in the 1971 symposium "Inter-Ethnic Conflict in South America" hosted by the World Council of Churches in Barbados. At that meeting, Chase-Sardi helped draft and was a signatory to the Declaration of Barbados: For the Liberation of the Indians—a cornerstone of the emergent international Indigenous rights movement that would later result in the multicultural turn that followed democratization across the region.[17] Chase-Sardi's team traveled to select ranches across the Chaco to spread the news of rights and incite a process of knowledge transfer intended to spur Indigenous action.[18] Not entirely unlike the evangelism of Anglican missionaries that sought to "liberate" Enxet and Sanapaná from savagery while also clearing the way for settler colonialism in the Bajo Chaco, the Marandú Project can be read as an evangelical endeavor whereby liberation rested in the promise that political rights would disrupt the throes of racial capitalism. Drawing from Paraguayan labor law and the principles of the 1971 Declaration of Barbados, Chase-Sardi used Marandú to connect the struggle for Indigenous rights in Paraguay with burgeoning international rights movements, thus preempting Paraguay's multicultural turn.

In November 2015, I met with Marcelino López, one of four leaders of Xákmok Kásek, who broke with the community when sixty-three families decided to forcibly reoccupy their ancestral lands in February that year. Instead, he and his family stayed in 25 de febrero, a small parcel of land ceded to the people of Xákmok Kásek by another Indigenous community after Xákmok Kásek was forced to leave Estancia Salazar in 2009. We sat in the dappled shade of young algarrobo trees next to a one-room brick schoolhouse and a 5,000-liter, cracked, fiberglass water-storage tank emblazoned with fading white spray paint that read "Oxfam." The elementary school chairs we were sitting on wobbled under our weight as we passed tereré to one another. Towering thunderheads grew as oscillating waves of cicada song built to a shrill, near-deafening sound, underscoring the increasing summer heat and humidity. I furtively watched storm clouds building above the trees as we sat, while the palpably increasing humidity manifested in the sweat beading on both our brows eventually dripped to the ground. Marcelino spied my worry about the weather and laughed out loud, shaking his head slowly while sharing his scarce but generous smile. "Ndokymo'ai koa [This won't rain]," he said, gesturing to the sky. Marcelino knew the prospect of rain made me nervous. When it rains, the 50-kilometer dirt road to the community turns to deep mud, slick as wet ice, that can render travel impossible for a day or a week at a time depending on the severity of the storm. Marcelino and I had been trying to meet for this interview for about ten months. Due to a series of events—principally rain, road conditions, Marcelino's work as ranch capataz that takes him away from 25 de febrero for weeks at a time, and my work commitments in different communities—finding a time to sit down for an interview had been challenging. The impending rain threatened to cut our opportunity short. Still, we sat, drank tereré, swatted mosquitos, and talked like the rain would never arrive.

Recounting his view of the key moments in Xákmok Kásek political mobilization, Marcelino reframed the story of the struggle in a way that few others had done. At one point, he looked me directly in the eyes to say, "Marandú changed everything." He paused, letting the words sit in the air between us. "Before that, we just worked and lived on the ranch. We did not know that we had rights—we did not even know what rights were. . . . Then Chase-Sardi came with Marandú and he did workshops. He taught us about the law and what rights were, that we had labor rights, and that the ranchers had to respect them. I learned a lot from Chase-Sardi. I listened and watched and really listened. I thought about it and understood what he was saying." I passed him tereré, which he drank with a long, slow draw on the metal straw before snapping his head back to laugh loudly and flash a large smile. "We were crazy [*tavy*] before, but then we learned we had rights and that they had to give us better working conditions. Later, things changed, and we learned about other rights."[19] One of the most fundamental changes he referenced was adoption of Law 904/81. With the 1981 adoption of Law 904, "the Indigenous Communities Statute," Paraguay begrudgingly began to open avenues for Indigenous peoples to claim legal rights. Law 904/81 established the framework for state recognition of Indigenous peoples and adjudication of the rights they are guaranteed, including the process for land restitution that communities could use to regain access to portions of their territories. "We didn't know about ancestral territory, but we learned about it, that we had rights to it.[20] Then we demanded the state give us our land back. That is how the *lucha* [struggle] began. Chase-Sardi taught us about rights. And so we tried to get better working conditions. Esteban Kidd taught us about land rights, [Law] 904, and we decided that we should fight to get our land back. That is when I became a leader of the community."[21]

As Marcelino spoke those words, I was struck by how his story denoted a stark threshold—a before and after that changed Sanapaná political subjectivity vis-à-vis the state and ranchers. For him and many others from Xákmok Kásek, Marandú represented an opportunity to learn a language of rights that incited new political possibilities and fields of struggle.[22] I mean this literally because, as noted above, *marandú* means both "news" and "knowledge" in Guaraní. The new knowledge of rights, that they existed and insinuated a specific relationship with the state and other actors, created new epistemologies Enxet and Sanapaná peoples leveraged to forge strategies that advanced their visions of the future. It is no surprise then that Xákmok Kásek's claims originated from demands for better working conditions on Estancia Salazar and later evolved into demands for land rights as the Paraguayan state adopted new legal instruments.

The Stroessner administration stopped the Marandú Project in 1975, when officials arrested, jailed, and tortured Chase-Sardi and four of his colleagues. Amid the Cold War and Paraguay's brutal dictatorship, the state criminalized much collective mobilization and direct challenges to the political economic order of the landed elite.[23] Furthermore, Chase-Sardi's activism intersected with the work of the German anthropologist Mark Münzel and the Danish solidarity NGO, International Working Group on Indigenous Affairs (IWGIA), alleging that the Paraguayan state was culpable for acts of genocide against the Aché people who live in southeastern Paraguay.[24] The genocide claims originated in response to Paraguay's state policy of integration from 1958 to 1966 that involved coercing Aché to settle on reservations where many succumbed to disease, were sold into child slavery, or abused in other ways.[25] Whereas Marandú was principally a domestic affair, the Aché case advanced to the Inter-American Commission on Human Rights and shone a bright light on the Stroessner regime's abuse of Indigenous peoples. The

Aché genocide case was not proven in court, and the Stroessner administration was never found guilty, but the resulting international pressures led by the US government and action by domestic solidarity organizations prompted Stroessner to take the first steps to formalize Indigenous rights.[26] Despite its brief existence, Marandú was integral to the political formation of many Enxet and Sanapaná who, like Marcelino, became leaders in their respective communities and struggles.

Paraguay's legal framework provided no robust protections for Indigenous peoples prior to the passage of Law 904/81. As Chase-Sardi, Brun, and Enciso write, "In relation to the fact that the white colonists occupied the lands of the natives, they [Indigenous peoples] cannot protest due to the letter of the law, because there is none. The law gives rights to force undesirables from property, and if necessary use force to achieve this. . . . The indians suffer most in this situation because they have no rights or possibility for legal defense."[27] Given the legal lacuna, Chase-Sardi and colleagues sought to leverage labor law to improve Indigenous well-being. Indeed, the strategy they used was not unique to Paraguay. The International Labor Organization (ILO), formed in 1919, played an early, albeit vital, role in fostering intergovernmental and international frameworks for the protection of Indigenous well-being vis-à-vis labor law. In response to the widespread prevalence of using forced Indigenous labor or egregious labor exploitation arrangements that denied adequate pay or safety, the ILO was formed, in part, to "address directly the political and economic disempowerment of indigenous peoples."[28] And while the Forced Labor Convention of 1930 and Convention 107 in 1957 were intended to protect Indigenous laborers, they failed to respect Indigenous self-determination insofar as Convention 107 was unabashedly integrationist, despite having an origin in the antislavery abolitionist society.[29] Marandú did not have assimilationist intents like ILO 107 or the Anglican resettlement project La Herencia, but the project did resonate with burgeoning international efforts to use labor rights as the vehicle to develop exclusive rights for Indigenous peoples.

PARAGUAY'S MULTICULTURAL TURN

Across Latin America, and certainly in Paraguay, the purported fight to stave the spread of communism throughout the Cold War resulted in the evisceration of democratic norms, as evidenced by the prevalence of authoritarian dictatorships. The wave of torture, extrajudicial killings, and "disappearances," acts often directly or tacitly supported by US policy, are not relics of the past; they continue to shape struggles for justice across the region.[30] As evidenced by myriad examples too numerous to cover here, Indigenous peoples were often regarded with direct or tacit suspicion as vectors for the spread of collective organization and socialist political mobilization.[31] Exemplifying this, the first state agency created to address Indigenous issues in Paraguay in 1958, the Department of Indigenous Affairs (DAI), was operated by the Ministry of Defense. DAI deemed Indigenous peoples wards of the state and advanced an integrationist policy by promoting Indigenous settlement and agricultural production to contribute to the predominant economic activities driving state-led development in its rural frontiers. There was, however, a clearly anticommunist imperative to this work. Harder-Horst writes, "Whenever peasants challenged the existing land-tenure system, Stroessner, to legitimate repression, publicized a 'Communist Threat.' Given such paranoia, it should not be surprising that his generals feared that isolated native settlements' communal lands were actually hotbeds for potential Communist infiltration."[32] The suppression of Indigenous collectives throughout the Cold War exposes the politics of resource control used to legitimate long-standing projects of racial stratification based on the distribution of land rights.[33]

However, the democratic opening that swept Latin America in the late 1980s through the early 1990s seemed to reverse course by rejecting assimilation and the "indian problem" through new rights regimes based on principles of recognizing and respecting difference.[34] In the wake of long-standing genocidal policies and violent assimilation tactics that sought to erase Indigenous presence across the Americas, the "acceptance" of ethno-racial difference through official multicultural policies promised to fulfill liberal ideals of equality, liberty, and morality by improving Indigenous well-being.[35] In short, Indigenous dispossession is incongruent with imaginaries of liberal democratic states that "should" foster societies that accept and allow spaces for socio-cultural difference.[36] The official turn to multiculturalism by many state governments in Latin America brought with it a newfound body of rights to protect populations that have been historically dispossessed of land, recognition, and political inclusion, specifically, Indigenous and Afro-descendant communities.[37] From regionwide constitutional reforms to the 1993 adoption of Law 70 in Colombia that legally codified Afro-Colombian collective rights, the multicultural turn initiated a wave of new political demands across the region.[38]

Given that labor laws were the principal tool used to advocate for better living conditions on the ranches during the Marandú era, the multicultural turn created a specific body of Indigenous rights laws that promised to reverse historic inequalities and wrongs wrought by land dispossession. The laws created the juridical possibility that Enxet and Sanapaná peoples could take back the same lands stolen from them where they had labored "practically as slaves," as Eulalio recounted to me. The multicultural turn thus references a historical conjuncture when states across Latin America embraced a vision of Indigenous rights as vital to democratization and the enduring policy framework used to govern ethnic difference. That is to say, in the context of Paraguay, the codification of Indigenous rights is inherently, albeit tenuously, tied to a rejection of authoritarianism.

Nevertheless, in practice, multicultural policy has reinforced racial boundaries, particularly through the adjudication of Indigenous land rights. As Coulthard argues, "Instead of ushering in an era of peaceful coexistence grounded on the ideal of reciprocity or mutual recognition, the politics of recognition in its contemporary liberal form promises to reproduce the very configurations of colonialist, racist, patriarchal state power that Indigenous peoples' demands for recognition have historically sought to transcend."[39] Although Coulthard is writing of Indigenous experiences in Canada, similar power relations permeate Indigenous-state politics in Latin America. Radcliffe captures this dynamic in her work on postcolonial development policy in Ecuador, arguing that "multiculturalism did little to challenge, let alone overturn, entrenched colonial [read racial] hierarchies, as it tended to regulate expressions of difference while retaining forms of privilege and stigmatization."[40] Rather than alter colonial forms of power, multicultural rights most often advance a political agenda that (de)limits the range of possibility and acceptable "difference" of Indigenous lives that is fundamental to how settler colonialism operates socially and spatially.[41]

Here I am not arguing against efforts to increase equality and social justice. The adoption of Indigenous rights coupled with constitutional and policy reforms have created new politico-juridical means that Indigenous communities around the world have used to advance self-determination and territorial autonomy.[42] Proponents of multiculturalism suggest that ethnic rights can alleviate dispossession and create more equitable, just societies.[43] Constitutional reforms and the ratification of new legal instruments, such as the ILO Indigenous and Tribal Peoples Convention 169, were therefore common aspects of regional efforts to develop multicultural rights frameworks.[44] However, as I have argued elsewhere, the liberal, statist legal framework is an aporia where the pursuit of justice is necessary but always out of reach because such laws reaffirm the authority of the settler state.[45] Where multicultural reforms have been adopted to ensure Indigenous rights, there is a pervasive and persistent gap in the implementation of the laws and policies that those reforms produce, with highly uneven effects on Indigenous well-being.[46]

RECOGNITION AND LEGAL PERSONHOOD

Law 904/81 created the legal process to adjudicate land restitution to Indigenous peoples as collective property but with very specific prerequisites to attain legal recognition. That law defines Indigenous communities as "a group of extended families, clan, or group of clans with culture and their own system of authority that speak an autochthonous language and live together in a common habitat."[47] Though the Law 904/81 does mention Indigenous self-determination (*autodeterminación*), there is no mention of Indigenous peoples, only "communities," "clans," or "groups." Further, Law 904/81 defines communities as settlements of at least twenty families (i.e., separate households) and entitles those in the Chaco to a *minimum* of 100 hectares per family. By that calculus a community of twenty families is guaranteed at least 2,000 hectares within their ancestral territories with titles administered collectively, in the name of the community, not individual families.

Once titled, Indigenous lands cannot be rented, subdivided, or resold, thus fixing them as static entities within a dynamic propertized landscape. Even though Law 904/81 was a major advance for Indigenous rights in Paraguay and is fiercely defended by Indigenous peoples from the regular threats to dismantle or weaken its content, the law truncates Indigenous collectives through its mandate about the form and limits of community rights.[48] Nevertheless, it is the operational legal framework necessary for land restitution. Communities must therefore attain *personería jurídica* (legal personhood) to legally reclaim their lands.

Recognition as a personería jurídica is a complex process. It requires conducting a community census with a registry of all family names and demographic data (gender, marriage status, age, etc.), providing the specific geographic location, identifying and naming leaders, then presenting all of this information to INDI. Here I focus on naming leaders. The act obligates INDI officials to visit communities and attend a meeting where community members approve the new leadership. Everything must be documented in writing and signed by all community members and the INDI officials in attendance. The whole process is repeated with any subsequent change to official leadership. This is not only a cumbersome procedure, but one that reasserts the centricity of the state's authority by mandating its physical presence in collectives that pursue official recognition as communities or seek to change leadership within them. In March 2016, I witnessed the process unfold in Sawhoyamaxa when a young man, Eriberto Ayala, was slated to be named a new leader of the community. Eriberto was born on the Loma Porã ranch that Sawhoyamaxa claimed 14,404 hectares of land from. He spent most of his childhood living on the side of the highway that passes in front of the ranch after several families were expelled from Loma Porã for demanding land restitution. Unlike most other members of Sawhoyamaxa, Eriberto has attended some college, has traveled to the United States and Europe to represent Sawhoyamaxa, and is a deft, multilingual orator and highly skilled negotiator who has played a leading role advocating for his community. As such, he has catapulted to the fore of the community's struggle.

"We have been wanting to hold this meeting for a long time," Eriberto told me as we drove from his *aldea* (smaller village within the community) to Leonardo's, where the INDI officials had been instructed to visit. We arrived to find a few cows resting in the shade of a large tree but no one else. Leonardo left his house and walked across the pasture to join us when he saw us start carrying chairs from the nearby schoolhouse to the shade. "Where are they?" asked Eriberto. Leonardo replied, "I just Whatsapp'ed with them. They are on their way from Concepción." Eriberto had been awaiting this day, when he would be recognized as a leader of his aldea and therefore one of the primary leaders of Sawhoyamaxa. "We'll see," he said. "Call your people, Leonardo. I'll call Marecos. Let's get everyone ready for when they get here so this doesn't take too long." After setting up six small wooden chairs and a small desk, we sat and waited. Over the next hour people from

Leonardo's aldea, mostly women and young children, joined us under the tree, walking from their homes, some up to 2 kilometers away. Carlos arrived from his aldea on a well-worn motorcycle. Notably, no one from Eriberto's aldea joined the meeting. Although sharing a single communal name—Sawhoyamaxa—the years of conviviality, struggle, and life together have created tensions and subdivisions within the broader "community."[49] As a result, each aldea is a smaller subcommunity often based loosely on family ties. Yet being elected and officially recognized as a leader by INDI empowers each leader with the ability to represent the Sawhoyamaxa collective in official state negotiations and proceedings. Sitting in the grass, some women drinking tereré questioned, "Why aren't there more people here? Picking a leader is important. We should be over there." They thought it strange that this meeting was not being held in Carlos's aldea, often referred to as Sawhoyamaxa Central for its location and fact that he is the community's longest acting leader. Before anyone attended to this concern, the rumble of a truck approaching on the lone dirt road that stretches a straight 3 kilometers from the highway to where we sat alerted us to the arrival of the INDI officials. Eriberto stood, walked to my car, and grabbed the black blazer he brought with him for the occasion.

"Sorry that we took so long." Three INDI functionaries got out of their truck as Eriberto and Leonardo greeted them. They shook hands and chatted for a few minutes before gathering their things—a clipboard and a worn folder full of documents, as well as a thermos with water for tereré—before walking over to the small group that had gathered for the meeting. "Mba'eichapa pende ka'aru"—How are you this afternoon?—asked one official as she looked around to assess the group before sitting at the desk and setting up her supplies. "Ore tranquilopa," we are doing well, replied one person in attendance. "Good then. I understand we are here because you would like to name a new leader." She pulled out a community census and a small notebook to write the *acta*—official minutes of the proceedings—that would record the events and be stored at the INDI office in Asunción. Carlos then started speaking from his chair: "We are here to add new leadership to our community. Eriberto has grown up in the lucha and has done a lot of work for the community. His people want him to be a leader of 16 de agosto with Bascilio. Leonardo, Bascilio, and I agree. What do you all think?" As these meetings often go, people were reluctant to talk at first, but eventually one woman spoke out. "Iporã. Good. Eriberto has done a lot." With that, others joined in to share thoughts.

The INDI officials sat, listened, and took notes throughout the discussion but offered no interventions until it was time to officiate the change. Then one of the officials spoke: "We will need to record the names of those in attendance and check them against our census.[50] Please show me your identity card when you come to the desk." Leonardo had already gathered the documents from the thirty or so people in attendance and handed them to the functionary, who then copied each name onto the acta after checking them against her census. Once done, she called each person forward to either sign under their name or place an inky thumbprint on the page if they did not know how to write. The whole affair lasted just over an hour once things began, a short and uneventful meeting given the consequences of naming a new leader who will generally have the role for life.

Choosing new leaders, even though community members name their leaders, often changes internal power relations. The state's requirement to name and recognize leaders has several immediate effects. First, it facilitates state governance of Indigenous peoples by rendering communities legible in a specific manner that aligns with state dictates. The use of censuses, birth and death registries, demarcation of lands as a form of property, and recognition of specific leaders all serve to order people and land in a manner convenient for the state. Alternatively, when people are not recorded on such "official" records due to several structural factors like lacking identity documents, that also serves as a de facto mode of governing life, through erasure. Second, by assuming that one person or a small handful of people will effectively represent their communities, the process imposes a hierarchical political organization in communities that may, or often do, operate according to other forms of social organization. Naming political leaders may challenge the power of other "unofficial" leaders, such as shamans or spiritual guides who play an important role in historical and traditional social organization, if the selected leader(s) do not traditionally map onto customary power structures within communities. Third, communities often select leaders who can speak and understand the lingua franca necessary to negotiate with the state: Spanish. Until recently, relatively few Enxet and Sanapaná spoke Spanish well, as Guaraní is the lingua franca on the ranches and is widely spoken in Yakye Axa, Sawhoyamaxa, and Xákmok Kásek. Limited literacy rates are still quite high as access to formal education is sparse, with less than 5 percent of young people having access to classes beyond fourth or fifth grade and most classes being taught in Guaraní locally. Language and literacy thus limit who has access to political power and influence beyond the communities.[51] Taken together, these three factors in practice work to delimit how communities choose their leaders and also place a great deal of power in individuals to gain and access resources that other community members cannot because of their status as recognized leaders.

In the weeks following Eriberto's recognition as a leader, I heard comments from members of Sawhoyamaxa who raised concerns about the process and its potential effects, for example: "He speaks Spanish well and is smart. He has done many things for Sawhoyamaxa, but I do not know if he is the best person to be a leader. We didn't know about the meeting so could not debate this. Those leaders have things that we don't have." Comments like these point to tensions and unequal relations within communities that are exacerbated by the imposition of new social and political orderings that facilitate the aims of the state but are presented as respecting Indigenous self-determination. Law 904/81 is a tool to defend Indigenous rights but creates a uniform model to which Indigenous peoples must conform to access state services or attempt to act on the rights they are legally afforded. That is, communities can technically decide their leaders, but they must do so within the specific constraints of the state's mandated process and not necessarily according to social or community norms. Despite these limits, recognition of leaders in this manner is necessary because it creates the opportunity to gain personería jurídica, the vital step toward demanding land restitution.

TO TAKE BACK THE RANCHES

Law 904/81 created the legal avenue to reclaim portions of ancestral territories lost to ranchers. Many of my Enxet and Sanapaná interlocutors refer to this process simply as "the lucha," in Spanish, "fight" or "struggle." When people refer to la lucha they mean not just the process of demanding land from the state but the generations-long struggle to fight for self-determination as a people whose rights, however, continue to be violated. One cold morning Anivel Flores and I sat next to a small crackling fire in the cold predawn light at his home on the site where the Yakye Axa community has lived since their land claim began—the margin of a highway in front of the lands taken from his forebears—when he reflected on his community's lucha.

> Our case, *ore lucha*, has been very long. The people have tried in many ways so that they can overcome the lucha, but they could not. There came a moment when our leaders were tired. They died. You know? Esteban López and Tomás Galeano. They were the first leaders in this place. The lucha has been very long. We have experienced so much. They were so tired, and there was no response from the state. There came a moment when they were so tired and the people were losing faith. The state officials gave us no answer. There was little hope. They didn't give. With the passing of time the leaders got sick. That illness killed them. I don't know what kind of illness came. But they died. First Tomás, then Esteban. As far as I understand, they knew something. Something is extremely important about this place. . . . The first thing, the way the lucha began was that the people first demanded the Loma Verde ranch land. They claimed what the law says. What I understand is that the law says the Chaco was Indigenous territory. For that reason the people claimed, they claimed one original territory. That is Loma Verde.[52]

The lucha that Anivel refers to here began at a very specific moment, when the Yakye Axa community demanded that the Paraguayan state return 18,188 hectares that had first been appropriated for the Anglican industrial ranch El Paso and later sold to the owners of the Loma Verde ranch. Following Esteban López and Tomás Galeano's initial petition for personería jurídica status and land restitution in 1993, in 1996 the state finally recognized Yakye Axa as an Indigenous community. Community recognition should take a maximum of thirty days per Law 904/81. However, significant delays in securing formal recognition regularly occur and are commonly explained by state officials as a matter of bureaucratic procedures.[53]

Such explanations falter because a clear pattern of state neglect to adjudicate Indigenous rights is plain to see across the Yakye Axa, Sawhoyamaxa, Xákmok Kásek, and Kelyenmagategma cases. As I discuss in depth in the next two chapters, not only did the effects of these delays on human rights impel the Inter-American System to hear each of these cases, but they are also indicative of how the politics of recognition spur environmental racism that is rendered visible through Indigenous land claims. However, here I focus on how and when each land claim began and tease out some common threads across each case.

Whereas Anglican missionaries in the Bajo Chaco purchased lands for some Enxet, Sanapaná, and Angaité communities through La Herencia and other Indigenous settlements were established at El Estribu (the Tribe) and La Patria (the Fatherland) in the late 1970s and early 1980s, many other communities sought land restitution via Law 904/81. Rather than resettle on land purchased by the church, members of Sawhoyamaxa, Yakye Axa, Xákmok Kásek, and many other communities chose to pursue the promise of the law and make the state return portions of their ancestral lands. In Tierraviva's archives I traced each claim to their initial filing dates: Xákmok Kásek in 1986, Sawhoyamaxa in 1991, and Yakye Axa in 1993.

State officials have resisted returning Enxet and Sanapaná lands for decades. As a result, members of the Yakye Axa, Sawhoyamaxa, and Xákmok Kásek communities endured what Nichols might call "recursive dispossession," manifested here in the denial of land rights, ensuring material impoverishment, human rights violations, and epistemic violence.[54] Enxet and Sanapaná peoples mobilized concerted campaigns with support from organizations like Tierraviva to pressure the Paraguayan state to address the state's failure to resolve each community's land claims. Instead of resolving the claims, administration after administration has made minor gestures in attempts to placate community members despite egregious human rights abuses. Rather than govern by upholding the law, several successive state administrations have instituted a near-permanent state of emergency, first instated by the decree President Luis González-Macchi issued in 1999 to provide food and water services to Yakye Axa and Sawhoyamaxa.[55]

The IACHR highlighted the state's rationale for issuing the emergency declarations in its 2005 Yakye Axa ruling. The deprivation of land rights thwarted "access to the traditional means of subsistence associated with their cultural identity, because the owners [of surrounding ranches] do not allow them [i.e., members of Yakye Axa] to enter the habitat that they claim as part of their traditional territory."[56] The states of emergency declared in Yakye Axa, Sawhoyamaxa, and, later, in Xákmok Kásek explicitly reference the material life conditions created by land dispossession, specifically, the lack of access to reliable water sources, the prohibition of entry onto private properties for subsistence activities like hunting or firewood collection, and acknowledgment that the communities had no land that could be used for agricultural production. In other words, the emergency declarations show that state officials were aware of the grave circumstances in each community. The declarations' core provisions include orders to provide monthly emergency food rations, potable drinking water, regular access to medical care, and assurances that basic housing and education needs are met until resolution of land restitution. Yet the state of emergency, like the lucha, has become the norm.

The lucha has taken so long that many Enxet and Sanapaná interlocutors do not recall exactly when it began, instead discussing it as the condition of everyday life. During a conversation with a group of women from the Santa Elisa aldea of Sawhoyamaxa about the community's land claims, Gladys Benitez stated, "I don't remember well what year we began *ore lucha*. I think it was the year 1998 when we started *ore lucha*. That is when we started our claim. You will have to ask Carlos. He knows well. He has been leader the whole time."[57] She paused, mulled the question further, and pointed to the ground. "This is ours. We lost our people here. This is our real territory [Ko'a ha'e ore tekoha voi]. Our grandfathers and our grandmothers came here. They were with us when the lucha began. They ended here during the lucha. Now they are no longer with us." Gladys paused again and looked at the group, eleven women, three small kids, and one infant, gathered under the small porch of a home constructed on lands Sawhoyamaxa had recently reoccupied.

> We have endured suffering for many years. Kids have died. Elders have died. Young men and young women have died. They all died throughout the lucha. Hunger. Exposure to the cold. We have experienced much here. There is no way to make money. We have so much suffering. We have been sick. There are no doctors. There is no medicine. So we have experienced much and lost many of our people throughout the lucha. We cannot lose this land. They must title it to us. They know that it is truly ours and that we have the right to claim it. That is all I have to say.

Gladys's words make clear that when exactly the lucha began matters less than the recurrent effects of the epistemic and affective violence of withholding lands.

I do not suggest that Yakye Axa, Sawhoyamaxa, Xákmok Kásek, and Kelyenmagategma have had the same experience navigating their respective luchas. The specific histories and details of the four cases are distinct. But there are important trends that resonate across the cases. Among these, state officials and responsible institutions have failed to provide due process of law in several key areas: (1) adjudicating community recognition in a timely and meaningful manner; (2) ensuring community members have basic identity documents, including birth and death certificates, so they can access necessary state services; and (3) resolving legal matters on which land restitution hinges. These trends are plain to see in the narratives shared above but also in the legal process each community has endured through the lucha. Beyond merely filing petitions for land restitution, each community pursued all domestic legal avenues to advance their claims, before eventually losing their respective appeals for land restitution before the congress in the late 1990s. Another important common thread in these cases is that each community began working with Tierraviva shortly after it was founded in 1994 by Anglicans and Paraguayans upset with the Mission's legacy in the Bajo Chaco and the state's refusal to adjudicate its Indigenous rights law. Lawyers and staff from Tierraviva have worked closely with each community, playing an influential role in shaping the legal strategy used in the Enxet and Sanapaná dialectics of disruption. Rather than recite a story of centuries-long resistance or a claim to radical alterity that animates indigenism across many sites in Latin America, my Enxet and Sanapaná interlocutors maintain a sharp focus on demands based on political rights—first for better working conditions, then to reclaim lands taken from them on which they had been forced to labor.

Political rights and the normative assertion that the state is responsible for ensuring those rights have long animated much Enxet and Sanapaná activism.[58] Using the phrase "ore derecho" (our rights), my interlocutors often articulate their demands in specific terms that clearly denote this point. In Paraguayan Guaraní the word *ore* connotes an exclusionary expression of the English-language concept "we," signifying only the group associated with the speaker.[59] "*Ore derecho* says that the state must provide land in sufficient quantity and of good quality for free to the Indigenous. But not any land, land we choose, our ancestral land." Clemente Dermott, one leader of Xákmok Kásek, would regularly explain this to me, making clear that Indigenous rights to communal land supersede individual private property rights. On the other hand, when Veronica Flores from Yakye Axa said, "The state doesn't see *ore derecho* because they have left us here without doing anything to stop our suffering," she made clear that Indigenous rights are discretionary. And when Leonardo González, a leader of Sawhoyamaxa, said, "*Ore derecho* is clearly stated in Law 904 and the constitution but they choose to do nothing," he was pointing to Paraguay's primary Indigenous rights laws that are irrefutable on paper but elusive in practice. Thus saying "ore derecho" in these contexts means the rights of/for the Indigenous peoples, exclusive of non-Indigenous people. The discursive appropriation of ore derecho inverts the exclusionary logic of multiculturalism by explicitly denying access to non-Indigenous peoples. In this way, Enxet and Sanapaná engagements with multicultural politics of recognition have been strategic acts that seek to disrupt settler and state power through subtle but clear forms of refusal to abide by the status quo.[60]

"I WANT TO BE SEEN AS A HUMAN"

The first time Eriberto and I met, it was a damp winter day in 2013, overcast with flat gray clouds. We sat together drinking tereré on the back patio of the Tierraviva office in Asunción for just over three hours. The Tierraviva office is a hub of legal advocacy that also serves as a site for Indigenous collaboration and exchange. The organization provides a small hostel-like space where Indigenous peoples from across the Chaco can stay free of charge while they attend to necessary community business, like attending meetings at INDI, trying to ensure that the Ministry of

Health provides medical services, petitioning the Ministry of Education for a schoolteacher, or other similar affairs. The hostel is a site where people meet, wait for their meetings, talk, and build relations.

Eriberto and my conversation traversed many topics. But some two hours in and long after the yerba mate in our tereré had lost its flavor, he said something that has remained with me: "We have been fighting for so long. The community fights and suffers on the side of the road, but we won't give up. We are just fighting for what is ours, our land, our rights. I am Indigenous. But I am also human. *I want to be seen as a human.*"[61] Eriberto's words suggest that to be Indigenous is to be afforded certain rights and privileges that are simultaneously *more and less* than those of non-Indigenous. Elsa Ayala, an elder who is Eriberto's grandmother, expressed a similar sentiment to me, albeit in other terms, one afternoon in 2016 while we talked in Sawhoyamaxa.[62]

> Our family suffered so much at the Loma Porã [ranch]. I also worked at the Loma Porã ranch. I did not get anything except for the accident that I had there. For thirteen years I lived inside the ranch and our children suffered. Then they changed the administrators. They changed them. Then they had no more work for our people, and we all had to leave to live on the side of the road. They [those removed from the ranch] looked for a place to survive on the road because there was no more work at the ranch. They did not give us any more work. The innocents [children] suffered. They suffered so much. So there was much that we did. We went to the palms. We went to the vines. There was nothing else we could do to feed our families. Now the same thing is happening again here. No one [from the state] comes here to see us and they know where we are. . . . They treat animals better than the Indigenous.

Mundane, routinized forms of dehumanization recall the specter of the Indigenous "other" who occupies a "savage slot" through which difference is defined, studied, and ultimately maintained.[63] This "slot" exists beyond academic theorization; it permeates the settler narratives I assessed in chapter 1, narratives that named Enxet and Sanapaná as "savage" while calling for Indigenous peoples to abandon their traditions such that they might become Christian capitalists—in effect, more human.[64] Such discourse indexes the partitioning of Indigenous life from non-Indigenous that occurs in long-standing racial tropes and juridical practice.[65] Further, a sort of "savage slot" is manifest in multicultural policies that define difference in ways that reinforce the very racial hierarchies that precipitated the creation of such policies. The "savage slot" is thus rendered a juridical relation with the state through which people and land are organized and perhaps governed. This dynamic is plain to see by assessing the process of becoming a legally recognized Indigenous community with legal personhood and the outcomes of efforts to recover stolen lands. And while many scholars have assessed the politics of recognition in Latin America through the lens of neoliberal multiculturalism, I have taken a different approach.

Much of the academic debate—particularly emanating from US-based scholars of Latin America—takes aim at the uncanny confluence of neoliberal political-economic reform and ethnic rights. No scholar has been more influential in advancing this critique than Charles Hale, whose concept "neoliberal multiculturalism" has shaped years of subsequent analysis.[66] Hale's book *Más que un indio* analyzes how the rollout of neoliberal political economic reforms in the 1990s ran parallel to, and indeed motivated, the adoption of limited multicultural rights for the Indigenous peoples of Guatemala, particularly the Maya. Whereas analysts suspected that the evisceration of state services and promotion of the individual over the collective, which often defines neoliberal practices, would produce antagonistic relations between Latin American states and Indigenous peoples, Hale incisively observed the opposite to be true.

> The point is, simply, that neoliberal economic reforms have embodied great flexibility in regard to indigenous cultural rights; this follows because the key defining feature of neoliberalism is not strict, market-oriented individualism, as many contend, but rather the restructuring of society such that people come to govern themselves in accordance with the tenets of global capitalism. Compliance with the discipline of the capitalist market can be individual, but may be equally effective as a collective response.... As long as cultural rights remain within these parameters, they contribute directly to the goal of neoliberal self-governance.[67]

Hale's analysis is persuasive, and neoliberal multiculturalism is clearly a powerful framework that resonates across the Americas. Indeed, his work has greatly informed my thinking on Indigenous politics in Latin America. Hale is attentive to historical continuities and has recently argued that the era of neoliberal multiculturalism may be coming to an end.[68] But I fear during years of circulation many scholars (and students) use the concept of neoliberal multiculturalism as a "black box" that privileges contemporary political economic dynamics over the legacies that shape them. My point is not to disregard the utility of neoliberal multiculturalism as an *analytic* but to suggest that in many instances, such as the cases discussed in this book, the concept never fully captured the complexity of struggle or the nuances of Indigenous demands.

The Enxet and Sanapaná struggles that animate this book precede multicultural and neoliberal reforms in Paraguay, as do the prevailing modes of racialized governance established by the missionaries and cattle ranchers who have long controlled land and livelihoods in the Bajo Chaco. In the previous chapter I outlined how settler colonialism, expressed through the establishment and spread of cattle ranching, produced distinct racial geographies. Those very geographies endure to the present day, manifested in the biophysical landscape that is now a highly altered system designed to support one form of life: cattle. Yet this biophysical, more-than-human landscape is also simultaneously the product of distinct social and juridical relations. Thus, as interlocutors like Marcelino López, Elsa Ayala, and dozens of other Enxet and Sanapaná I have spoken with from across the region have recounted, the racial hierarchy of land control that shapes ongoing struggles for land rights was forged not by neoliberalism but by a form of racial capitalism that operates today much as it did in the early 1900s.

It was within this conjuncture that the Yakye Axa, Sawhoyamaxa, Xákmok Kásek, and Kelyenmagategma communities all embraced the promise of rights and, later, the politics of recognition to make their respective land claims. Yet, returning to Marcelino's recollection of the Marandú Project, "We were crazy until we learned we had rights," and reading it alongside Eulalio's statement, "We were practically slaves until we learned we had rights," I aver that long-standing patrón-peon relations forged in the first waves of racial capitalism in the Bajo Chaco shaped Enxet and Sanapaná political struggles through the present. These issues intersect with neoliberal reforms and multicultural politics but are not predetermined or inherently bound by either. This is not to say that nothing has changed, but rather that the effects of the neoliberal conjuncture have amplified existing forms of oppression spurred by racial capitalism. Enxet and Sanapaná struggles not only precede neoliberalism and notions of multiculturalism, but they promise to outlive them and cannot be constrained to that specific analytic. While it is undeniable that engaging the law and comporting with the state constrained the scope of Enxet and Sanapaná political struggles for decades, the actual dynamics of land control and settler-Indigenous relations reveal the limits of the neoliberal multiculturalism analysis in this context. Instead of working as an ethnic spatial fix to facilitate resource governance by making "empty lands" legible to the state by advancing private property regimes, the cases discussed in this book all revolve around a different dynamic. None of the land in question was "empty" or actively controlled by Enxet and Sanapaná at the time of their claims. Each case centered on taking land from private property owners—ranchers—whose use was predicated on economic productivity, then returning that land to Indigenous communities who would hold it collectively, and ultimately diminishing the economic productivity of the land vis-à-vis the legal tenet of "rational exploitation" established in Paraguay's Agrarian Statute.[69]

Attending to the entwined operation of racial capitalism and settler colonialism provides a better analytical frame to explain how and why Indigenous dispossessions persist on extractive frontiers that are not-quite-neoliberal. Penelope Anthias's *Limits to Decolonization* provides an important critique from which I build: "By locating the limits of cultural rights in a particular governmental paradigm—a kind of 'recognition trap' that indigenous peoples fell blindly into—critiques of neoliberal multiculturalism obscure the deeper structures of coloniality and capitalism that condition indigenous struggles for territory in the present."[70] I agree that there is too great an emphasis on neoliberalism as the primary proponent of Indigenous dispossessions. Neoliberal policy and practice are struck through with enduring colonial power relations and always racialized, but the organizing principle of settler colonialism is Indigenous dispossession—first of land, then of all forms of autonomy.

The Indigenous activists, academics, and lawyers who have played vital roles in creating Law 904/81, pushing the Paraguayan state to include a chapter in the 1992 constitution to codify Indigenous rights as a foundational charter, and who continue to demand the state respond to their claims did and do not intend to police Indigenous difference.[71] Indeed, these are important legal gains. Nor can we diminish the vital influence of Indigenous movements to challenge historical and ongoing oppressions by trying to hold the state accountable. But the discretionary ways Paraguayan state officials apply the law have radically violent effects; they upend the dreams of a democratic utopia that many Indigenous peoples and their allies held in the wake of the Stroessner regime. I want to be clear that I am not suggesting that the problem is merely one of getting the policy and law "right." The problem lies in settler colonial appropriations of Indigenous lands and the racial capitalism that drives such processes.[72]

In/Visible

On October 22, 2015, I joined members of Yakye Axa and Sawhoyamaxa at the opening of the exhibition *El Grito Enxet* (the Enxet Cry) at the Centro Cultural Paraguayo Americano (CCPA; Paraguayan-American Cultural Center) in Asunción. Upon arriving, I immediately noticed that almost all the members of Sawhoyamaxa and Yakye Axa who came to the event were waiting outside the gallery, talking quietly with one another. There was a small table with artisan wares that women from the communities brought to sell, but there was not much business. Inside the gallery were perhaps ten to fifteen *asuncenos*—non-Indigenous residents of Asunción—who appeared to be upper-middle class, based on their nice clothing, behavior, and exclusive use of Spanish. Asuncenos milled about looking at the portraits, reading descriptions that accompanied them, and made comments condemning the living conditions and human rights violations the artwork exposed.

The exhibition featured paintings by the local artist Diego Schäfer and was part of a multiyear advocacy campaign organized by Tierraviva and Amnesty International on behalf of the Yakye Axa and Sawhoyamaxa communities. The campaign was called "Hacer visible lo invisible," Make the Invisible Visible. To make the invisible visible in this context is to cast light on the human rights violations and environmental harms that the Yakye Axa and Sawhoyamaxa communities are experiencing due to the state's failure to restitute land and implement judgments handed down by the IACHR. An underlying narrative animated the campaign and exhibition: state neglect effectively renders Indigenous rights and well-being invisible. Schäfer makes the invisible visible by painting black-and-white portraits that depict daily life. He uses another layer of paint that is only visible when exposed to ultraviolet light to reveal what was otherwise hidden in plain sight: human rights abuse caused by the negligence of the Paraguayan state. *Doña Florencia* is the title of one of the paintings.

FIGURE 6. *Doña Florencia*, digitally enhanced painting by the artist Diego C. Schäfer from the 2014 exposition *Hacer visible lo invisible*. Florencia's portrait appears with the missing identity document transposed over her face, visible only when ultraviolet light is applied to the painting.

The painting highlights the fact that prior to the IACHR judgments, few people from Yakye Axa and Sawhoyamaxa had identity documents. Under normal lighting the viewer only sees Doña Florencia's face. But the ultraviolet light reveals her face on a ghostly, albeit elusive, state-issued identity document. State officials required that community members make a trip of several days to Asunción to get an ID, impossible for most because of the expense. Lack of state-issued identity documents, including birth and death certificates, negated the Enxet full rights as citizens by denying them the ability to vote and access some state services. It is a de facto form of juridical erasure that expunges Enxet life from the settler state, existing perhaps only as a number on a census but not recognized or identified in any state registry. The IACHR found that the state neglected to effectively issue

ID documents to members of Yakye Axa and Sawhoyamaxa, which was, in part, a denial of their right to due process and fundamental rights as Paraguayan citizens. Moreover, during adjudication of each case before the IACHR, community members could not prove to the court exactly how many people died while awaiting due process of their land claims because many of them had not been issued birth or death certificates. Despite ample testimony, those lives could not be counted, nor could the state be held accountable for their deaths. Thus settler colonialism in the Bajo Chaco erases Enxet in life and death. The Paraguayan state recognized both communities as legal entities, even though many community members did not officially exist on any state registry. Documents with thumbprints in place of a state-issued ID number are lasting witness to the lack of official documentation.

Doña Florencia was one of thirteen portraits. Another painting depicted a young child playing with a bucket that under ultraviolet light turns out to have been previously used for toxic chemicals. Mobile vendors often sell the buckets cheaply, and many people in the communities use them to gather and store water from the stock ponds. Another painting depicts an older woman weaving a basket from *caraguata'y* fibers. The fibers change to thread woven from plastic bags, evoking the fact that community members have little access to forest resources necessary for cultural practices. However, Tomás Galeano's portrait stood out. Tomás was one of the original leaders of Yakye Axa who helped initiate the community's land claim but had recently passed away. Tomás wore glasses. Under ultraviolet light, his glasses reflect an ethereal image of the lands that Yakye Axa claimed, the island of palms, lands he was never able to return to.

The act of making visible is a denunciation of the Paraguayan state. Making visible challenges official narratives that claim the state is working to ensure Indigenous rights and implement the IACHR judgments. Schäfer's artwork creates a discursive space where community members and their allies can advance their political goals through claiming and shaming. The strategy involves publicly mobilizing memories of violence to shame states for human rights abuses and thus claim rights from those states. "Making the Invisible Visible" is a clear example of that strategy.

Despite its widespread use and appeal across social movements, I suggest that the very acts of shaming and "making visible" can have contradictory effects. The strategy can re-victimize subjects of human rights abuses by requiring them to recite their pain publicly. Shaming the state to claim rights often requires that victims of human rights abuses relive memories of those abuses publicly as a necessary political strategy—both a cathartic and a traumatizing experience. The CCPA reception and the *El Grito* exhibition illustrate the multiple effects of making visible in subtle but clear ways.

A reception followed the inaugural events. Waiters in formal attire brought glasses of wine or soda to attendees. The thirty or so people milled about and mingled. None of the people from Yakye Axa or Sawhoyamaxa drank wine, but

FIGURE 7. *Don Tomás, leader of Yakye Axa*, digitally enhanced painting by the artist Diego C. Schäfer from the 2014 exposition *Hacer visible lo invisible.*

they did drink soda. Asuncenos drank wine and shortly thereafter began talking about the fact that Paraguayan politicians were "sin vergüenza" (shameless) for their behavior toward Indigenous Paraguayans. As the night progressed and people drank more wine, the conversation seemed to shift to other quotidian things pertinent to life in the capital city: potholes, new shopping malls, and plans for post-reception gatherings. There was a clear social differentiation between the asuncenos and the Enxet in attendance, with little interaction between the two groups. Many people from Yakye Axa and Sawhoyamaxa left shortly after the opening ceremony to sit outside with their wares and talk with one another.

At one point, I was looking at the portrait of Tomás Galeano and his large glasses. Anivel, one of the Yakye Axa leaders, walked up and asked if I knew who Tomás was. I told him I had never met him but that I knew of Tomás. Looking at the picture,

Anivel told me Tomás had encouraged him to become a leader of the community, though he was quite young at the time. Until Tomás's suggestion, Anivel had been an *estancionero*, driving cattle on nearby ranches.[1] "I learned much from Tomás," Anivel said. We stood looking at the painting in silence for several minutes. Then he said, "It is good that they did this [made the exhibition]. But it is hard to look at these and think of the suffering. When I see these pictures [*fotos*] they make me think, make me remember a lot of painful things. Tomás fought for years but was never able to see the end of the fight."[2] After that, Anivel left the gallery.

Anivel's comments about the images on display at the exhibition highlight one of the many processes of re-victimization that making visible entails. Making visible is an arguably necessary political strategy but can objectify mundane forms of violence. The images, while starkly beautiful denunciations, are disassociated from the context they were abstracted from. Inviting community members from Yakye Axa and Sawhoyamaxa to the reception was intended to further humanize and render visible the issues the portraits depict, Schäfer told me. Yet, based on what I observed that night, I was not sure that was the effect.

The organizations coordinating the "Hacer visible" campaign contend that the only way to confront injustice is to expose it. The campaign's goals are "to denounce the historical discrimination faced by Indigenous peoples in Paraguay, educate in Human Rights and encourage participation in the defense of the Human Rights of Indigenous Peoples in Paraguay."[3] The campaign has raised the profile of the Yakye Axa and Sawhoyamaxa cases both within Paraguay and internationally, even garnering support from the renowned Puerto Rican reggaeton band Calle 13. However, in making the invisible visible in the way that was done that evening, it was clear that new erasures were produced. Some of the people depicted in the portraits, including Doña Florencia, were in attendance, yet mostly silent: present as living images and stories rather than people who live the images framed on the gallery walls. Indeed, most members of Yakye Axa and Sawhoyamaxa only briefly looked at the paintings, and there was a clear racial divide inseparable from the objectifications the campaign sought to overturn. Still, it is clear that making the invisible visible has increased pressure on the Paraguayan state to act. Without such pressure, state officials could very well do nothing but let community members languish on the margin of the highway. Making visible is one strategy to disrupt the official state narratives of care for Indigenous citizens and its facile commitments to implement the IACHR judgments. Through optics of care, officials intend to control the image of how the state handles Indigenous affairs but does so in a way that obscures what is hidden in plain sight: legal abandonment and the environmental racism that results.

CHAPTER 3

Biopolitics of Neglect

Ruta 5 is a 145-kilometer stretch of highway that connects the towns of Pozo Colorado and Concepción while simultaneously bisecting Yakye Axa and Sawhoyamaxa. Roughly following the early Anglican supply lines route, the highway is bordered to the north and south by ranchlands with a landscape defined by pastures and palm trees. Given the long history of ranching in this area, the only settlements along the highway aside from Yakye Axa and Sawhoyamaxa are a handful of houses populated by landless campesino families trying to make a living working as hired hands for local ranchers. Here cattle outnumber humans many times over. There is little to reveal that people also occupy the region, save for the residents of the roadside communities who display wares such as freshly skinned animals, honey in repurposed plastic soda bottles, and fans woven from palm leaves near the highway's edge. The goods serve as markers that call to the eye because they break with a settler landscape overwhelmingly populated by cattle, barbed-wire fences, and the remnants of a once-extensive palm and scrub forest. Other markers break the pattern of fencerows adorned with signs reading *propiedad privada* (private property). Makeshift memorials commemorate lives lost to the everyday violence of roadside life, whether from traffic accidents or lack of access to medical services or transportation. It seems that most traffic passes without taking notice of the homes, people, and lives on the margin of Ruta 5.

Yet from the margin it is impossible not to notice each passing car, bus, or semi speeding by. Where Ruta 5 passes through Yakye Axa and Sawhoyamaxa, the road surface turns from asphalt to a mixture of packed earth and pebbles used as fill.[1] When vehicles pass, they kick up clouds of orange dust that coats everything with a fine grit, from the plants whose green leaves appear yellowed to the clothes left to dry on the barbed-wire fences that mark the limits of the Loma Verde ranch, and permeates the air community members breath every day. On one of my first visits to Yakye Axa, I awoke startled in the night by the semis lumbering over the road's many potholes. The heavy trucks make the ground tremble like a low-grade earthquake as they pass, to say nothing of the sounds of their creaking chassis, the loud music, and the cattle mooing in protest. The traffic passes day and night, while most people in Yakye Axa and Sawhoyamaxa have little to no access to transportation other than their feet, something often referred to as "línea once." This literally translates to "line eleven," referring to bus route 11, yet it is also a metaphor for the two legs whose silhouettes evoke the number 11. Línea 11 means you will be walking instead of taking a bus.

Life on the side of the road in Yakye Axa is pedestrian. In contrast to the traffic, the pace of life is slow. Kids either play on the cracked, dry earth or in the mud, depending on the season. Some families go to the small Pentecostal church, while others still believe in what many community members refer to as "cultura indígena."[2] Women wash clothes in a pond dug into the margin. Men often look for sparse day-labor opportunities on nearby ranches. People sit together to share tereré, watch the traffic pass, and talk about life on, and possibly off, the margin. In many ways, everyday life on the margin of Ruta 5 is not that different from living in other rural communities across the region that are subject to the challenges posed by Paraguay's agro-export development model. Wage labor is often sparse, as is access to state services, and struggles for land rights abound.

The circumstances through which Yakye Axa and Sawhoyamaxa both came to inhabit the margin of Ruta 5 and remain there for over a generation are distinct. After both communities refused to give up their respective legal struggles to reclaim portions of the Loma Verde and Loma Porã ranches that had enclosed their lands, the owners of those ranches forced them from the properties by making life untenable—restricting hunting and access to water and firewood, among other acts. Given the history of land enclosure in the Bajo Chaco, two options remained: move to join another indigenous community on lands not their own or stay and demand restitution of their ancestral lands. After years of unsuccessful attempts to achieve land restitution, the Yakye Axa left the Loma Verde ranch to live with relatives in El Estribo, a community located some 200 kilometers northwest. However, life at El Estribo was difficult because the small parcel of land was already home to over one hundred Enxet families, leaving little space for people of Yakye Axa to live. After several years, community members decided to return to their lands at Loma Verde, but ranch owners prohibited entry. In protest, community members established Yakye Axa on the margin of Ruta 5 in front of the lands they claimed; the community still remains there at the time of writing. Members of Sawhoyamaxa established their roadside community after being forced from the Loma Porã ranch in an effort to force the state to adjudicate their land claim.[3] Neither community anticipated the state claims would go unanswered for so long.

The dialectics of disruption involve working with and against the law; here I focus on the spaces and situations between those acts. Whereas chapter 2 discusses the evolution of Paraguay's politics of recognition by attending to emergent Enxet and Sanapaná indigeneity and the following chapters tease out extralegal actions community members take to disrupt the patrón, this chapter centers forms of liminality through which settler governance of human and other-than-human life operates to define contemporary Indigenous-state relations. The Paraguayan state's legal abandonment of Enxet and Sanapaná people exposes the aporia of simultaneous inclusion and exclusion as full citizens, revealing how the biopolitics of other-than-human life has profound impacts on Indigenous lifeways. Scholars often describe routinized forms of violence that are so common as to appear natural as structural, silent, and slow.[4]

This chapter argues that such violence is the outcome of a *biopolitics of neglect* and its manifestation as environmental racism, whereby specific social groups are forced to live the unfreedoms of dispossession so that others might live.[5] The Paraguayan state governs Indigenous affairs through forms of neglect manifest across several registers—from failure to adjudicate land claims to the imposition of states of emergency. This how many of my interlocutors have come to know "the state" and how many settlers blame environmental harms on "Indigenous culture."[6] In the broadest terms, Michel Foucault's formative notion of biopolitics posits an analytic to understand how states come to govern populations through initiatives that render them measurable and classifiable and seek to ensure particular health outcomes for the operation of a capitalist political economy.[7] States require legible subjects to ensure the governance of life—from human populations to land and natural resources.[8] Instead of focusing directly on state efforts to govern Indigenous life, I assess how neglect via legal abandonment is a de facto form of governance. In so doing, I point to how state actions, or the lack thereof, deny care to Indigenous peoples while simultaneously ensuring the well-being of cattle that graze on appropriated lands. Thinking with biopolitics beyond the human, I examine how the governance of cattle life, as a proxy for settler well-being, takes precedence over ensuring the basic human rights of Indigenous peoples.[9] Environmental justice scholarship has long viewed environmental racism along the registers of distributional, procedural, and representative processes or the lack thereof. I build from those approaches by attending to the literal and metaphoric margins that many of my interlocutors from Yakye Axa, Sawhoyamaxa, and Xákmok Kásek have inhabited.[10] There are clear problems of inadequate resource distribution, due process, and political representation that undermine Enxet and Sanapaná well-being. However, as will become clear later in the book, my interlocutors' actions move beyond these forms of (in)justice through restorative acts that drive transformative justice beyond legal remedies alone.

Legal abandonment is a facet of the biopolitics of neglect that simultaneously advances a tacit project of Indigenous erasure and distances the settler state from culpability. There is, however, an important discursive act that states employ to distance themselves from guilt. Some might call it plausible deniability. I call it the optics of care. State actors use videos, press releases, public acts, declarations, and the like to create the imaginary of a pastoral state that seeks to ensure Indigenous well-being, when in reality the optics of care normalizes everyday forms of racialized violence because they do nothing to fundamentally change inequity. In effect, then, state officials maintain their ability to govern Indigenous affairs through discretionary acts that maintain uncertainty as the norm. Through uncertainty, the biopolitics of neglect becomes the quotidian means of eliminating Indigenous life where vital resources like emergency aid and legal protections always come without guarantees.[11]

RUMINATING ON BIOPOLITICS OF THE MORE-THAN-HUMAN

A growing body of literature critiques the political ecology of the soybean industry and its profound impact on life in Paraguay; cattle capitalism receives less attention.[12] Here I want to shift attention from the bean to the bovine to think about biopolitics and the governance of life. An incipient soybean economy can be traced to the influence of Japanese immigrants who arrived in Paraguay after World War II and cultivated relatively small plots of land with soy in select sites in central Paraguay. However, it was not until the late 1980s that Brazilian émigrés began to introduce soybean production in a significant manner along the Paraguay-Brazil borderlands, and later, in 1993, the first genetically modified (GM) soybeans were smuggled into the country from Argentina. The introduction of GM soybeans in Paraguay initiated a series of distinct social-ecological ruptures that ushered in new modes of governance over life and territory.[13] Despite the importance of soybean production and its effects on politics and life in Paraguay, cattle have long been the cornerstone of rural development across the country and drive development in the Chaco.

From the seven cows and one bull discussed in chapter 1, Paraguay's herd has grown to more than 15 million head of cattle, and the country is among the top ten global beef exporters.[14] In the first quarter of 2020, the National Service for Animal Quality and Health (SENACSA) reported that 137,000 people tend to 14,026,143 cattle in 103,946 "establishments" (farms, ranches, etc.) across all seventeen administrative departments in the country.[15] Moreover, the level of detail recorded and made publicly available about the status and composition of Paraguay's cattle herd is remarkable. At any point, producers can evaluate the total number, classified by specific age group and gender, of cattle living in any given department and/or establishment size. In early 2020, there were, for example, 299,802 cows (female) living in establishments containing 1 to 20 animals, whereas 2,838,170 cows were living in establishments with more than 1,000 animals.[16] SENACSA provides the same level of detail for steers, heifers, bulls, recently weaned calves, calves, and oxen because it maintains a rigorous and regular process for tracking cattle health and production across Paraguay. These processes require that all producers report any births, deaths, sales, or transfer of ownership of cattle. SENACSA uses this data to create biannual production reports and control cattle movement via checkpoints on all major roadways where trucks transporting cattle must stop for inspections to ensure that all animals are appropriately registered with current vaccinations and documentation of ownership. The framework for cattle governance is supported by legal doctrine, economic policy, technical support for producers, biosecurity measures, and everyday inscription devices like cattle brands and ear tags that mark lives as owned, ordered, and accountable.[17]

State imperatives to support cattle life are in stark contrast to the state's lack of support for Indigenous well-being, something that the governance apparatus created for both populations underscores. A dedicated minister of ranching works within the Ministry of Agriculture to command an army of field technicians, veterinarians, and scientific research to advance the industry in support of cattle life and death. Meanwhile, the state agency dedicated to the governance of Indigenous affairs is only an institute with far less political clout than a ministry and an abysmal budget to adjudicate the services it is tasked with providing.[18] Indeed, Indigenous peoples have long been denied basic identity documents due to the lack of state funds to maintain updated census information and registries. Whereas industrial cattle production in the United States often revolves around a concentrated feedlot model that requires extensive nutritional inputs, such as the soybeans grown in southeastern Paraguay, cattle are almost exclusively pasture raised in Paraguay.[19] It comes as no surprise, then, that supporting a herd of 15 million cattle requires an extensive land area—all of which is unceded Indigenous territory. Herein lies a critical point. The Paraguayan state's biopolitics of caring for cattle life reveals the neglect to provide basic forms of care for the lives it considers to be in the way of cattle capitalism.

Here I want to pick up on Foucault's influential calculus of making live and letting die. For Foucault, this calculus centered on making specific human populations live and letting other human populations die. Indeed, Li elaborates on this very point when she ponders "why governing authorities would elect not to intervene when they could, or select one subset of the population for life enhancement while abandoning another."[20] I work with Li's analysis of "surplus populations" to show why governing authorities would select one population for life enhancement while abandoning another. Bringing this provocation into conversation with approaches to the biopolitics of the other-than-human, I ask why Paraguayan state authorities would choose to support cattle life—lives destined to be killed—over its Indigenous citizens living on the margins of the cattle economy.[21]

"WHAT A PRIVILEGE IT IS TO BE A COW!"

Agrarian politics and rural social movements continue to grapple with the legacy of corrupt and illegal land acquisitions that stem from Stroessner-era land reforms. The former promise of land reform that fueled much of Stroessner's populist agrarian message had long faded, just as the once-stable incomes provided by traditional crop production that many campesinos relied on disappeared with the collapse of the country's cotton market, mechanization of sugarcane production, and introduction of GM soybeans.[22] Shifts in global and regional commodity trading driven by increasing demands for soybeans and the influence of the MERCOSUR regional trade agreement radically altered campesino livelihoods.[23] These macroeconomic shifts directly influenced the local political economies of agrarian life, something I witnessed during the two years (2006–8) I lived in central Paraguay working with non-Indigenous campesino families on issues of food security and soil conservation.

Here I take a pause from the Chaco to draw from my previous experiences working with campesino families in Barrero Azul because those experiences reveal insights into how the cultural politics of food and racist tropes influence popular imaginaries of Indigenous peoples that circulate in everyday conversation. The cultural politics of beef consumption that I became aware of through my work amid the global food crisis resonate with Indigenous land struggles in the Chaco. Beef has become part of Paraguayan national identity; thus challenging the status quo of the ranching industry can be read as an affront to deeply held traditions.

One of the main concerns in Barrero Azul was the fact that prices for the goods campesinos produced had fallen through the floor while prices in the local stores for staple goods like wheat or rice had simultaneously gone through the roof, squeezing campesino families at both ends. Such concerns were reflected by the growing disquiet reported on the nightly news. Sitting on the porch at my host family's house on hot, humid summer nights in early 2007, we watched news reports showing that Australia was suffering through its worst drought in centuries, a slow-moving disaster that destroyed its wheat production, causing prices to rise around the globe. By all measures, this was the start of the global food crisis of 2007–8, when prices of major staple food commodities rose around the world, intersecting with the subprime housing market financial crisis of 2008 that resulted in what many now call the Great Recession. With the subsequent collapse of global financial markets, many investors turned to more stable financial instruments and spurred the global land rush.[24] As a result, Paraguayan soybean production dramatically expanded to fill the increased demand for flex crops, and the price of land in southeastern Paraguay soared, displacing many large-scale cattle ranching operations to the northern Chaco, where lands were much cheaper. Indeed, young campesino men who I worked with left Barrero Azul to take temporary jobs clearing land and building fences on the new ranches. Kai Mario, my dear friend, debated going but ultimately decided to stay in Barrero Azul because of his family.

Kai Mario, his wife, Ña Barbara, and their four children lived in a 4-by-5-meter single-room house on a small plot of land hemmed in between two cattle pastures. Mario paid no rent to live on the land, though he was responsible for caring for his patrón Silvio's small herd of about thirty-five cattle. Raising four school-aged kids while making the equivalent of about US$3 per day, in addition to whatever he could earn doing side jobs, was extremely difficult. During the two years that I lived with Mario and Barbara, I gained intimate insight into how the politics of land inequality in Paraguay impact smallholders and their families in highly uneven ways. I also learned how important cattle, particularly the ability to eat beef, is to national imaginaries of identity. Indeed, many people I have worked with across the country do not consider something a meal unless it contains meat, preferably beef.[25] When we ate meals of only beans, my teenage host brothers would often choose not to eat in protest. Beans marked a culinary class politics that they would not abide. Before walking off to sulk out of sight, the eldest son would stand up from the table and declare in his crackly pubescent voice, "Nda'u mo'ai pe tembiu. Mboriahu peguarã" (I won't eat that food. It is for the poor). In his view, a lunch without meat was a meal that only the truly destitute would eat. He preferred to go hungry rather than succumb to the embarrassment of such intimate food politics.

Beyond the question of class, food names can reveal how racialization works through everyday practices. Meat at the local butcher was expensive. The modest stipend I received for my work and funds I shared with Mario and Barbara did not cover the cost of quality meat cuts. Instead, my host family purchased "puchero avá." *Puchero* is stew meat. *Avá* is Guaraní for "Indian." At the local butcher, puchero avá—Indian stew meat—consisted of the leftover cuts from the butchering process: small hunks of bone with bits of meat, ligaments, and chunks of fat, or the cow's entrails. When lunch contained these cuts, we savored a few bits of meat and then gnawed on cartilage, sucked the marrow out of bones, and chewed hunks of fat.

The everyday politics of beef consumption reveal more than mere food preference. They reveal the deeply ingrained relationship between cattle capitalism and settler colonial life, even for those dispossessed from that system and alienated by it daily. The Paraguayan anthropologist Margarita Miró Ibars traces the history of the dish puchero avá to the front lines of the Triple Alliance War, where food for soldiers was scarce and the need for protein-rich foods was great.[26] After butchering higher-quality cuts of meat, the leftover cuts were also necessary to maintain soldiers' lives. Despite the lifesaving significance of the dish, the equation of these cuts of beef with the avá, the Indian man, shows how the everyday processes of racialization position Indigenous lives as necessary leftovers within settler society. Puchero avá thus stems from a racial food geography and is a quotidian reminder of the social order of Indigenous life in settler imaginaries. Yet it is also a bridge between the class politics of poor campesinos and Indigenous peoples, whose lives have limited value in cattle capitalism.

What happens to the surplus populations who now inhabit the margins of political economic, social, and ecological processes required to convert vast expanses of Paraguayan territory to soybean fields and pasturelands? The answer is not without its contradictions. Many landed elites and state officials view such populations as left over, yet acknowledge that they play an important role in feeding national imaginaries, like puchero avá. Imaginaries of Indigenous heritage fuel an important source of Paraguayan identity politics. Guaraní is one of two official languages, the other being Spanish. And though Guaraní is an Indigenous language, some Indigenous peoples of the Chaco consider it equally as colonizing as the Spanish or German spoken by settlers across the country because of how it is also used in official state discourse and among non-Indigenous Paraguayans. Guaraní also marks clear class divisions, associated with rural spaces of those with lower levels of education—a legacy of Stroessner-era efforts to promote Spanish by banning Guaraní language instruction. The endurance of the Guaraní language and its recognition as one of two official languages in Paraguay is a source of national pride and identity for many. Indeed, populist leaders often use Guaraní to appeal to rural Paraguayans, as demonstrated by the former presidential candidate Lino Oveido's 2008 campaign slogan *ikatu lo mitã!* (The people can do it!). In these ways, the Guaraní language comes to shape national identity and allows many speakers to selectively articulate a connection to Indigenous heritage, the "sangre y tierra" (blood and land) Guaraní, when or if it is advantageous. On the other hand, state narratives created the imaginary of the campesino who settled the "empty lands" of southeastern Paraguay during the Stroessner-era agrarian reforms as the cornerstone of national development, hardworking agrarian people with the courage to pioneer a new life for the promise of a better future.[27] Yet that imaginary has tarnished with time. In the context of laser-leveled fields and precision agricultural methods to maximize yields from monocrops, the discourse about campesinos has changed; they are seen more like weeds and akin to Indigenous peoples, both of which are the disorderly leftovers who have become an obstacle rather than a vehicle to development.[28]

Whereas the Jesuit Miguel Chase-Sardi advocated for Indigenous rights that were trampled by the ranching industry in the Chaco, the Jesuit priest Pa'i Oliva defended campesinos whose human rights the soybean industry threatened. A Spaniard who first traveled to Paraguay in 1964 during the dictatorship, Oliva was immediately expelled from the country, only to return in 1994, gain citizenship, and draw from liberation theology to maintain ardent critiques of agro-extractivism until his death at the age of ninety-three in 2022. Throughout his life, Oliva argued that the valuation of export commodities, both soy and cattle, over those of the rural poor facilitated state violence. From 2009 to 2016 he published his thoughts in a personal blog, from which I quote his short essay, "The Privilege to Be a Cow."

> The privilege to be a cow.
> And what a privilege, my God!
>
> For their nutrition, there exists 17 million hectares of land dedicated to cattle ranching in Paraguay. And, given that we have 11 million cows, each one has more than a hectare to eat from. All the while in Paraguay, there are more than 300,000 campesinos who do not have even one hectare.

> In our country, there are more veterinarians for cows than doctors for humans. Worse yet, the veterinarians are not afraid to go to the countryside to care for the little cows. Meanwhile, many doctors prefer to stay in Asunción, abandoning the sick in the countryside.
>
> What a privilege it is to be a cow!
>
> Our campesinos, united by good faith with Paraguayans, we mobilize today to yell to everyone that we also want a solution to the ill-gotten lands. They must examine the property titles and place appropriate taxes on the lands according to their size, type of production, and the manual labor employed.
>
> In the production of soy, only one person works for every 500 hectares planted. In one garden, a family of four works.
>
> Between cattle with privileges and virtually untaxed lands accumulated in very few hands, we live poorly in Paraguay.[29]

Pa'i Oliva's words reference the reality of many rural poor who have been driven off their lands to live on the margins of the country's primary agro-extractivist industries. Whether it be the literal margin of Ruta 5 in the Chaco where Yakye Axa has been located for more than a generation or the edges of soybean fields where campesinos *sin tierra* (without land) or the Mbya Guaraní of the Yapo community in Paraguay's southeast now live, the biopolitical imperative to support cattle and soybeans for export takes precedence over the lives of leftover, "surplus" populations.[30]

As Pa'i Oliva wrote, the Paraguayan state invests far more to facilitate care for cattle than it does to facilitate care for "surplus" campesinos and Indigenous peoples. Veterinarians will readily travel to the *campo* (countryside) to administer vaccinations; indeed, the ARP history of Paraguayan cattle ranching boasts, "In 2011, 12,600,000 head of cattle were vaccinated two times, something incomparable nationally. This would be equivalent to vaccinating the entire population of Asunción against the flu annually for 40 years without missing one of its inhabitants."[31] Meanwhile, it is no exaggeration to state that Indigenous peoples and many campesinos live without any viable access to even basic health services. Several independent assessments have demonstrated this trend. The IACHR judgments that address the Yakye Axa, Sawhoyamaxa, and Xákmok Kásek cases each detail the repeated failure of the state to provide health services to community members. Moreover, the 2015 report by the United Nations Special Rapporteur on the Rights of Indigenous Peoples reiterates these concerns and argues that the life conditions for Indigenous peoples across the country should be treated as an emergency.[32] These are the fundamental rights, the privileges of citizenship, that most rural poor who live in the spaces between the dialectics of soybean production and cattle ranching do not enjoy. The state's biopolitical priorities to ensure care for the life of soybeans and cattle at the expense of its most marginalized citizens reveal the biopolitics of neglect and how extraordinary violence becomes routine.[33]

THE EMERGENCY

The sun was already low in the sky when the brand-new white Mercedes cargo truck emblazoned with bold black capital letters reading Secretaría de Emergencia Nacional arrived in the 16 de agosto aldea of Sawhoyamaxa. Eriberto and I, along with everyone else in the aldea, had been waiting all afternoon for the truck to arrive with the month's ration delivery. Hearing the rumble of the truck drawing near, Eriberto jogged to the side of Ruta 5 and flagged down the delivery. SEN workers steered the truck to a flat spot just off the highway, and shortly after that, two state functionaries stepped out of the cab, one with the community census and the other to supervise the food provision. The functionaries recruited a handful of Enxet men to offload the cargo. Working fast in the setting sun, the men lifted nearly 2,000 kilos of goods out of the truck bed while the functionary sat and observed. Each product, from bleached white flour to salt, was wrapped in 20- to 30-kilo bundles and had to be lifted up and over the top of the truck bed before being lowered down onto someone's waiting shoulder. From there, each person carried the load a few meters before setting it on the ground, where another group of people opened the packages and organized all the products into piles on the dirt. After community members unload the rations under the supervision of SEN functionaries, who also verify community census information to ensure that only registered families receive food, they fill one plastic bag provided by SEN with 40 kilos of products. Since rations are only delivered to one location per aldea it is each family's responsibility to carry the goods to their homes, which many have to do by walking several kilometers because few have motorcycles or working bicycles. The thick plastic bags often later serve as makeshift housing materials or to store clothing at home.

A few days before the SEN ration distribution, Gladys, a key figure in the Sawhoyamaxa land struggle who lives in a different aldea from Eriberto, had invited me to her home to talk about the implementation of the IACHR ruling in favor of the community, but she also shared her view of the SEN food deliveries.[34] She was tending to a recently planted bed of lettuce when I arrived, explaining that an NGO recently held a food-security workshop in the community and encouraged families to plant gardens. She set down her hoe and invited me to drink tereré while we talked. "We get food from *the emergency*," she said as we sat in front of her house. "They bring us food every month. Sometimes they are late. We don't know exactly when it will come"—her words hung in the air before she looked toward her neighbors' houses—"but everyone here gets food from them." Counting on her hand, she listed the inventory they usually receive. "They bring flour, yerba, sugar, rice, coquitos, oil, salt, and pasta. Five kilos each. They used to bring vaka'i and soap, but they don't anymore." She pulled over the bucket where she had been drawing out cups of water for the tereré to show me the yellow-tinted liquid gathered from a nearby pond and said, "Sometimes they used to bring water in a truck. It is supposed to be good water. But it was just pumped from a stock pond

FIGURE 8. The SEN truck and ration distribution in the 16 de agosto aldea of Sawhoyamaxa. A SEN functionary sits atop the truck watching community members hoist and unload the provisions. Photo by author, 2015.

because they didn't want to pay for the gas to carry clean water from Concepción. The trucks are heavier when full of water, so they use more gas. The drivers were sneaky. They would fill the trucks with dirty water on a ranch nearby and keep the extra money for the gas. They haven't given us water in a long time."

As the conversation continued, Gladys talked about being a single mother and the challenges of raising kids while doing basic domestic chores like gathering firewood or tending to the few animals she had.

> There is nowhere to work. Only ranches. They won't hire me. It is really hard. Without the land, there is no food. So we need the emergency. The food they bring isn't good. Sometimes it has bugs, or the flour is old and hard. The beans are bad. The yerba tastes bad. But it is all we have. What can we do? We eat it. But it is not enough for a family. Can you feed a family of six people with five kilos of rice for a month? My neighbor's family eats all that in a week. There is never enough food.

The provision of emergency services has been a necessary, yet always inadequate, source of food for members of all three communities. Indeed, in the seventy-one household surveys I administered in Xákmok Kásek and Sawhoyamaxa, every household indicated that the food rations had provided a necessary source of nutrition in the context of the land dispossession they encountered. This near-monthly ritual of emergency deliveries repeated hundreds of times since 1999 exemplifies how the Paraguayan state does the bare minimum to demonstrate "care" while abandoning legally binding commitments to restitute land.

Over the course of my research, many people from Sawhoyamaxa, Yakye Axa, and Xákmok Kásek did not equate the food provisions with a legal state of emergency but instead referred to the service only as "the emergency," as though emergencies are quotidian, normalized. That is because the emergency is everywhere. Every month the emergency makes its presence known when trucks loaded with sacks of food arrive to make a delivery. Emergency looks like food rations lined up in piles and draped in large, heavy-duty plastic bags emblazoned with the Paraguayan flag, the SEN logo, and then-President Horacio Cartes's governing mantra in Guaraní, "jajapo oñondivepa tape pyahu" (together we are building a new way). Emergency literally emerges from the ground because many of the beans that arrive get poured on the ground, where they are left to sprout later. In Xákmok Kásek, several people told me they deliberately pour out the beans in protest. "Indigenous don't want to eat beans," one person told me, "and they won't bring us something different to eat. They treat us like we are all the same, beggars who have to accept what they give." Emergency smells like stinky pasta that is questionably edible, but you eat it because there is nothing else to eat. It also smells like flatulence from those who keep their beans, which don't cook well because they are old and thus hard to digest. Emergency tastes like stale, dry crackers that are sometimes so hard they crack brittle teeth. It also tastes like bitter, dusty yerba mate of a quality not sold in stores. Often emergency doesn't taste like anything because the rations run out shortly after being delivered. Emergency sounds like the soft murmur of conversation and the sometimes-audible rumble in hungry bellies as people stand or sit and watch the food rations organized in piles on the ground before they can take them. It sounds like male community members joking and laughing as they unload 25- to 30-kilo packets of flour, salt, or yerba mate from the back of the SEN truck onto people's shoulders waiting below to carry the food to its designated pile. It sounds like a roll call of names as the SEN employee reads the census to call recipients forward one at a time to choose their pile of food. Emergency feels like brief relief from hunger, a welcome delivery of aid. But it also is the backbreaking strain of carrying 40 kilos from the drop-off point to your home.

Yet emergencies are not normal conditions of life. They are inherently temporal phenomena. *Merriam-Webster* defines emergency first as "an unforeseen combination of circumstances or the resulting state that calls for immediate action" and second as "an urgent need for assistance or relief."[35] In this regard, an emergency must be understood as a momentary rupture when conditions radically change in ways that threaten life. Yet the protracted states of emergency Paraguayan officials have declared in response to the conditions in Yakye Axa, Sawhoyamaxa, and Xákmok Kásek run counter to the normative temporalities of emergency. Rather than the unforeseen combination of circumstances that creates an immediate need for relief, the reorganization of life to support ranching was, and still is, meticulously planned by state agencies and private interests. The spatiality of land enclosure and systems of racial capitalism that enabled extensive cattle ranching, first in the Bajo Chaco and later across the entirety of that territory, required creating spaces for specific forms of life. Those spaces—pastures, retiros, enclosed Indigenous communities—ordered life in clearly biopolitical terms, "defining who matters and who does not, who is *disposable* and who is not."[36]

However, it is important to note that the biopolitics of life in this space is not only about the racial geographies of *who* matters, but the other-than-human geographies of *what* matters. The prioritization of cattle life over Indigenous life renders clear a different ordering of zoe and bios from what Agamben conceived in the state of bare life.[37] Instead of rendering the human subject animal and thereby justifiable to kill, such as with the "indios bárbaros" of the US-Mexico borderlands,[38] the demarcation of lands to manage other-than-human lives, in this case cattle, and the demarcation of emergency to manage Indigenous life materially separates the zoe (animal) from the bios (human) while effectively rendering Indigenous life neither fully human nor animal vis-à-vis the settler state. In this context, state acts deny Enxet and Sanapaná peoples their humanity by negating their rights while also drawing them into a liminal condition between subjecthood and personhood through protracted legal processes.[39] Governing by emergency is not an immediate response to provide relief to an unforeseen condition. It is a form of biopower that maintains liminality and environmental racism through neglect.

OPTICS OF CARE

The states of emergency declared in Enxet and Sanapaná communities are, at first glance, "make live interventions."[40] Yet their duration and subsequent normalization reveals the state's intent is not to make live but to create the image that it is providing care. Paraguayan functionaries use press releases, reports, and institution websites to create an optics of care that presents state actions as munificent when in practice they are anything but. Take, for example, the text from the SEN website that discusses the agency administering food rations in systematized ways to populations in need.

> Families from the Xakmok Kasek [*sic*] Indigenous community will receive more than 3,400 kilograms of food staples. . . . An operational team from the Secretariat [SEN] will head to the Puerto Pinasco district this afternoon to assist the inhabitants of the Indigenous community who will receive 72 food kits, each weighing 48 kilos. These goods will be very useful for the natives [*nativos*] whose principal foods are from hunting and fishing. Each family will receive the following nonperishable foods: oil (4 liters), rice (5 kg), sugar (5 kg), flour (5 kg), pasta (5 kg), yerba (5 kg), beans (5 kg), breads (5 kg), peanuts (3 kg), conserved meat (4 packs), soap (2 units), and salt (1 kg). The National Emergency Secretariat periodically assists Indigenous communities in the Chaco territory in agreement with the Court [IACHR] rulings that oblige the Paraguayan state to process land restitution and provide diverse services from its institutions.[41]

A close reading of this text reveals much about the state as patrón. Claiming to deliver 3,400 kilos of rations to Xákmok Kásek provides an impressive statistic that suggests a large quantity of food. At the time of that reporting, about 250 people lived in the community. Assuming the rations are evenly distributed across the population, 3,400 kilos ensure 13.6 kilos of emergency goods per person per month, or 0.45 kilo per day. If a person eats only two meals per day, the rations equate to one-quarter kilo per meal. The total edible kilos per person is considerably less if one accounts for the fact that salt, yerba mate, cooking oil, and soap factor into the total kilos provided to each family. Furthermore, this does not account for the nutritional and caloric value of the food, which, apart from the beans, is composed of highly processed starches. An overwhelming majority of household survey respondents across the three communities agreed that the quantity and quality of rations were insufficient. This was especially true for large families, who received the same quantity of food as a family of three. Respondents commonly replied, "michi'eterei" (very small) or "sa'i" (a little/too little), when I would ask about the quantity of rations. State officials I interviewed suggested that the food provisions are not supposed to be the sole source of food for a family for a month, hence the limited amount. Yet the state's repeated neglect in resolving the three cases, and hence the reliance on the state of emergency over the course of several decades, left the communities little option other than to rely on the rations.

The SEN text also builds on racialized discourse about Indigenous peoples in Paraguay. In Paraguay, *nativos* (natives) is often considered a pejorative term, along with *indio* (indian).[42] Indios are often equated with nonmodern or "backward" figures, whereas indígenas (Indigenous) are rights-bearing subjects.[43] The SEN text also harkens back to lasting tropes that Enxet and Sanapaná are hunter-gatherers by stating that the communities' primary food source "come[s] from hunting and fishing." Many Enxet and Sanapaná do still hunt, fish, and gather foods from the forest, but they do so out of necessity or preference rather than strict adherence to cultural practice.[44] As one woman from Yakye Axa commented to me, "If we don't go fishing, we won't eat. There is no money to buy food from the *makatero!*"[45] Although Enxet and Sanapaná traditions of hunting and gathering played an important role in their legal efforts to reclaim land, none identified themselves as hunter-gatherers and many openly rejected the term. As we sat by a fire cooking eel after our fishing trip that day, Clemente once told me:

> We are modern people. We know the law and our rights. We are professional ranchers, tractor drivers, teachers, leaders, butchers, and health workers like anyone else. We are not hunter-gatherers. I don't like it when people call us that. Enxet used to live that way, but not anymore. If I go hunt, or fish, or get food from the forest it is not because I am a hunter-gatherer. I like that food better. It is healthier. Beef is full of chemicals and medicine. Forest meat [*so'o ka'aguy*] tastes better and is natural. People who call us hunter-gatherers are ignorant. They don't know Indigenous people.[46]

Clemente's comments illustrate the Faustian bargain of strategic essentialisms.[47] Evoking the image of the hunter-gatherer, indigenistas have long lobbied the Paraguayan state to restitute large expanses of land to support traditional Indigenous practices. However, the image of the hunter-gather freezes the idea of Indigenous peoples in time and practice.[48] For SEN to reproduce the hunter-gatherer trope on its website in the year 2017 is telling. It demonstrates a lack of care and awareness of Indigenous issues, despite purportedly intending to do the opposite. The difference is important. Providing emergency services to ensure populations live or can sustain a temporary shock is arguably a positive intervention, yet providing such services to create an image of care that does nothing to address structural issues exacerbates Indigenous dispossession.

Finally, the suggestion that SEN "periodically assists Indigenous communities in the Chaco" is vexing. If nothing else, SEN's framing of the assistance program is dehistoricized and promotes an image of problem-specific care rather than systemic neglect. SEN has been responsible for providing food aid every month since 2009 for Xákmok Kásek and since 1999 for Yakye Axa and Sawhoyamaxa. There is nothing periodic about that; it is a routine and normalized activity. The only thing periodic about the emergency is that while rations are supposed to come every month, many people report they never know when or if they will come.

Periodic Assistance

I want to pause to think through one ramification of "periodic assistance." State actors—official representatives of the state—only periodically appear or are present in any of the claimant communities. Community members often express feelings of neglect due to this absence, stating that the officials have "forgotten about the Indigenous," "only care about the rich and not poor Indigenous," or "never come to check on our case." But the "periodic" visits to Yakye Axa, Sawhoyamaxa, and Xákmok Kásek evoke the way that many patrones govern their ranches. The patrones periodically visit to distribute goods, payments, and monitor ranch conditions. Often they fly in on airplanes or arrive in new Toyota Hilux trucks. The long-term effects of "periodic"—read: irregular—assistance to Indigenous communities creates predictable unpredictability, a form of power that, in this example, skews in favor of the state-as-patrón and ensures that state actors maintain a position of authority over resource access and distribution. Periodically, people wait on a scheduled day for food rations that never arrive. Periodically, SEN does not deliver the rations one month and the next month brings double rations. Periodically, spoilage or bugs ruin the rations. Veronica, a woman from the Santa Elisa aldea of Sawhoyamaxa, described it to me in the following terms, echoing Gladys' observations:

> Sometimes the drivers don't bring enough food. I think they take them [the rations] and sell them in Concepción [a town 70 km away]. If it rains or they think it will rain they don't come. We never know when the food will come. And then there are

times when it [the food] is bad. The flour is full of bugs and the pasta stinks so bad. But what can you do? We eat it. We have nothing, so we must eat it. Sometimes we complain, but then they don't bring it to us and make us wait. So we take it when they bring it, and eat it.[49]

Across all three communities, Enxet and Sanapaná interlocutors reported similar issues about rotten food and inconsistencies in delivery quantities and times, as well as the occasional conflict with delivery drivers. Perhaps most telling from Veronica's comments, however, is the fact that despite these issues, particularly the quality of the food rations, most people eat what they get because they have no other option. Care does not look like bread with weevils or hardened bags of flour. Photos and text on government institution websites and reports do not reveal these details. They construct an image intended to position the state as a benevolent patrón dutifully caring for its subjects. Yet the image of care occludes the fact that the state is reacting to conditions of its own creation.

If, as I have argued in the preceding pages, the biopolitics of cattle ranching intends to make cattle live (until they are chosen to die), then the corollary is to let the people on the margins of that system die. Both Povinelli and Melamed have argued that liberal democracies that ostensibly uphold the sanctity of human rights cannot openly allow the death and suffering of Indigenous peoples.[50] The death that results from a biopolitics of neglect thus occurs under the guise of an optics of care. By creating an image of comporting with human rights, Paraguayan state officials make calculated care acts directed not at the named recipients of such care but at other actors with which states interact, such as international human rights institutions and civil society monitors. Settler states strategically use statistics, imagery, and infrastructure to build a fetish of care that masks broader structural factors that ensure recurrent neglect of Indigenous rights.

Ordinary Emergencies

In my time working with and in the Yakye Axa, Sawhoyamaxa, and Xákmok Kásek communities I have witnessed several health emergencies and heard numerous testimonies that attest to the neglect. I want to highlight one stark but commonplace example. Tierraviva lawyers were making a trip to visit Yakye Axa and Sawhoyamaxa as part of their regular on-site monitoring of human rights conditions, and I was invited to join them. Upon arriving in Yakye Axa that afternoon in March 2015, we sat with Anivel and Anibal in front of the community's small Pentecostal church to drink tereré and catch up. Maybe thirty minutes after we arrived, a man with a concerned look walked quietly up to Anibal and whispered in his ear before stepping aside. We continued to talk for another few minutes, before Anibal mentioned, "There is a woman who is in labor over there, in the school. She is having problems. We called the hospital in Concepción four or five hours ago, but no ambulance has come." With that we all walked to the school, while José, one of the Tierraviva lawyers, drove their pickup to the site. As we approached, a woman moaned in agony from inside the small schoolhouse. She lay on a thin foam mattress on the dirt floor, surrounded by women from the community who were helping with the labor but unable to do any more because the baby was breeched, a life-threatening situation. As José backed down the embankment of Ruta 5 toward the school, six of us grabbed the mattress, each taking a corner and side to hold the mother as stable as possible while we lifted and moved her from the school through the door and into the bed of the truck. The baby's father climbed into the truck bed with two midwives to care for mother and child during the 90-kilometer trip down Ruta 5 to the hospital. The Tierraviva lawyers then drove off while I stayed behind.

Back in our seats near Anivel's house, we waited for news. "We have an agreement with the Ministry of Health," he said. "The [IACHR] judgment says that the state has to provide medical services. The ministry made an agreement to provide ambulances from the hospital in Concepción for the community." At that time, no one in Yakye Axa owned a vehicle, except for a few people who owned motorcycles. The only other option is to call the ambulance and hope that it actually arrives. "But most of the time they don't come," I was told. "They say that there is no gas or no money for gas to come all the way here. We often call them and they don't come so we do what we can." Only by a stroke of luck, José and Óscar happened to have arrived in Yakye Axa in time to shuttle the woman to the hospital in the Tierraviva truck. When José and Óscar returned late that evening, they reported that mother and child survived after an emergency cesarean section, though not without first being scolded by the medical staff for having waited so long to come to the hospital.

This birth is an example of the ordinary emergencies that regularly threaten Enxet and Sanapaná well-being. Indeed, on a trip to Yakye Axa in July 2016, I had to drive a man whose arm had been crushed during a logging accident to the same hospital in Concepción. The ambulance the community requested to take him to the hospital never arrived. All households I surveyed in Sawhoyamaxa and Xákmok Kásek reported having limited access to medical attention, medicine, and/or emergency services in the communities despite state agreements to provide such services in accordance with the respective IACHR judgments on each community.

A Senseless Building

Here I dwell on the Inter-American System attempts to improve health care access for Enxet and Sanapaná by mandating that the state provide reliable access to medical services and construct health posts in Xákmok Kásek and Kelyenmagategma. To Paraguay's credit, state officials complied with the mandates and constructed two, nearly identical, large health posts, one in each community. Each building is outfitted with six rooms—a reception area, two general checkup suites, a childbirth suite, a room for minor surgery, and a place for overnight stays—as well as the necessary medical instruments for such procedures. The buildings have large rainwater catchment systems and two-way radios to communicate with regional hospitals, and the one in Kelyenmagategma is outfitted with a state-of-the-art solar array to generate power. Construction and outfitting of each building cost approximately US$100,000, a significant sum given that very few equivalent quality health posts exist in the whole of the Chaco. On paper and in the concrete foundations of each building, the state complied with the Inter-American System to ensure the fundamental human rights of Enxet and Sanapaná. Yet the buildings are little more than a facade of care that masks a pernicious truth behind their walls.

Doctors and trained medical practitioners do not regularly receive and treat patients at the health posts, nor are they regularly supplied with medicine. On visits to Kelyenmagategma,[51] there was never any medicine save for two vials of antivenin, kept in a full-size refrigerator, but no syringes to administer the potentially lifesaving serum. The Xákmok Kásek health post built not on the community's land but in 25 de febrero, on the other hand, was full of medicine, but most of it had expired. Community members in Xákmok Kásek and Kelyenmagategma unanimously reported to me that they never know when doctors will be present in the facilities, if one is coming, and how long they will stay to treat patients. Despite having health posts in both sites, more often than not, community members must either find a boat to travel 70 kilometers downriver from Kelyenmagategma to Concepción or a truck to travel from Xákmok Kásek to Rio Verde or beyond. An Enxet first responder trained in basic community health told me, "There is no reason that this [the health post] is here. It looks nice. It has solar panels. We use the tanks [rainwater collection system] for drinking water. But the building is basically empty. No doctors are ever here to treat the sick. It is just a senseless building [*haéte edificio rei*]."[52] A Ministry of Health informant who spoke with me on condition of anonymity due to fear of reprisals, explained Indigenous health provision to me in different terms.

> It is shameful how the state treats the Indigenous. We join this line of work excited to try to make a difference. But it is really hard. They barely give us any money for gas. The people who are dedicated do their rounds on their own motorcycles and pay for their own gas. But most people can't do that. They don't have the money. Who pays when the motorcycle breaks? The roads are dirt and really tough. So even though we want to help we often stay in the health posts in town. That means we can't provide the care we should. But what can you do? The ministry does not give us the support we need to do our jobs. That means the Indigenous don't have the access they deserve. . . . I know the Xákmok Kásek health post. It is really far out there. You have to go far down the dirt road. If it rains you might be stuck for a week or two. There are lots of mosquitos and nothing to do. It is really hard to get people to agree to go work out there. Kelyenmagategma is even worse because the only way to get there is by boat.[53]

Over the course of our two-hour conversation, this Ministry of Health functionary indexed the frustrations of some state employees due to structural limitations and how those limits intersect with the provision of health services.[54] Instead of providing care, the health posts create an optics of care that suggests rights are being guaranteed. Behind each building's facade lies a "senseless" health post because state authorities fail to provide the resources needed to ensure they can provide the care they promise. Everyday forms of unpredictability exact a violent toll on the physical and psychological well-being of people who need medical services but only find antivenin with no way to administer it, expired medicine, or an ambulance that never arrives.

NEGLECTING CARE

Neglect serves as a form of biopolitics because the provision of "care" obscures the de facto denial of due process and other rights instead of addressing the root causes of Indigenous dispossession. Morgensen's analysis of settler colonialism as a globalized form of biopower vis-à-vis the fundamental logics of elimination manifested in and through "Western law" provides a helpful framing of how states of exception simultaneously include and excise Indigenous peoples from settler society.[55] And while the forms of biopower inherent in settler colonial processes of Indigenous erasure are fundamentally necropolitical in their intent to eliminate via direct violence or assimilation, I suggest that attention to the biopolitics of neglect adds another fold to studies of settler colonial practice. For Membe, "the subjugation of life to the power of death" is the essence of necropolitics.[56] In his theorization of necropower, Membe frames the subjection of life to the power of death through intentional actions—the Israeli occupation of Palestinian territories, chattel slavery on the plantations of the Americas, and Nazi concentration camps.[57] There is a clear self/other binary in each formulation that legitimizes the state of exception and its conjoined forms of violence. In the context of multicultural politics of recognition, the intentional strategy is not one of bulldozing houses to make way for new settlements per se. It is often a subtler form of legal abandonment that opens spaces and situations for neglect to act as a form of biopower that limits life choices.

The concepts of slow violence and structural violence have helped describe the temporalities of harm that do not have a precise locus or specific responsible actor.[58] While both forms of violence shape living conditions for Indigenous peoples across the Chaco, I suggest that settler colonialism and the forms of resource extraction that drive it must be understood not only as forms of environmental injustice, but as fundamentally authoritarian in the ways they condition life—defining what lives have value and what lives do not. The state of emergency is thus a project less concerned with controlling life than creating an image of caring for Enxet and Sanapaná life. In that way, it is a perverse spectacle, a fetish intended to shift attention from the structural causes of violence against Indigenous life to the actions of a state responding decisively to human suffering. The state of emergency also maintains the liminal legal status of communities that seek to take back their lands in acts that slowly chisel away at the vast territories now occupied by cattle ranches. Maintaining Enxet, Sanapaná, other Indigenous peoples, and campesinos on the margins of highways in front of the ranches or at the edges of soybean fields thus ensures a surplus labor population for landholding patrones should they want to hire while also supporting a broader narrative of agrarian politics that values "production" over noncapitalist social organization.

The geographies that Yakye Axa and Sawhoyamaxa have inhabited over the decades of their struggles show that community members are rights-bearing subjects who are subject to the abandonment of their rights. Moreover, the life conditions that many of my interlocutors grapple with give credence to the popular saying, "Cows live better than the Indigenous in the Chaco." Though destined for slaughter, cows have access to top-quality medical care, have a functioning governing apparatus that ensures their well-being during life, and are seen as vital to national identity—both as a form of sustenance and as the foundation of the political economy. On the other hand, the legislative measures taken to purportedly support Indigenous self-determination and well-being are plagued by chronic underfunding, to say nothing of popular tropes about "lazy Indigenous who don't want to work." I suggest that the topological dissonance between the prioritization of cattle life and the neglect of Indigenous well-being indexes the condition of legal abandonment—of simultaneously having and not having rights, which is the condition of never being banned or entirely included. Pratt's analysis is illuminating: she argues that legal abandonment is akin to "being neither inside nor outside the juridical order. The difference between exclusion and abandonment turns on the fact that abandonment is an active, relational process."[59] The states of emergency and the facade of care are active acts that maintain a specific social and spatial order. Rather than alleviate suffering, the states of emergency have created dependence on the state to provide food rations—a power relation whereby state actors provide, or do not, necessary life-supporting services that are always inadequate. They are now a regular feature of life that many young people in each community have always known.

The regularity of emergency feels like the normal rhythm of life, a delivery that marks the passage of time. But emergency also feels like a reminder of what could be but is not. Emergency is now mandated, not by the president of the republic, but by the IACHR, which maintains that Paraguay must continue to provide such services to Yakye Axa, Sawhoyamaxa, and Xákmok Kásek until each land claim is satisfied. Instead of dealing with structural issues that have created the need for emergency care, the Paraguayan state neglects to act because doing so could enable Enxet and Sanapaná to marginally challenge the structure of agro-export capitalism by taking "productive" lands back. Biopolitical programs such as these illustrate a pernicious valence of multicultural politics that leverage an optics of care to mask structural conditions that limit Indigenous land access, ultimately recentering the state not only as the arbiter of rights but also as the arbiter of who gets to live and how. Making live in the current conjuncture is thus not merely a question of which human population should thrive while others are left to perish, but which life-forms should exist and how.

Prison

Between the hard earth, winter's humid cold that chills to the bone, and sounds of semis passing intermittently in the night, I had not slept well. When I heard Anivel open the door to his home and start gathering wood to start a fire, I rolled out of my sleeping bag, unzipped my tent, and joined him in the dawn light. A small, battery-powered radio played a treble-saturated Paraguayan polka song about the Chaco War. "How did you wake?" Anivel asked. "Iporã," good, I replied. He said the same when I repeated the question. As Anivel lit the fire, I prepared tereré. We sat near the flames, talked, and squinted through the algarrobo smoke that occasionally wafted our way on the morning breeze, stinging the eyes and conjuring tears. The heat of the small fire on our faces was a welcome break from the cold morning. Soon, Veronica, Anivel's wife, joined us. We woke up slowly as the sun broke through the forest on the other side of the fence that separates us from the community's traditional lands. As we were starting our second pitcher of tereré, a young man who I had not yet met, Belfio, joined us.

This visit to Yakye Axa was different from some of my previous ones. I was conducting research as part of a global study about the strategic litigation of Indigenous land rights, the findings of which would be presented at the United Nations Permanent Forum on Indigenous Affairs and inform an Open Society Justice Initiative special report published in 2017.[1] Belfio was excited to talk with me and wanted his perspective included. When he arrived, Veronica stepped away from the fire. Belfio took her place on the broken brick where she had been sitting. We drank tereré and talked with Anivel for a few minutes. Then I took out my recorder, and we began our conversation.[2]

> *Joel*: Can you please introduce yourself for the recording?
>
> *Belfio*: My, my name is Belfio Gómez Benitez. I am twenty-five years old. I grew up on the side of the road, and I have experience.
> And we began.
> Much suffering [*heta sufrimiento*]. Much [*heta*].

FIGURE 9. A semi hauling cattle kicks up dust as it speeds through Yakye Axa on Ruta 5. Photo by author, July 2016.

It is a well-known story. They know of it all over.

I have a lot of experience.

Like I said, I grew up on the side of the road, and there has been a lot of suffering.

And this.

In the middle of this suffering, I have knowledge.

We will one day achieve what we want.

As I understand in normal terms, the normal person, as I understand it, no one wants the past suffering.

Do you understand?

For that reason, I say that I have the experience from the middle of the suffering, the crisis, the persecution.

I say that to you because we live like we are isolated, like we are in prison, in the desert.

So I have the experience of how we have lived, and I want to teach that so that we do not live it again as we did in the past . . .

Joel: Why do you say that you have suffered?

Belfio: And that is why I say I have the experience.

I wake up, and I see our suffering.

Our crisis, of the community, that we have already passed from the little to the big, the young to the old.

On that side, I have experience.

The land they gave us is not the land we originally requested.

But I have experience and knowledge so we can achieve something . . .

Joel: How do you see your future on the land? What is your wish for that land and Yakye Axa?

Belfio: I have many thoughts based on my experience.

From age three or four, I remember growing up on the side of the road without land.

I have many wishes that I would like to do. In this time, if we had the land, I would, I have ideas. But they are not everyone's.

We all have ideas of how to live well.

But for that moment, there is a but [*hay un pero*].

There is a but.

For the moment that we have the land, many people ask what we will do? What will we go and do?

There is one but [*hay un pero*] that we want the state to remember.

There is the community development fund that we can use so that we don't live there as we have lived here.

The state looks at other [Indigenous] communities and has doubts. They get land and don't do anything. That is because they do not have a fund to help them develop. To help them advance. For that, there is much we can do.

There is much we can do if they give us our development fund after we move so that we can progress so that we don't live as we have.

We lost the original fight for the land.

Much time passed, and we fought.

But we lost that fight and took the other land.

Now the second fight is for our alternative land.

That I don't fully understand, but we have it.

But now we continue to suffer.

There has been much suffering since they bought the land.

Time has passed.

The people here heard they purchased the land for the community.

But.

Now today, much time has already passed. I don't even know how much, three or four years. The community has suffered a lot.

We, for example, me like a young person. I am a young man. I see my elders in the middle of these four years. Some, some elders wanted to put their feet on the ground of our land.

But, in those four years they have left us.

And that is the suffering.

That is the suffering.

So that our elders can step on the land, the land of the future of the community.

But that is the fight.

The fight of the community.

There is the entry.

Today there is the entry. That is to say the road, so that one day the community can go.

Go, and know, and live, and project their future.

I grew up on the side of the road, in the midst of the suffering.

Akakuaa rutacotare, en el medio del sufrimiento.

CHAPTER 4

Restitution as Development?

Three hundred sixty-seven kilometers from Asunción, a nondescript dirt road branches off of Ruta 5. An old wooden gate limits passage near the highway's edge. Seemingly countless similar roads lead off the highway. Some of them are hundreds of kilometers long, but most just lead deep into ranches that span thousands of hectares. I had been keeping an eye out for this dirt road since the bus made the turn east off the Trans-Chaco Highway at Pozo Colorado. The dirt road enters Estancia Michi, which is part of the 14,404 hectares that members of Sawhoyamaxa had been trying to reclaim for years. As I peered out through the dusty bus window, I could see a retiro with faded white walls, adorned in red trim, and a large wrap-around screened porch. A corral just east of the building looked ready for use, but tall weeds signaled that it had not seen cattle for quite some time. There were also some small houses a hundred meters or so from the retiro that looked like they had been recently constructed, with a handful of people sitting in front of them drinking tereré in the waning sun. Speeding past the entrance to Michi, as it is locally called, I knew that Sawhoyamaxa Central was close, so I readied my bag and headed to the front of the bus to depart. Minutes later, the bus decelerated on the degrading asphalt, kicking up red dust that mixed with the warm colors of the setting sun to let me off in front of the roadside market where I was to meet Leonardo.

Ruta 5 runs east to west, bisecting Sawhoyamaxa's land as it does Yakye Axa. Though a vital transportation link, the highway has long been considered a space that robbed vitality from Sawhoyamaxa. For decades, the highway hemmed Sawhoyamaxa into its margin as the community fought for land rights in a history like that of Yakye Axa. In both communities, watching traffic pass was a big part of daily life on the side of the highway. Bascilio once told me, "What else is there to do when you live in that little area between the fence and the road? The majority [of people] had no work, no place to go. Sometimes they would sit all day watching buses, cattle trucks, and cars pass. . . . The traffic passes here fast. Sometimes people got hit. Sometimes they [traffic] killed one of our animals. The road is

FIGURE 10. The entrance to Sawhoyamaxa. Community members painted over the sign that once read, "Estancia Michi," to proclaim the lands recovered. The retiro that ranchers refused to cede and that was used to surveil community actions can be seen at the right. Photo by author, February 2016.

dangerous."[1] Despite its latent threat, Ruta 5 now has a different character. After reoccupying their lands in 2013, almost everyone in Sawhoyamaxa moved away from the roadside, although a few stayed to operate small stores. Whereas many people once viewed the roadside as a carceral space, for many in Sawhoyamaxa it is now a shared space for social exchange and diversion.

The roadside was full of life when the bus left me in a cloud of dust and exhaust. It was early evening, and crowds had gathered to hang out at the end of the day. Loud *kachacka* music played from the speakers of a car parked in front of the main store. People gathered to watch a game of volleyball and wait their turn to play on a court where a wire fence that once forbade entry to the land had stood. Teenagers congregated on the road in groups, talking, laughing, and checking out the scene. The smell of frying empanadas and wood smoke lured some folks to a small shop. Among those watching volleyball, Leonardo saw me depart the bus and waved me over. After shaking hands, I jumped on the back of his motorcycle, and we drove to Santa Elisa, one of Sawhoyamaxa's aldeas.

It was dark by the time we arrived but still hot, so we sat and drank tereré on the front porch of Leonardo's house—a brick and tile building painted red, in the color of the Loma Porã ranch. We first met in 2014 while waiting to attend a pretrial hearing at the Supreme Court in Asunción. That day, the former president of INDI, Rubén Quesnel, was awaiting trial for embezzling roughly $500,000 destined for community development projects in Sawhoyamaxa and Yakye Axa. The funds were part of the IACHR rulings on behalf of each community's case against the Paraguayan state. Both communities worked independently with Tierraviva to petition the Inter-American Commission on Human Rights in the 1990s to negotiate land restitution from the Paraguayan state after having exhausted all domestic legal options to recover their ancestral territories via the state's Indigenous rights framework (see table 1 for a summary). After several years and complex legal proceedings that I detail later in the chapter, the IACHR ruled in favor of each community. Yet, despite the unprecedented legal victories in 2005 and 2006, community members are still fighting the state to ensure implementation of the rulings. That day at the Paraguayan Supreme Court was just one of countless efforts taken over decades of struggle to advance restitution. Unfortunately, however, Court officials postponed the pretrial hearing for a future date due to a "technicality." Little did we know then that that would be one of nineteen postponements before Quesnel would be tried and found guilty in 2018. Such routine breaches of justice in the Enxet and Sanapaná cases discussed throughout the book are indicative of how legal abandonment is manifest through neglect, something Leonardo lamented about the stalled land expropriation.

The Paraguayan Congress passed Law 5194 in 2014 to expropriate 14,404 hectares of land to Sawhoyamaxa after nearly three decades of legal struggles. Nevertheless, state officials had yet to fully enforce the law more than a year after its passage. "How can there be two landowners?" Leonardo asked. "They [state officials] approved the expropriation and say that the land is ours, but Rodel's people won't leave the retiro. He still has the title." Leonardo's new home—formerly a Loma Porã ranch retiro owned by an influential landholder in Paraguay—was a testament to the quandary. More surprising was the fact that neither state officials nor company employees used physical force to remove the people of Sawhoyamaxa from the lands.[2] Given the history of political patronage driven by tight relationships between landed elites and elected officials, it was hard to fathom how Sawhoyamaxa could have taken de facto control of the land while Rodel's company had not ceded ownership. The quandary exemplifies various forms of legal liminality that beset Enxet and Sanapaná land struggles.

Here I use the notion of legal liminality to draw attention to the spaces and situations produced through legal processes that lie simultaneously within and outside the law.[3] Such spaces and situations are liminal in the literal meaning of the word: "occupying a position at, or on both sides of, a boundary or threshold" or "relating to a transitional process."[4] The condition of legal liminality is charged with political potential but always oppressed by unpredictability, an inherent effect of the limits of settler law to advance Indigenous justice.[5] The predictable unpredictability created by legal liminality, like waiting for food deliveries that may not arrive or having constitutional rights written that may or may not manifest

TABLE 1 Summary of main legal proceedings that precipitated the IACHR judgments

	Yakye Axa	Sawhoyamaxa	Xákmok Kásek
Year of state recognition	1996, though petition was initially filed in 1993.	1993, though petition was initially filed in 1991.	1986
Year land claim began	1993	1991	1986
Area of initial land claim	18,188 hectares	8,000 hectares. Claim expanded to 15,000 hectares after recognition.	200 hectares, but evolved to 6,900 hectares, then to 20,000 hectares.
Major domestic legal proceedings	After exhausting all legal options during 6 years, an appeal to Congress for land expropriation was denied in 1997. A state of emergency was declared in 1999.	After exhausting all legal options during 6 years, an appeal to Congress for land expropriation was denied in 1997. A state of emergency was declared in 1999.	After exhausting all legal options during 13 years, an appeal to Congress for land expropriation was denied in 1999. A state of emergency was declared in 1999.
Petition to Inter-American Commission	2000	2001	2001
Inter-American Commission findings	IACHR recommended land restitution and other measures in 2003.	IACHR recommended land restitution and other measures in 2003.	IACHR recommended land restitution and other measures in 2008.
Year IACHR judgment issued	2005	2006	2010

in practice, is a hallmark of the epistemic violence of selective neglect in liberal states. Bureaucratic procedures that produce legal liminality rather than resolve legal disputes regarding Indigenous self-determination legitimate the denial of Indigenous sovereignty.[6] An iterative process often ensues: legal liminality creates the condition for new legal processes that intend to alleviate problems that legal abandonment created.

This is evident in Paraguayan state implementation of the IACHR judgments mandating land restitution for the Yakye Axa, Sawhoyamaxa, and Xákmok Kásek communities. These cases demonstrate how legal liminality plays a dual function in settler-state governance of Indigenous life. First, legal liminality is a central, though tacit, strategy settler states use to manage Indigenous dispossession—a strategy that attempts to assuage concerns about the forms of neglect I discussed in chapter 3 by shifting attention to bureaucratic legal processes.[7] Take, for example, the requisite processes that Indigenous peoples must comply with to gain state recognition or to change official leadership within communities. In practice, the acts create barriers to resolving land claims because they require INDI officials with scant resources to be present in communities or community members with even fewer resources to travel to the capital city, Asunción, to follow up on administrative processes. Land restitution guaranteed in the law is delayed, but this is done in such a way that allows state officials to suggest such delays are a matter of process rather than structural limitations. Second, legal liminality naturalizes Indigenous dispossession by foregrounding bureaucratic processes instead of addressing actual conditions that undermine Indigenous well-being. Throughout the published IACHR judgments on each of the Sawhoyamaxa, Yakye Axa, and Xákmok Kásek cases, a common state narrative is evident. State officials repeatedly claimed that they are complying with Paraguay's legal procedures that uphold private property rights and that Enxet and Sanapaná claimants should choose alternative lands within their ancestral territories. Such a position effectively shifts the blame for protracted Indigenous dispossession onto communities themselves by suggesting they are refusing an equivalent resolution by taking other lands. Despite IACHR's intentions to remedy the state's rights violations against members of the Sawhoyamaxa, Yakye Axa, and Xákmok Kásek communities, the politics of implementing each IACHR judgment make clear that social-spatial relations of settler colonialism cannot be undone by law alone.

IACHR JUDGMENTS: PROPERTY AND DEVELOPMENT AS HUMAN RIGHTS

Since issuing the "landmark decision" in favor of the Mayagna (Sumo) Awas Tingni community versus the state of Nicaragua in 2001, the IACHR has played an increasingly important role arbitrating Indigenous territorial claims in Latin America.[8] The IACHR's judgments produce jurisprudence widely used to support Indigenous peoples' collective property rights. In the Awas Tingni case the IACHR argued, "The concept of 'property' as articulated in the American Convention includes communal property of Indigenous peoples that is defined by their customary land tenure."[9] The Awas Tingni decision consequently created new opportunities for Indigenous communities across the Americas to advance land claims by articulating property as a communal, not solely individual, right. At the time of this writing, jurisprudence established in the Awas Tingni case has influenced at least eleven subsequent IACHR decisions in favor of collective property rights for Indigenous peoples of Latin America, three of which pertain to communities in Paraguay.[10]

The IACHR has the authority to arbitrate cases of alleged human rights abuses between victims and countries party to the American Convention on Human Rights.[11] However, the Court's mandate does not provide a mechanism to enforce the implementation of judgments. Thus the IACHR relies on the political will of guilty states to implement judgments in favor of victims of human rights abuses. The structure of issuing legally binding judgments with no enforcement mechanism other than voluntary state action is, in and of itself, a liminal legal arrangement. Because of this, moving from the issuance of an IACHR judgment to its implementation in situ has been a persistent challenge for Indigenous communities that have received favorable decisions from the Court.[12] Paraguay is not an outlier in this problematic trend of state resistance to IACHR authority but an emblematic case of chronic malfeasance.[13]

In each judgment, the IACHR argued that the protracted denial of communal property rights violated Article 21 of the Inter-American Convention on Human Rights, which enshrines the right to property.[14] The state's violation of Article 21 resulted in several subsequent human rights violations against members of Yakye Axa, Sawhoyamaxa, and Xákmok Kásek: denial of the right to life, humane treatment, personal integrity, and a guarantee of rights without discrimination, among others (table 2). The IACHR found that state officials knowingly perpetuated the dire living conditions of community members by refusing to remedy their land claims effectively. It is, therefore, through the prism of private property rights that the IACHR viewed all other human rights violations against the three Enxet and Sanapaná communities.[15]

The IACHR works from a premise of universal human rights but employs a pluralistic approach to adjudicating Indigenous land cases by working with Indigenous legal traditions and norms.[16] Given this, IACHR interpretations of human rights law and the reparations often required by IACHR judgments can be used to challenge the political-juridical norms of settler states that govern Indigenous rights. This is by no means a guaranteed outcome or the express intent of the IACHR, but it has created a new field of political possibility for Yakye Axa, Sawhoyamaxa, and Xákmok Kásek. In each judgment, the IACHR ordered that Paraguay restitute land to Enxet and Sanapaná peoples and accompany land restitution with development measures that ultimately advance environmental justice. The IACHR's role in advancing Indigenous land rights across Latin America creates political-juridical openings that many communities with favorable rulings use to challenge extractive development. In this regard, the IACHR judgments on Indigenous land rights cases have been polemic, with many Latin American states and affected private industries resisting the Court's reach and its recommendations for land restitution and rights-based development.

Aside from the IACHR, NGOs and other international human rights organizations have increasingly promoted rights-based approaches to development in the past two decades.[17] The UN's Millennium and Sustainable Development Goals (SDGs) are arguably the most well-known efforts to promote the human rights–development nexus by creating a purportedly inclusive and environmentally benevolent vision of development. Skeptics argue that a focus on growth-oriented development lacks a meaningful vision of justice and, therefore, will fail to mitigate inequality, broadly construed.[18] However, the IACHR judgments on the Yakye Axa, Sawhoyamaxa, and Xákmok Kásek cases chart a vision that attempts to rework the human rights–development nexus by squarely focusing on

TABLE 2 Summary of the IACHR judgments on the Yakye Axa, Sawhoyamaxa,
and Xákmok Kásek cases

Community	Judgment Year	American Convention on Human Rights: Articles Violated	Deaths Attributed to the State by IACHR
Yakye Axa	2005	1(1), 2, 4(1) 21 2; 8(1), 8(2 d-f), 25	16
Sawhoyamaxa	2006	1, 1(1), 2, 3, 4(1), 5(1), 8, 19, 21, 25	18
Xákmok Kásek	2010	8(1), 21(1), 25(1), 1(1), 2, 4(1), 5(1), 19	14

Details About Convention Articles
– Article 1(1): Obligation to respect and guarantee rights without discrimination
– Article 2: Domestic legal effects
– Article 3: Right to juridical personality
– Article 4: Right to life
– Article 5: Right to humane treatment
– Article 5(1): Right to personal integrity
– Article 8: Right to a fair trial
  – (2) d–f: Innocence until proven guilty. Accused have right to defend against accusations; state
    will provide free legal counsel; defense may examine witnesses and call expert witnesses
– Article 19: Rights of the child
– Article 21: Right to property
– Article 25: Right to judicial protection

NOTE: The IACHR provides publicly available records about its cases via the "Jurisprudence Finder" on its website: http://www.corteidh.or.cr/cf/jurisprudencia2/index.cfm?lang=en.

actions that support Indigenous environmental justice—specifically, though not exclusively, through land restitution.

Every Indigenous land rights case the IACHR has ruled on to date—from Argentina to Honduras—shows a similar strategy that I call *restitution as development*. Rather than merely find states guilty of human rights violations against Indigenous peoples in instances such as these, the IACHR requires that states title land and couple it with other forms of development. The core goal is to end Indigenous dispossession by returning stolen lands to each community per the law. There is an important caveat, however. The IACHR recognizes that land restitution alone will not assuage the social, economic, and political marginalization that drives human rights violations. The approach in these cases asserts that development initiatives must accompany land restitution to support Indigenous self-determination and the pressing health, education, and housing issues created by sustained land dispossession. Restitution then becomes more than a question of merely returning land but one of enabling Indigenous communities to harness what Engle calls "the elusive promise of Indigenous development."[19] While development drove and perpetuated Indigenous land dispossession in each of the cases, it seems IACHR judges view restitution as development as a path to ensure Indigenous self-determination.

Restitution as development is not without contentiousness. Indigenista NGOs in the 1980s and 1990s, including Tierraviva, embraced a "hunter-gatherer paradigm" to argue "that only large tracts of land could ensure the maintenance of this indigenous way of life and, in addition, ensure the protection of the environment."[20] Based on historical fact, the leaders of Yakye Axa, Sawhoyamaxa, and Xákmok Kásek leveraged this hunter-gatherer paradigm, a strategic essentialism, to file claims for lands within their respective ancestral territories. Such essentialisms do not come without drawbacks, even though they can work as a legitimate legal strategy. Not surprisingly, state officials and area ranchers objected vehemently, arguing that the claims were predicated on an expanse of land necessary to support hunter-gatherers, not settled Indigenous communities. The ARP began a concerted counter-effort that advocated assimilation and agrarian development to deal with the Chaco "indian problem."[21] ARP members, many of whom are elected state officials, argued, and some still do, that the Indigenous peoples of the Bajo Chaco live as peons who do not need access to large areas of land based on historical occupation and use. This logic reduces life to a class relation mediated through property (i.e., peons don't need land) rather than understanding life as based on dynamic relations that supersede the limits of class relations.

One former head of the ARP Indigenous Affairs Commission and co-owner of Estancia Salazar told me, "There is no need to purchase large tracts of land for the indians! They are not hunter-gatherers and do not need large extensions of land. They are peons! Campesinos! If anything, INDI should teach them how to work, buy some cattle, and find a small piece of land to make a community where they can live. They can work on ranches or do other things to make money. The indians would take that, but the NGOs won't let them because they make money off of indian suffering!" After our extended interview, he lent me a photocopy of an old presentation that he regularly gave in the 1990s and early 2000s. Comprising 108 slides, the presentation argues for assimilation. One of the slides is titled with the question, "Can they return to the forest?," and displays an Indigenous man on horseback in front of an estancia building. The notes below the image state that the man depicted is an "Indigenous office worker" who, like his colleagues, "wears Adidas shoes" and "dances in the best discos of the capital city." By asking, "Can they return to the forest?," the author suggests a teleological notion of social change inferring that the Enxet and Sanapaná peoples who labored on his ranch were bound to wage labor as the basis for social reproduction instead of other pathways community members might choose for themselves if given the opportunity.[22]

The influence of the ARP and its arguments about hunter-gatherers on state responses to Enxet and Sanapaná land claims is evident in the proceedings of the IACHR judgments. The state's legal counsel argued against returning the lands specifically claimed by Yakye Axa and Sawhoyamaxa because they were occupied by ranches. Instead, the counsel suggested the mobile traditions of many hunting and gathering societies negate their rights to claim any specific site and that they should accept any land within their broad territories.

> It is remarkable that while both Yakye Axa and Sawhoyamaxa indigenous communi-
> ties belong to the same ethnic group, the Enxet-Lengua,[23] they each claim territories
> so very distant from each other. When each group separated from the other to form a
> different community, they "chose" particular land spaces as belonging to "their
> ancestors," based on little more requirements than their own whim. Historically, the
> areas they moved about cover a much larger area within the Chaco territory, for
> which reason their stubbornness in claiming estates that have been declared ratio-
> nally exploited and held under lawful property title is a token of intolerance and
> shows their willingness to hinder the endeavors of Paraguay.[24]

I want to underscore several points made by the state's legal counsel in the Sawhoyamaxa hearing. First, the argument rejects the material fact that the lands claimed by Enxet peoples of Sawhoyamaxa and Yakye Axa have specific historical and cultural importance to community members, a core premise of Indigenous rights in domestic and international law. Enxet land claims evoke the multiple relationalities that community members have with specific sites, something lost in the state's purely political economic rationale. Second, the dismissive language suggesting that the claims are merely stubborn, whimsical, or intolerant map onto racist tropes used to frame Indigenous peoples as acting without intentionality or purpose. Third and finally, how the state's language about Enxet mobility hinder-ing development resonates with early Anglican missionary imperatives to stem the "wandering instincts" of Indigenous peoples through the imposition of private property to facilitate ranching.[25]

In its ruling on the Sawhoyamaxa case, the IACHR roundly refuted the state's arguments: "The Court considers that the fact that the claimed lands are privately held by third parties is not in itself an 'objective and reasoned' ground for dis-missing prima facie the claims by the Indigenous people. Otherwise, restitution rights would become meaningless and would not entail an actual possibility of recovering traditional lands, as it would be exclusively limited to an expectation on the will of the current holders, forcing indigenous communities to accept alterna-tive lands or economic compensations."[26] Further, the IACHR elaborated on the fact that Enxet peoples had not voluntarily ceded their lands or made the lifestyle changes they had adapted to but were forced to make them given the coloniza-tion of the Bajo Chaco and near-total usurpation of their territories by settlers. Following a similar legal argumentation in the Yakye Axa, Sawhoyamaxa, and Xákmok Kásek cases, the IACHR thus ordered Paraguay to demarcate each com-munity's land, transfer property titles, and then implement a series of measures within three years of titling to meet specific goals: the payment of predetermined community development funds alongside the provision of basic medical services,

TABLE 3 Summary details about restitution measures ordered by IACHR

Community	IACHR Judgment Year	Compliance through 2022	Community Development Funds to Be Paid	Other Notable Reparations
Yakye Axa	2005	Partial	US$950,000	No payment issued for death of community members.
Sawhoyamaxa	2006	Partial	US$1,000,000	Land demarcation and title to be issued within three years of judgment. US$380,000 paid for the deaths of 17 community members. Provide identity documents to all community members.
Xákmok Kásek	2010	Partial	US$700,000	US$260,000 paid for the deaths of 14 community members. Provide identity documents to all community members. State will incur a US$10,000 fine for each month of delay, to be paid to community members. Construct community health center.

NOTE: In all three communities, the IACHR ordered Paraguay to provide delivery of potable water and food rations, basic medical services, protection of the claimed lands until claims could be resolved, and public admissions of guilt by state officials, among other measures.

potable water, and food rations until state officials could satisfy the demands for land restitution (table 3).

That the IACHR employs a vision of Indigenous well-being that is more comprehensive than land restitution or economic development is laudable. Despite these intentions, the actual implementation of restitution as development by Paraguayan state officials is highly problematic. The temporal condition of restitution as development—that the state should implement all measures within three years—intends to create dramatic change over a short time frame. The three-year window also created an expectation in the three communities that their long-standing dispossession of land would soon be resolved. Yet at the time of this writing more than fifteen years have elapsed since each judgment, and restitution as development is still unresolved. This protracted process of legal abandonment produces spaces and situations of liminality in which rights-bearing subjects are denied those rights yet always promised that resolution will soon come, ensnaring Indigenous peoples in veritably endless bureaucratic and juridical processes that deny the ability to live without everyday forms of environmental violence.

RATIONAL EXPLOITATION
AND RACIAL GEOGRAPHIES

In March 2013, after twenty years on the margin of Ruta 5, the people of Sawhoya-maxa cut the fence and crossed onto the lands they had long claimed. Carlos, the longest-serving leader of Sawhoyamaxa, reflected on the decision during a workshop Tierraviva facilitated in Xákmok Kásek that brought leaders from Yakye Axa, Sawhoyamaxa, and Xákmok Kásek together to share lessons learned. Sitting under a grove of algarrobo trees on newly constructed benches, Carlos, Anivel, Clemente, and Serafin talked candidly about their luchas. In total, about forty people from Xákmok Kásek sat and listened to the conversation that Óscar, a lawyer for Tierraviva, facilitated. Talking with Anivel about the fact that Yakye Axa remains on the margin of Ruta 5, Carlos said, "For me, living on the side of the road for over twenty years was prison. Until we reoccupied our land, we lived in prison." His words echoed those of Belfio, whose entire life has unfolded on the margin of the highway. "People got sick. They died. We suffered. . . . The state didn't do anything. We had to reoccupy our land. We don't have the title yet, but now we are free from the road."[27]

The reoccupation was a risky but well-calculated strategy to pressure state officials to implement restitution as development. As Ireneo, a former Tierraviva lawyer, once told me, the community grew tired of waiting and decided to "implement the [IACHR] judgment themselves."[28] Self-implementation was an act of self-determination intended to change the liminal state of being on the side of the road that had long plagued Sawhoyamaxa. The reoccupation contests the normative social-spatial order of cattle ranching while impelling the Paraguayan state to adjudicate the law—either in favor of the community or in favor of the ranchers. One year after the reoccupation, the Paraguayan Senate voted to approve Law 5194/14, the expropriation of 14,404 hectares to Sawhoyamaxa in the name of "public interest." The expropriation was a historic act. Indigenistas hailed it as a watershed moment for Indigenous rights in Paraguay.[29] Never before had state officials moved to force a Chaqueño rancher to cede private property in favor of an Indigenous community. An irrefutable crucial legal victory, it also unexpectedly created new legal liminality.

The 14,404 hectares expropriated to Sawhoyamaxa are part of a 60,000-hectare ranch owned by Kansol S.A. and Roswell S.A., subsidiary companies of Grupo Liebig, a Paraguayan cattle ranching, timber, and real estate consortium with landholdings across the country. At the time of my field research, however, state officials had yet to enforce the expropriation fully or issue title to Sawhoyamaxa. The resulting condition is persistent uncertainty that draws ranch staff and the Sawhoyamaxa community into conflicts over land control. Beyond merely reoccupying the land, community members built homes, gardens, and soccer fields, and each aldea has a small schoolhouse with state-licensed teachers. Each aldea purchased a small herd of cattle using some of the community development funds awarded in the IACHR judgment. Without doubt, Sawhoyamaxa is a lively community of several hundred people who are actively working to rebuild relations with their land. However, at the time of this research Kansol and Roswell still owned the property, technically. The company had not ceded title, refused to accept payment, and, through early 2019, still occupied the main retiro at the former Estancia Michi. Sawhoyamaxa is now the de facto landowner, yet does not legally own the land because the community does not hold the title.

The situation draws to light ambiguities in Paraguayan property law that produce legal liminality. The 1964 Agrarian Statute that dictates the governance of property rights in Paraguay vis-à-vis Article 109 of the Constitution states that "rationally exploited" land cannot be expropriated without landowner consent. Land actively used for economic gain, particularly livestock and agricultural production, is the crown jewel of so-called rational exploitation in Paraguay, but so are lands with "improvements."[30] In this view, improving land means making investments by building infrastructure or enacting other activities geared to generating income. Without explicitly stating as much, this constitutional clause fundamentally enshrines property rights along class-based and, therefore, racialized lines by establishing a principle of economic production as the pinnacle of rights to property in land. The dispossession of Enxet and Sanapaná coupled with efforts to produce a landless, disposable labor force to work on ranches all but ensures that Indigenous peoples of the Chaco are excluded from the economic means to purchase land, let alone invest in extensive "improvements." The structure of property rights as such ensures the recursive dispossessions that juridically and spatially situate Indigenous peoples simultaneously within and outside the protection of the law.[31]

Unsurprisingly, Kansol and Roswell representatives have long contested the law of expropriation, arguing that the land is rationally exploited, thus not subject to usurpation without consent to sell. During an interview, the company's then-acting chief administrator and legal representative explained to me how the company identified an alternative parcel of land, Estancia Pedernal, owned by the Paraguayan military, that his company wanted Sawhoyamaxa to accept instead of the land at Michi and Santa Elisa. Citing Law 904/81, the administrator argued Pedernal would be easy to transfer because it is state-owned land, whereas Michi was "rationally exploited, productive land." He gave me several documents detailing the investments that the company had made to "improve" the land by constructing stock ponds, fencing, pastures, and retiros.[32] As we discussed the case, the administrator grew increasingly animated, his voice rising in frustration. "The anthropologists say that the people of Sawhoyamaxa are Chanawatsan 'of the river' with a 250,000-hectare territory. Pedernal is 12 kilometers from the river, where they can fish. Michi is 40 kilometers from the river and is ranching land. The only reason they are there is because NGOs trucked them there in the nineties and manipulate them to make money." His last point reiterates a common talking point about the Enxet and Sanapaná land claims—that they were only made because NGOs guided the process and prolonged Indigenous dispossession to make money. The administrator then pivoted: "We are not against the rights of the Indigenous but are against an expropriation that we view as a breach of justice. How is it just to expropriate rationally exploited land the national constitution of the Paraguayan Republic states is inviolable?" The administrator's argument echoes those that the state's legal counsel made in the IACHR hearings—that the selection of Michi and Santa Elisa is arbitrary and thus all lands within the territory are interchangeable.

IACHR interpretations of Indigenous rights, however, challenge the supremacy of private property over the collective property rights of Indigenous peoples, if upholding the former violates the latter. In its interpretation of Paraguayan property law and the rights guaranteed by the American Convention on Human Rights, the IACHR unambiguously rejected the notion that privately held land cannot be expropriated to Indigenous communities: "This argument [about rational exploitation] lodges the idea that Indigenous communities are not entitled, under any circumstances, to claim traditional lands when they are exploited and fully productive, viewing the Indigenous issue exclusively from the standpoint of land productivity and agrarian law, something which is insufficient for it fails to address the distinctive characteristics of such peoples."[33]

Without saying as much, the judgment flags the racialized and classist logics that privilege economic production and assume that Indigenous peoples use land irrationally—a long-standing trope employed to undermine Indigenous land claims across Latin America.[34] "Rational exploitation" concerning Indigenous land claims operates on a discursive register that situates Indigenous peoples outside of activities that are, or could be, economically productive, a reductionist stereotype that effectively frames Indigenous peoples as prior to capitalism to justify a politics of exclusion.[35] The notion of rational exploitation also erases the history, and present, of Indigenous labor in such so-called productive systems. This is precisely why I focused on the role of Indigenous labor exploitation in earlier chapters of the book. On its face, the discourse of rational exploitation upholds the "productive pioneer" and "intolerant" Indigenous trope so often used to justify taking Indigenous lands. The IACHR judgment can be read as charting an alternative legal geography of property that exposes the reticence of Paraguayan law to reconcile the liberal rationalities of "productivity" used to defend racialized regimes of land control and dispossession.

Tensions between interpretations of property as an economically productive resource or as a communal good in Paraguayan law intersect with what Stocks argues is a significant obstacle to Indigenous land restitution in Latin America, that it is seen as "too much [land] for too few [people]."[36] While working in Sawhoyamaxa, however, I frequently heard community members ask a rhetorical question that evokes the inverse of the problem Stocks discusses: "Why does one [white] man need 60,000 hectares of land when we are a community of over one hundred families that have no land?" The notion of rational exploitation, in this case, frames Indigenous communities as actors not worthy of the land rights they are legally guaranteed, further upholding the primacy of settler land control while exacerbating legal liminality for Sawhoyamaxa. The lack of resolution regarding expropriation has led to physical violence, to which I now turn.

The morning of June 17, 2015, was gray and brisk, like many winter days in the Bajo Chaco. The cold, damp weather made it difficult to leave the tent where I was staying in Xákmok Kásek. However, Serafin and two journalists had to make it to Pozo Colorado by 8:30 a.m. to meet with folks from Tierraviva who were headed to Sawhoyamaxa for meetings about the expropriation. The four of us soon loaded in the little-used SUV I had recently purchased and set off, talking about the progress of both communities' ongoing land claims. We met with Ireneo in Pozo Colorado, where Serafin and the journalists got out of my truck, then loaded into the Tierraviva pickup to head off for Sawhoyamaxa. I returned to Xákmok Kásek to attend a meeting I had been asked to record. During the meeting, Serafin texted to say that things had not gone well in Sawhoyamaxa.

Accompanied by their legal counsel and Paraguayan police officers, two Sawhoyamaxa leaders, Carlos and Bascilio, approached the retiro at Michi to request that the ranch staff who were occupying the building vacate the property. During the exchange, the manager of the Loma Porã ranch owned by Kansol and Roswell drew his pistol, aimed it point-blank at Bascilio, and refused to leave. Fortunately, he did not pull the trigger, and the event was captured on film by one of the journalists that accompanied Serafin. Yet despite more than forty witnesses and the video recording of the lethal threat, the police did nothing to reprimand the ranch manager. Moreover, the local district attorney never pressed charges against the administrator, despite community requests and ample evidence.[37]

The incident clearly shows the impunity with which many ranchers in Paraguay's Chaco violate state law by creating their own social-spatial order based on the logic that rational exploitation foments.[38] Law 5194/14 upholds communal property as the assumed solution to Enxet dispossession. But expropriation in and of itself fails to alter the underlying power relations that perpetuate the legal abandonment of Sawhoyamaxa and supports settler colonialism and white supremacy. State authorities claimed they had done "everything possible" to advance the case by passing Law 5194/14, upholding the constitutionality of the law, and arguing that Liebig is responsible for accepting payment and ceding the property title.[39] I disagree. State officials have not enforced the expropriation because many of them seek to maintain a social-spatial order amenable to landed patrones. Indeed, many elected state officials have direct ties to the ranching and soybean industries. Failing to enforce the expropriation maintains legal liminality where Sawhoyamaxa rights are unstable, the Janus face of inclusion/exclusion on which legal abandonment operates.

When I visited Sawhoyamaxa for this research, particularly between 2015 and 2017, many community members would ask if I thought the state or Kansol and Roswell staff would forcibly dispossess them of the land again. I never had a ready reply. The question had long been an open one, with little to indicate any sort of viable resolution on the horizon. The state's failure to uphold the law of expropriation or resolve either party's claim to the land produced uncertainty and the de facto suspension of Sawhoyamaxa rights. At the same time, failure to expropriate the land emboldened Kansol and Roswell by tacitly indicating their claim to the land was valid despite the ratification of Law 5194/14. The situation resulted in two parties each with a legal position to claim ownership, both entitled to own the land but neither being able to fully use it as they intended. In many ways, the Yakye Axa community has navigated a similar type of legal liminality, simultaneously owning land but not being able to access or use that land and thus remaining incarcerated on the margin of Ruta 5.

"AN ISLAND SURROUNDED BY PRIVATE PROPERTY"

Members of the Yakye Axa community first learned to be ranch laborers on the Anglican mission station El Paso that was established on these lands before they changed hands to become the Loma Verde and Maroma ranches. Despite this long connection with the land, armed men patrolled the boundaries of Loma Verde in the 1990s after the community claimed the lands. Inocencia Gómez recalled these men in her testimony to the IACHR: "At Loma Verde estate, an individual was stationed as the place's 'matador,' who walks alongside the wire fence with a shotgun, threatening the children and women, because he is under orders to not allow anyone to enter for firewood or water."[40] The *matadores*—literally, "killers"—no longer patrol the fences. Yet memories of that violence haunt community members, who still need to cross the fence to get drinking water from stock ponds, collect firewood, or hunt game on the ranch property. "We suffer on the side of the road. We used to suffer even more because they prohibited us from entering the private lands to get water or hunt," Veronica Flores explained. "They would shoot in the air over our heads if we entered their land. We could not get water or even wash clothes. They made us stay on the side of the road. It is so painful some people cannot even think of it."[41] Crossing the fence is a necessity because there is no viable agricultural land, no place to hunting or to collect firewood, let alone get drinkable water, on the highway's margin.

Yakye Axa is only 56 kilometers from the Paraguay River as the *tuyuyú* flies.[42] The entire area that comprises this part of the Chaco is a vast, flat alluvial plain that is subject to seasonal flooding and droughts. Consequently, Ruta 5 is constructed on a small levee to protect it from the floods that regularly inundate the region. The marked differences in precipitation regimes between the wet and dry seasons convert the predominantly clay soils to a surface that is either baked rock hard by the relentless sun or quickly turned to slick mud by rain. The elevated road ensures that traffic can pass during the rains but effectively limits the flow of surface water, exacerbating flooding along the side of the highway. The homes built in the margin

FIGURE 11. The fence that separates members of Yakye Axa from the lands that contain the site of yakye axa. Photo by author, July 2016.

are regularly flooded. On one wet day, I spoke with Inocencia, who described the effect of the rains: "You see? When it rains, there is mud everywhere. My house fills with mud. Just like pigs. That is how they [state officials] think of Indigenous people, like we are animals. They leave us here to suffer instead of giving us what the law says is ours, our land."[43] The cargo trucks that careen down Ruta 5 hauling cattle, *carbón*, and contraband pose a lethal threat to the people of Yakye Axa. Passing traffic has struck, killed, and maimed several people during Yakye Axa's tenure on the margin. Unlike the fast-moving traffic, there is a commonplace slow violence. Basic illnesses become grave threats. The promise of leaving the road one day brings hope but also the enduring trauma of uncertainty. Despite the urgency of the challenges that confront Yakye Axa, which are well known, state authorities have only haltingly implemented restitution as development.[44]

ALTERNATIVE LAND FOR WHICH THERE IS NO ALTERNATIVE

Following the 2005 IACHR judgment, the Paraguayan state repeatedly failed to negotiate the purchase of the Loma Verde ranch for Yakye Axa. The IACHR foresaw this as a contingency, stating: "If for objective and well-founded reasons the claim to ancestral territory of the members of the Yakye Axa Community is not possible, the State must grant them *alternative land*, chosen by means of a consensus with the community, in accordance with its own manner of consultation and decision-making, practices and customs."[45] Seven years after the IACHR judgment, in 2012, members of Yakye Axa had grown weary of waiting on the margin of Ruta 5 and agreed to accept an alternative parcel of land to resolve their claim because Loma Verde ranch owners would not sell and the Senate would not vote to expropriate. "It was a hard decision," Veronica Flores lamented. "But the Loma patrón did not want to sell. . . . We agreed to take the land because the state said they would build us an access road. Life on the highway is hard, and we suffer a lot here, so we decided to accept the alternative land."[46]

In annual reports to the Inter-American System, Paraguayan authorities touted the purchase of the land as part of their compliance with the IACHR judgment.[47] Yet state reports did not mention that the alternative land is 60 kilometers from where Yakye Axa is located on the side of the highway. The only way to access the alternative land is by private roads that cross a patchwork of ranches demarcated by a grid of fences with locked gates that render the new site for Yakye Axa effectively inaccessible. If the community were to relocate to the land without the construction of a public access road, they would not be able to leave, because at least 20 kilometers of private property enclose the land in every direction. As Marciano, the man whom I later took to the hospital because his arm had been crushed in a logging accident, told me in March 2015, "In the Enxet language *yakye axa* means 'palm island.' The state couldn't buy us the land we originally claimed where Yakye Axa is, so now we have a different island. It is an island surrounded by private property."[48]

In March 2015, I was invited to join leaders of Yakye Axa along with a handful of other community members and two lawyers from Tierraviva on a trip with state officials to investigate and map a potential route to construct an access road to the alternative land.[49] After departing Ruta 5, it took three hours to complete the remaining 35-kilometer trip. Subject to flooding and only transited by ranch staff traveling on motorcycle or horse, the forest closed in around most of the roads. Our trip required crossing through five locked gates, a feat we could only achieve because of court orders mandating the investigation. To pass through each gate, we had to stop, then search for and negotiate with someone who had the keys. Ranch gatekeepers were hesitant to give us passage because the presence of state officials or anyone not associated with the ranches is rare in these parts.

The final ranch we needed to cross to access the Yakye Axa land, Tamarindo, was the most resistant to our requests. The Tamarindo patrón argued with Tierraviva lawyers for an hour as we all stood in the sweltering sun. He threatened to deny us passage and proclaimed he was the authority in the area—not the state. Extolling his rights as a private property holder, he declared that he would fight the construction of an access road across his property at all costs. Throughout the conversation, our police escorts were silent. Their silence echoed loudly. It reflected the legal abandonment of Enxet rights as the police seemed ambivalent about enforcing the court orders that granted us unimpeded access to the Yakye Axa property; instead, they relied on community leaders and their legal counsel to negotiate passage. Eventually, the patrón conceded, with the condition that his lawyer, who happened to be at the ranch, accompany us. Before we left, the patrón declared that he would not give "indios, indigenistas, or anyone else" permission to cross his land in the future no matter what state authorities said. The patrón's defiance underscored the fact that ranchers have for the most part operated with little state interference since the Anglican-led colonization of the Bajo Chaco. While many people decry the absence of the Paraguayan state in the Chaco, ranching patrones have long established and operated through their own social-spatial order. Challenging that order is always a fraught act.

With the patrón's lawyer joining our group, we drove the final 12 kilometers across the ranch to the southern boundary of the alternative land. Aside from the two leaders of Yakye Axa, this was the first time the other community members on the trip had set foot on the alternative land. The mood was a mix of excitement, anxiety, and procedural banality as we walked a couple of kilometers from our trucks to the property line, then crossed onto the alternative land and made our way to an old retiro. The site was overgrown with waist-high grasses and the material traces of bygone infrastructure erected by conscripted Indigenous labor in the service of cattle capitalism. Taking refuge from the sun in the shade of the porch, Anivel and Anibal discussed the logistics of building the road to the land with representatives of the Ministry of Public Works and Communications (MOPC), INDI, and their legal counsel. At the same time, other community members surveyed the surroundings and dreamed about how to rebuild the community in that place unknown to them. A couple of us walked about the area surveying old fruit trees and speculating about the quality of the soil for gardening. Community members talked with cautious excitement about finally being liberated from the margin of Ruta 5. Though the trip was years in the making and took hours to complete, the quickly fading sun cut our time short.

On the return to Ruta 5, I sat in the back of a pickup with a couple guys from Yakye Axa. We bounced down the dusty dirt track in silence, tracing our path across ranch after ranch. Unspoken but likely on all our minds was the question of when the community would be able to occupy their land. Three years had already passed since the state bought the land, leaving Yakye Axa stranded not on an island but on the margin of Ruta 5, where a generation of children had grown up watching cars pass but having nowhere to go themselves. The visit to the alternative land was a clear reminder of how "the practices of legal abandonment do not simply happen anywhere; they are always accomplished through particular material and symbolic geographies."[50] The physical spaces of exclusion on the margins of cattle ranches and the laws that the state itself regularly violates contradict the symbolic geographies and imaginaries of liberal democratic states that protect their Indigenous citizens through multicultural policies. The valences of legal abandonment are multiple, connected across counter-topographies of ethnicity, labor, and racism across the Americas.[51]

Several months after our visit to the alternative land, in July 2016, I sat with a group of eighteen people on the side of Ruta 5 in Yakye Axa.[52] The goal of the

FIGURE 12. Walking from the trucks to the alternative land. Photo by author, March 2015.

discussion was to consider how things have changed for community members since the IACHR issued its judgment in 2005. At one point in the conversation, people reported that since the state purchased the alternative land, several community members have died or been seriously injured as a result of living conditions on the roadside. Throwing her arms in the air, Jorgelina Flores made this clear: "We set up here because we thought that we would get the lands that are truly ours. But now we have to go to another place. That is what hurts me. I am no longer at peace because our family members who have died are here. There are many. Many are in our cemetery here. That is why we don't want to let this go, that is why I don't want to let this land go." Her voice cracked as she spoke, until she began sobbing. "My father died here. I can't do it!" Jorgelina yelled. "How can I leave my father here on the side of the road? To this day I hurt so bad just thinking of it. I will not go once the community moves because I cannot leave him here. That is why I don't want to go to another place! There is no cure for the patrones [Ndairemedioi pa la patrónkuera]. They just want to take the Indigenous lands!"[53]

With each passing year that state officials do not comply with the IACHR or implement restitution as development, feelings of neglect, destitution, and indignity among affected community members grow. Another participant proclaimed, "They [state officials] bought us land but never built a road. We watch them drive by on the highway all the time while we are here on the side of the road. . . . One thing that we have learned is that they do not care about the poor or the Indigenous. If they did, they would have built the road a long time ago."[54] That the Paraguayan state has not dedicated the resources necessary to complete the road is more than bureaucratic malfeasance. It is a pedagogy with a clear lesson: Indigenous lives matter less to the state than the political economy of cattle ranching and export-oriented development that many other roads in the Chaco facilitate.

Over the years I have worked with Enxet and Sanapaná peoples, it has also become clear that the psychological and emotional toll of having rights while being continuously denied those rights is often more pernicious than direct physical violence. Legal abandonment exacerbates this violence by ensnaring Enxet and Sanapaná peoples in perpetual states of liminality, without resolution: people live as the dispossessed owners of land, on margins between roads and fences, and with rights at the heart of the nation's founding creed that are never guaranteed. Frantz Fanon's *Black Skin, White Masks* elucidates the epistemic, embodied violence of colonialism in its operation on the psyche of the colonized. Building on that work, Fanon later argues, "The colonized world is a world divided in two."[55] Settler colonization produces racial geographies that delimit different worlds where a constant but unresolved tension between inclusion and exclusion marks the condition of being a subject of rights whose rights are actively denied.

The recognition of rights and the constant denial of those rights produce suffering and shame, exemplified by Inocencia's assertion, "That is how they [state officials] think of Indigenous people, like we are animals." The indignity illustrated by such statements is accompanied by shame when people cannot live a dignified life or practice vital acts like burying their family members in accordance with their traditions because land dispossession prevents them from doing so. Shame is a tool, and product, of colonization. As Bessire observed of the colonization of Ayoreo territories in northern Paraguay, "Shame was . . . the testament to the fact that the conditions of life and being were never quite possible."[56] Occupying epistemic and ontological spaces between in/humanity and being the subject of rights whose status as such is never guaranteed is the dilemma of legal liminality and the aporia that the condition presents.

ARRESTED

In June 2016, MOPC began building a crossroads that links Yakye Axa and Sawhoyamaxa in new ways. "Crossroads" is often used to indicate a metaphorical conjuncture where change is imminent, albeit unknown. But it is also a synonym for an intersection. Postcolonial feminist geographers argue that intersectionality reveals how difference and oppression operate spatially.[57] The new road construction materially links Yakye Axa and Sawhoyamaxa land struggles to render visible intersections between legal liminality and environmental racism.

Instead of building on the route we investigated in early 2015, the new road bisects the land expropriated to Sawhoyamaxa. MOPC officials suggested the new route would be quicker to construct because it bisects Sawhoyamaxa, a community sympathetic to the Yakye Axa struggle, as opposed to the Tamarindo patrón.

Although promised to be completed in three months, construction of the Yakye Axa access road has proceeded at an excruciatingly slow pace. At the time of this writing, MOPC has yet to complete the road. The Payseyamexempa'a and Kelyenmagategma Enxet communities that border Yakye Axa's alternative land also stand to benefit from the access road. The annual rainy season regularly cuts both communities off from accessing needed services. Several people, notably children, from Payseyamexempa'a have died in recent years because they could not secure necessary medical attention due to the absence of passable roads during the rainy season.[58] For this reason, the Yakye Axa community refuses to occupy the alternative land prior to completion of the access road. Construction of the access road also sheds light on the liminal legal status of the Sawhoyamaxa expropriation. When initiated, it bolstered Sawhoyamaxa's de facto rights to the contested 14,404 hectares by legitimating expropriation insofar as the construction occurred with community approval and in opposition to Roswell and Kansol. The road opens new ways for Sawhoyamaxa community members to access hunting and fishing grounds deep within the property. However, the new road runs in front of the house that ranch staff occupied, allowing them to monitor and catalog Enxet activities the company deemed illegal in continued efforts to overturn the expropriation. Restitution as development is the IACHR's attempt to bridge the gap between de jure and de facto rights. In theory, this gap can be closed by new jurisprudence and requiring that guilty states make reparations and policy changes to improve the material conditions of life for victims of human rights violations.[59] Yet the piecemeal implementation of restitution as development is akin to what Radcliffe calls the "crumbs from the table" of poorly devised and practiced policies of participation, so often used to paper over development interventions on Indigenous territories.[60]

This chapter's title poses a question: Restitution as development? It is a question on the minds of many people who live in Yakye Axa, Sawhoyamaxa, and Xákmok Kásek. Anibal once noted, "It has been eleven years since the Court [IACHR] made the judgment. We are still here on the side of the road, suffering, waiting for the state to respect our rights."[61] Many years have passed since Anibal spoke those words. Meanwhile, the state has garnered nearly $2 billion in financing to construct new roads in the Chaco with much fanfare around the "Bi-oceanic highway" that will bisect the region from east to west, a duplication of the Trans-Chaco Highway, and the reconstruction of Ruta 5 that runs through Yakye Axa. MOPC pushed these new projects around the clock, even during the height of the COVID-19 pandemic. Meanwhile, construction of the short dirt road to Yakye Axa's alternative land has been arrested for over a year, just as the lives of those who have lived in the margin of Ruta 5 have been arrested for more than a generation.

Heart

Every time I stop by Ignacia's home, she takes me to the garden, and we see how things are growing. On this March day, things were growing well. The mandioca was tall. The sweet potato patch was covered in a tangle of vines and dark green leaves. A handful of small trees planted from seeds seemed well on their way— papaya, grapefruit, and even a mango. "I go to the pond to get water, then come back and give it to them," she told me. "See! They are growing well!" It was exciting to see how her yard had changed over the last year, from a grass-covered pasture to a home with a large garden and lots of flowers. "Do you see my flowers? They are very pretty! I am happy." With that, she told her son to get the photo album. We walked to the shade of some trees where two hammocks hung that she had woven from plastic rope. We each sat, and her son brought over the album.

She flipped through the pictures as her son and sister listened, occasionally adding comments to the stories. With each image, she shared memories from across the years. She paused when we got to one picture: a young woman wearing a navy-blue dress surrounded by other, older women holding sticks about three meters long with bells at the top. Ignacia reminded me that it was a picture of the *baile kuña*—an initiation dance done for women entering puberty. The picture was old, taken at Estancia Salazar before the community had to leave the ranch. I had seen a copy of the picture before and understood that Tierraviva used it as part of the evidence for the community's IACHR case. Ignacia recalled, "This was the last time a girl in Xákmok Kásek did the baile kuña. It is *cultura indígena* [Indigenous culture]. We used to do those things when we lived at Salazar because that was still our land. We were still on our land. Over time we did it less, but we still did it. People still knew cultura indígena. When we had to go to 25 de febrero, we stopped. I hope now that we are back on our lands, we will do it again." Ignacia and her sister Estela explained that while they were at 25 de febrero they could not practice cultura indígena because they were not on their land. It was familiar but foreign land. Now that they were again living on their lands they could, and would, begin again.

"The men were not happy when they had to work for Eaton. It is our land, but he owned it. We could not do what we wanted. They had to do what the patrón wanted." Ignacia talked about how some of the men worked near the retiro to plant peanut crops for Eaton on the best land in the area and how they built the old retiro there. "Eaton had lots of land. It went far that way and that way," she said, while gesturing with her arms to the east and south. "But Eaton loved this part of his estancia. He used to call it 'the heart of Estancia Salazar.'"[1] After that, she asked if I had ever been to Retiro Primero. "Yes," I replied. "It's over there where Yakare used to live." She laughed and shook her head. "Many people think that is Retiro Primero. It is just an old retiro. The real Retiro Primero is over there," she said, pointing in the opposite direction. With that, she stood up. "*Jaha*," let's go, she said. So we did, and Estela joined.

Ignacia led the way across one pasture, through two old wire fences, then into a stand of young trees next to a large old stock pond. "He built this pond for his cattle and his horses," she noted, as we surveyed the clearing in the forest. "Eaton had a lot of money. He used to fly here in a little plane. There is an old runway over there," she pointed. Estela nodded and listened. Then we pushed on into the shade of the trees. As we wandered through the forest, Ignacia and Estela recounted stories about the challenges of life on Estancia Salazar and labor exploitation on the ranch—stories I had heard from many people. Both women fell quiet as we approached a different stand of trees. In it were young mesquites and lots of brush, but there were also older trees that had not been cut. An old gray post stood among the bushes. Before I could ask, Ignacia announced, "This is Retiro Primero. When Eaton came here in his airplane, he would stay here. He loved this place." What was once a farmstead is now but rubble, the traces of history recalled in memories, rusty wires, and a few rotting wooden posts. As we walked to the post, Ignacia turned to me. "He [Eaton] said, 'I will never give even one centimeter of land to the Indigenous. I will never give them the heart of Estancia Salazar!' But now we have Eaton's heart in our hands. It has been a long time, and we have suffered a lot through the fight. Sometimes we didn't think that we would make it. Now we are here. We are never going to leave."

Five Years of Life

In February 2015, sixty-three families from Xákmok Kásek risked everything. Each family packed their belongings, then emptied and deconstructed their homes of palm wood and tin roofs in 25 de febrero. The old freight truck that community members had pooled scant resources to rent made trip after trip. With each journey a new set of families loaded all their material possessions into the back of the open-air truck bed: bags of clothing, old refrigerators, small orange satellite dishes and TVs, treasured photographs, bedding, and pets—everything. A dusty, hour-long trek bouncing in the back of the truck under the summer sun followed. Upon arrival at the Retiro Primero land, each family that crossed through the faded gray entrance gate walked down an uncertain path while simultaneously setting foot on lands most had never physically traversed. Yet many carried those lands in their hearts and minds throughout Xákmok Kásek's decades-long struggle to reoccupy Mopey Sensap—the place of the white hummingbird. Sitting with Clemente in the shade of his new shelter, a lean-to made of the weathered tin roofing material that had adorned his old home, we looked at grainy cell phone pictures in a WhatsApp feed he and others used to document the move while he recounted the story.

As discussed in previous chapters, the Xákmok Kásek community had challenged the Paraguayan state to restitute lands within their ancestral territories since 1986. The legal claims and court proceedings were troublesome to area ranchers and an annoyance to the state, as demonstrated in fierce resistance from both sectors in media campaigns intended to smear Tierraviva and cast doubt on movement leaders themselves. Leveraging the law to maintain pressure on the state was meant to break the patterns of land control that dispossessed Enxet and Sanapaná peoples. However, complying with the law and adhering to the dictates of state bureaucratic orders reaffirmed Paraguay's authority to set the terms of recognition and the social-spatial relations of land control in the region.[1] Refusing to fully comply with the state any longer, the Xákmok Kásek land reoccupation was a direct challenge to geographies of settler capitalism. This chapter traces how members of Xákmok Kásek have employed shifting strategies of engaging and refusing settler legal orders to force the Paraguayan state to reconcile the community's demands for land rights, actions grounded in a politics of reconstituting collectives.

Sanapaná and Enxet experiences fighting for land rights reveal the dialectical politics of selectively refusing and engaging the state. The Xákmok Kásek struggles, similar to those of Yakye Axa and Sawhoyamaxa, cannot be reduced to either absolute rejection or acceptance of state recognition. The actual practices employed over the long arc of Enxet and Sanapaná resistance shows that community members have leveraged *both* rejection/refusal and acceptance of recognition.[2] This subtle but important point brings nuance and texture to ongoing struggles for legal recognition and associated rights that many Indigenous communities in Latin America experience.

Here I want to pause to discuss comments that Anibal Gómez, a leader of Yakye Axa, shared that index subtleties of working with and against the law. Anibal lives by himself in a small home on the south side of Ruta 5 near his aging parents' house. We sat in the morning sun on twenty-liter plastic buckets turned upside down. During our conversation, we talked about the short trip we took the day before to evaluate the construction of the access road to the community's land when he reflected on the outstanding legal struggles Yakye Axa confronts. "We have fought for a very long time. But the patrones are very strong and did not help anything. Even now, from what I have seen they don't really respect the law. There is the law in reality [on paper], but you have to act in addition to that. Because with the law alone you can't do anything. You have to act in addition to that, in person, in order to be strong." He looked toward the highway as a car passing by kicked up dust. "Our legal proceedings went on for a while, but the parliamentarians just sat around and did little to help. Many times they came out against rather than in favor of, many came out against Indigenous rights. They left us like that and we saw what the situation was. So you have to act above the law [*ley ári*]."[3] Working in addition to, or above, the law involves many acts. When Yakye Axa and later Sawhoyamaxa and Xákmok Kásek took their cases to the Inter-American System, they acted in addition to Paraguayan law by scaling their struggles to the international sphere. When Sawhoyamaxa community members cut the fence that had long hemmed them in at the margin of the highway, they acted above the law to force the state to respond. Similarly, when Xákmok Kásek community members reoccupied Retiro Primero and later closed the Trans-Chaco Highway they worked with and against the law.

This chapter focuses on how Xákmok Kásek has worked above and with the law using extralegal strategies that disrupt histories of dispossession and thereby chart a new future. Earlier chapters assessed some early actions to comply with the law for remedy, like naming state-recognized leaders and navigating years of legal proceedings from Paraguay to the IACHR and back. I juxtapose the two strategies to illustrate how the dialectics of disruption work through efforts to employ a favorable judgment from the IACHR alongside extralegal actions to reconstitute the community as a place-based collective. By reworking recognition to force state officials to reconcile with Enxet and Sanapaná demands, community members assert their self-determination through embodied and emplaced practices that restore relations and build pathways toward more just futures. The restorative actions taken by Xákmok Kásek show that settler power is not total; such power can and must be disrupted. For all its limits, recognition did create a narrow political opening that Sanapaná and Enxet peoples have gradually expanded, like water dripping on a rock that slowly erodes a seemingly impenetrable barrier. Although rights should guarantee the ability of the subjects of them to enjoy their benefits, that is clearly never the case.

Time and again social movements show that rights are never given but must be taken through action. This is, in part, why I insist that right-based approaches alone are insufficient. Critiques of the politics of recognition discussed throughout the book show that relying on the state to uphold rights is Sisyphean. Theoretically and normatively, states should uphold the laws they create, but that is generally only done to uphold specific political economic and class relations. Anibal's comments about working "ley ari," above the law, show the paucity of rights-based approaches that do not disrupt settler modes of emplacement and replacement. Starting from a point where Indigenous rights simply did not exist, the decades-long struggle for labor and land rights led by Enxet and Sanapaná communities has tacked between strategically following and, now, strategically working above the law. The dialectics of disruption have become a powerful tool to challenge legal liminality as a logic of racial capitalism.

I have spent many years conversing with members of Xákmok Kásek and accompanied the community in its land reoccupation, attended negotiations with state officials, documented protests, and celebrated several anniversaries that mark new life on, and with, the land. Through the strategies of refusal and engagement, Xákmok Kásek community members have eroded the social-spatial control of settler patrones to re-create sovereign spaces for collective life.[4] So often, a focus on the politics of recognition or neoliberal multiculturalism centers on notions of indigeneity as a political-juridical relation with settler states and the myriad ways that relation revolves around dispossession. These are undeniably significant factors. I take this discussion further by arguing that environmental violence is inherent in the politics of recognition on extractive frontiers, something that does not reduce Indigenous movements to mere resource politics but that works with the complexity of justice struggles in this conjuncture. I reiterate a key point: Enxet and Sanapaná struggles for land restitution are struggles for Indigenous environmental justice. Returning land to Indigenous peoples creates the conditions of possibility for transformative justice based on restoring relations through self-determination.

Indigenous resistance and intellectual traditions, as well as a significant body of critical scholarship, make clear the importance of place, land, and relations to many

Indigenous peoples.[5] Aware of this, the IACHR has advanced jurisprudence that codifies the spiritual, cultural, and extraeconomic value of specific sites to Indigenous communities, arguing that land understood as "productive" within capitalist systems is not more sacred than Indigenous claims to lands that were taken without consent. And while much literature focuses on the defense of Indigenous lands against usurpation or the politics of land titling, fewer studies examine the politics of land restitution for Indigenous communities who were removed from their lands, let alone the process communities take to reconstitute collectives on those lands after restitution. If restitution is "the restoration of something lost or stolen to its proper owner" and land is more than a mere resource but a site of embodied relations, how do communities negotiate their reencounter with what has been stolen? By what means do people reconstitute their relations, both with one another and to other-than-human counterparts in place? In considering these questions, I draw from the first months of the Retiro Primero reoccupation to trace the contours on which members of Xákmok Kásek began to remake relations with their lands.

By explicitly drawing a concern for environmental justice into conversation with the politics of recognition, two important dynamics come to light. First, as several scholars have shown, the politics of recognition circumscribes a range of acceptable Indigenous behavior as defined by the settler state.[6] Many of these works focus on the limited range of actions, both socially and politically, that recognition and rights-based claims afford Indigenous peoples. These are important contributions to debates about the intimate relations between settler colonialism and law as a tool of social control or governance. Yes, many studies critically evaluate Indigenous land-titling initiatives, which literally circumscribe collective property within ancestral territories or sites beyond those territories.[7] The spatial ramifications of such circumscriptions are less explicitly discussed, however.[8] Second, if Indigenous environmental justice hinges on the capability of communities to maintain or reconstruct relations in and to territories, as Whyte suggests, the literal delimitation of those spaces vis-à-vis state-sanctioned property-rights regimes ultimately also constrains the spatial practices necessary to (re)constitute social collectives in territory.[9] By foregrounding how Enxet and Sanapaná resistance strategies rework recognition, this chapter shows how spatial practices are related to the operation of environmental injustice, on the one hand, and vital to the dialectics of disruption, on the other.

LAND BACK

As I write, seven years have passed since Xákmok Kásek reoccupied Retiro Primero. The tarp encampment where I spent several months with community members has long been abandoned. Homes, gardens, soccer fields, a school, a large community center, and much more now dot the land as you travel down the dirt road that leads from the entrance of the community to its terminus several kilometers away near Clemente's new house. What is more, the state acquiesced to

FIGURE 13. Milciades commemorating the "heroes" of Xákmok Kásek during the five-year anniversary of the land reoccupation. Photo by author, February 2020.

pressure from the land reoccupation and purchased 7,701 hectares that encompass Retiro Primero and Mopey Sensap for the community in 2017, partially complying with the community's claim and IACHR recommendation of 10,001 total hectares. With the purchase of the land, new state-led development projects that had not been envisioned in the IACHR restitution as development strategy soon followed. One project, by the National Service for Environmental Sanitation (SENASA), aims to provide greater water security via the construction of rainwater storage tanks at key sites in the community. Through a different project led by the Ministry of Urbanism, Housing, and Habitat initiative called Che Tapyi, nearly every family now has a two-room home constructed of brick with a tin roof and wired for the eventual arrival of electricity. While state officials like to suggest that they execute these projects to comply with the IACHR ruling, such claims are misleading. Che Tapyi is a national antipoverty initiative funded by Taiwan, whereas SENASA is leveraging a World Bank loan to improve water access in thirty-one Indigenous communities in the region.[10] On the other hand, community members have used restitution-as-development funds to purchase strategic shared resources like a truck that serves as an ambulance, a tractor and other necessary implements to maintain roads within the territory and till fields, a communal cattle herd, and sheep or goats for every family. However, one of the most symbolic acts to date is the reappropriation of the old retiro that Eulalio and other community members once helped build to accommodate Estancia Salazar's non-Indigenous peons.[11] The building has been refurbished with a new tin roof, a fresh coat of white paint, and electricity to power a large freezer and refrigerator; it now serves as a cooperative store where community members can purchase fair-priced food staples or offer their own goods for sale. Xákmok Kásek community members have rewritten the geography of Retiro Primero, reterritorializing it as Sanapaná and Enxet in the recent years of life living on lands once stolen from them and where many once worked for the patrones.

"There is much work to be done. There is still a lot of need in the community. But thanks to the strength of the community, to God's blessing, and for our sacrifice we have achieved much. We are here on the land and living in peace." Clemente's words cracked through the speakers of a portable sound system as he addressed a crowd of about fifty people who had gathered in the shade of the new community meeting space to commemorate the fifth anniversary of the land reoccupation. At the invitation of Clemente and other community leaders, I traveled from Florida to Xákmok Kásek to celebrate the occasion. It was a hot, late February day in 2020 with few clouds and a dry north wind. The event was held on the site of the new community church that was still under construction. A corrugated tin roof welded atop tall rebar pillars provided shade as we sat on small wooden benches listening to the day's program. Clemente, Serafin, Amancio, and Eulalio took turns speaking to the crowd, each recounting elements of the community's land rights struggle.

However, it was Milciades who orchestrated the event and prepared a special commemoration to close the formal ceremony. Milciades solemnly recounted a history of struggle to remind everyone not to take for granted the gains we had gathered to celebrate or forget the lives lost in the decades-long struggle. "We would not be here today if it were not for the heroes whose sacrifice and courage broke the locked gate and reoccupied this land, who left everything behind and faced the unknown. Living under tarps, passing hunger, suffering, and never knowing what could happen. We recognize the heroes today." He concluded by calling the names of every person who first agreed to reoccupy Retiro Primero and enter the land on the day the lock was broken. "Ignacia Ruiz-Dermott . . . Felix Dermott . . . Ramon Larossa-Dermott . . . Clemente Dermott . . . Serafin López . . . " As he called the names, each person slowly and solemnly made their way to the front and stood facing the crowd. Milciades, his wife, and his daughter were the last people to join. All told, a group of about forty people—from five to over seventy years old—stood in silence, reflecting on the significance of the moment. Behind the group, a blue tapestry had been tied up to create a backdrop on which gold letters spelled out a message that read, "Xákmok Kásek Cinco Años de Vida [Five Years of Life]."

The ceremony ended with little fanfare. Some people gathered in small groups to talk in the shade of an algarrobo tree, while others wandered over to watch the soccer tournament taking place. A small army of women worked feverishly to make a meal of chicken, goat, rice, and bread. Milciades and I sat under the tin roof, drank tereré, and talked. We have long shared a connection, as we are about the same age, are teachers, and spent time in Arizona—he for a leadership workshop and I during graduate school. Among other things, we reflected on the current struggles Xákmok Kásek faces, as well as the past five years, including my first visit to the community. Though a member of the Xákmok Kásek community, Milciades lives and teaches school in Paraiso, an aldea of the Angaité Indigenous community La Patria, about 70 kilometers from where we sat. He comes to Xákmok Kásek when school vacations allow. When I first arrived in March 2015, Milciades had already returned to Paraiso for work and wanted to hear my thoughts on those early months in the tarp encampment.

RECONSTITUTING RELATIONS

Things often work out as you least expect. In preparation for the research that informs this book, I traveled to Paraguay in 2013 and 2014 to build relations with members of Yakye Axa, Sawhoyamaxa, and Xákmok Kásek. I thought that I would most likely focus on the former two and devote less time working with the latter, based on proximity and other logistical issues. During my early fieldwork I met with representatives of Yakye Axa and Sawhoyamaxa, in addition to visiting both communities and gaining their feedback on the research design. Because of transportation limitations, I was not able to meet with members of Xákmok Kásek until I went with a lawyer from Tierraviva, Ireneo, to the site of the reoccupation in late March 2015. Shortly after arriving, I was drawn into a process that would redefine my research: the reoccupation of Retiro Primero.

After driving six hours from Asunción and making our way down the final 12 kilometers of dirt road, we arrived at the reoccupation just as the sun reached its apex in the late summer sky. Banners demanding compliance with the IACHR adorned the wire fence at the entrance to the Retiro Primero land. With permission from a man standing guard at the gate, Ireneo pulled in and parked in a small patch of shade under an algarrobo tree. A large semicircle of shelters enclosed the entrance to limit passage. Yet unlike the campesino encampments erected on the exposed landscapes of southeastern Paraguay's soybean fields, devoid of trees, most members of Xákmok Kásek had cleared underbrush below a low canopy of mixed trees to construct some thirty to forty shelters made of black plastic tarps largely hidden from sight. As Ireneo and I exited the truck, a group of men approached to greet us. In his characteristically generous way, Ireneo smiled and shook hands with everyone, introducing me in the process. Not more than fifteen minutes had passed, and folks were talking about one aspect of what Ireneo told them about me: "He is a geographer, knows how to map, and has a GPS unit." Maximiliano, one of three community members who traveled to Peru in 2009 to testify before the IACHR, had recently completed a community mapping workshop in Argentina and suggested that we immediately begin mapping the sites where each community member intended to build their house. I was reticent, thinking it necessary to discuss the process and methodology before embarking on counter-mapping. Such concerns were secondary, however, to the excited group that had formed and the imperative to "map or be mapped."[12] No sooner had we piled our bags and gear on the dirt than twelve men jumped in the back of the truck, with five more in the cab, and we were again driving, this time into the reoccupied lands.

Retiro Primero is located on a tract of land that at the time of the reoccupation was still operated by Eaton Cía and ARPA S.A. As we drove down a small dirt road inside the ranch, it was clear that few cattle were being run on the land: pastures were overgrown, not a cow was in sight, and forest stands had started to take over what was once previously cleared. Bouncing down the road, we heard two thumps on the cab's roof, indicating that it was time to stop. Everyone unloaded, and we walked to the first site, where a three-meter-square patch of land had been recently cleared and tilled. Stuck on a tree branch planted at the edge of the site, a green plastic soda bottle further staked a claim. Elijio looked at me and said, "Ape. Che mba'erã. Ogajapota ape [Here. This will be mine. I will build a house here]." With that, I turned on the GPS, took out my notebook, and recorded the site where Elijio intended to build his home. For the next four hours we walked or drove from site to site, using the GPS unit and notepad to record the location and names of nearly every family who currently lived under the plastic tarps at the entrance to the ranch. Each site was marked either by a small patch of land cultivated with sweet potato slips, a tree blaze, or an item like the soda bottle to claim ownership. Having only staged the initial reoccupation three weeks earlier, the people of Xákmok Kásek were clearly well into the process of rebuilding relations to the land and one another through such territorializing practices.

As we walked from site to site, some older members of our group recalled histories of where certain crops grew better than others, where they had once hunted certain animals, or where the land was more susceptible to flooding than other places. Yet this knowledge of the land was based less on recollection of occupation before the arrival of ranching than on experience working the land for ranchers. People were familiar with this land because they had spent countless hours building fences, herding cattle, or cultivating peanuts for Eaton and Cía, not because they personally recalled a time before dispossession of the land per se. Yet stories recounted and passed down from their parents and grandparents imbued the land with important meaning that animated a multifold process of unlearning Retiro Primero by reconstituting Xákmok Kásek through new encounters with place. More than marking the land to articulate a precolonial vision of territory, everyone who joined the mapping that day articulated visions for a new future shaped by an awareness of the past.[13] The process was part taking back and part reencounter. Before our collective action that day, families had staked out sites for their future homes while learning the land on their own. The mapping exercise was thus simultaneously one to begin legitimating each family's respective claims and an opportunity for those involved in the mapping to see, assess, and learn about other sites on the land. While noting GPS coordinates, I also took note of casual comments and observations members of the group made on our walkabout:

> "The earth here will be good for gardening. We will plant sweet potatoes and grapefruit."

> "This is *algarrobo blanco*. I remember when women used to gather its seeds and make flour. This will be a good tree to live by."

> "That tajamar has sweet water. It is big enough to last the long droughts."

> "Over there is *palo santo*. The ground is high here. I want to build my house here."

From that first mapping trip throughout the many months of the reoccupation, it was clear that the ability to reconnect with this land was a vital pedagogy for Sanapaná and Enxet renewal after generations of removal.[14] Through new connections to the land, Enxet and Sanapaná started creating a future of their own choosing rather than comport with a history not of their making. "We do this for our children and their children. We do not do this for ourselves. I am old. But this land is a place where they can live in peace. That is why we fight, so that they might have a future." Serafin López used to tell me this regularly when I stayed with his family. Here I want to bridge Serafin's comments with Whyte's observation that Indigenous environmental justice must be understood as the capability for collective continuance and Leanne Betasamosake Simpson's powerful assertion that Indigenous knowledges are grounded relationalities that come "through the land."[15] Returning to the land simultaneously asserted Xákmok Kásek self-determination and the community's efforts to ensure a space for collective well-being shaped but not determined by historical connections.

Reconnecting with foodways played an important role in rewriting the geographies of Retiro Primero during the initial months of the reoccupation. Through daily hunting and fishing trips, members of Xákmok Kásek began telling new stories of the land and making new histories that accumulate over time, covering the sedimentary traces of settler occupation but never entirely erasing their effects. Reestablishing relations by learning from the land and the new stories that result are everyday geo-graphing practices that enact a spatial politics of self-determination. Rather than static geographies, settler colonial appropriation of land is but a momentary geo-graphing that is, as Saldaña-Portillo suggests, part of "ongoing palimpsests of spatial negotiation amongst colonial, national, and indigenous populations."[16] Such acts of geo-graphing occurred not through the creation of new maps but through the formation of new social cartographies drafted through everyday life. Early in the morning, people would leave the tent encampment at the entrance to the Retiro Primero land on foot with a rifle or fishing gear to walk onto the land. Regardless of whether someone returned with something to eat, they always came back with a story of what they saw or learned.

"The pigs like it over there by the edge of the forest where the ground is low. I saw their trails."

"There are mountain lion prints by the northern boundary. I bet deer are there too!"

"Over at Alicia, the tajamar is great! We saw a lot of caimans and capybaras."

"At 25 [de febrero] I never saw tapirs. I know they are up past the retiro in the forest after the little paddock because I saw their fur stuck on a cactus."

"That land over by the big *samu'u* tree will be a good place for the community center. I remember when we used to plant peanuts there for Eaton. The land is good and does not flood as much. It is overgrown now, but we can clean it up."

During my time in the community, I joined several hunting and fishing trips. For all involved, the trips were about more than food. They were a form of pedagogical praxis enacted through embodied relations that slowly reterritorialized Retiro Primero as Enxet and Sanapaná space. With changing weather, the land, animals, and plants revealed how each reacted to drought or flood, crucial information that informed evolving decisions about where people would finally build their homes, if not at the locations we recorded during our first mapping exercise. Through these practices, community members collectively created a new vision for the future of Xákmok Kásek beyond one of mere reoccupation.

GEO-GRAPHING THE TEMPORALITIES OF RESISTANCE

Xákmok Kásek community members planned the geography of the reoccupation strategically, along several lines. Located at the main entrance to the Retiro Primero land, community members took control of the primary access point. They also occupied one of the few spaces on the property visible to passersby, an important site to hang signs demanding the state restitute the occupied land or receive any media interested in the conflict. However, there was also a palpable fear that state authorities or ranch staff would arrive to forcibly remove community members. The families closest to the entrance served as monitors who could warn others if a threat arrived, providing precious time to escape into the forest if need be. Being close to the road also offered access to traveling vendors who would pass through a couple times a week, offering scant access to commodity goods, from grapefruits and cookies to cigarettes and batteries. By the time I arrived, three weeks after the reoccupation, a small soccer field, two volleyball courts, a makeshift school, and a communal meeting space had been set up. From the entrance, shelters constructed from plastic tarps or tin roofing brought from 25 de febrero branched into stands

FIGURE 14. This school was one of the first structures built after the reoccupation of Retiro Primero. Photo by author, March 2015.

of algarrobo trees that offered shade and some protection from the elements. The temporary establishment was intimate. Shelters were constructed close to one another. Privacy was fleeting, as most shelters did not have four walls but were open to the air on each end like a quickly constructed tent.

Although community members anticipated a dramatic and quick response from state officials and ranch staff, the early months of the reoccupation were surprisingly calm. The ranch owners protested but did not appear. State officials took note and encouraged the community to leave but never forced them to do so or threatened them with police. When I first arrived, there was an energy in conversations about finally reaching closure in the case, about gaining title to the land. As Maximiliano told me one day, "Look around. Everyone you see took down their homes and came here because they were tired of waiting. We didn't know what would happen, if the police would come. But we came anyway. . . . It is important for our children to be here because now they are part of the lucha. You are also part of the lucha now because you are here."[17] That a decades-long lucha promised to be close to resolution imbued each day with the radical possibility that Xákmok Kásek would finally prevail. That energy fueled countless trips to different parts of the land where people would return at day's end tired but with more knowledge. Such knowledge was shared during daily conversations over tereré or while sitting watching a soccer game but also in regularly held community-wide meetings. Meetings often took the form of hours-long discussions that transited several topics in a focused yet open forum where men, women, and, to a lesser degree, youths would debate current events, future actions, and lessons learned on the land.

Initially, the meetings were charged with positive energy. People speculated that the landowners would sell soon because they were highly indebted due to purportedly low production on their ranch for several years. Rumors circulated in the tent encampment and on the streets of Asunción that the debt was held by one of then-president Horacio Cartes's banks, thus making it even more likely that the state would finally make the purchase.[18] Given this alignment of events, many community members felt that Paraguay would finally comply with the IACHR judgment not out of a commitment to Indigenous rights but because it would directly benefit the acting president. However, moods changed as weeks turned to months with little progress and the short days of the cold, damp winter set in.

I vividly recall one week in June that began with a heavy rain followed by days of unrelenting mist. The weather closed the dirt access road, turned the camp to mud, dripped into people's ramshackle shelters, and dampened the mood. Bronchial and sinus infections spread quickly through tereré sessions that sought to quench thirst and quell growing hunger. With the road closed, no mobile food vendors passed, and the scheduled delivery of SEN rations did not arrive. This was, perhaps, the darkest week of the reoccupation. An unfamiliar silence set in across the camp. Three days passed when almost no one spoke. With nowhere to go because of the relentless mist and slick mud that coated everything, nearly everyone stayed in their shelters. Sitting with Clemente's family on plastic buckets or a piece of wood near a smoldering fire, hours passed in silence. Looking across the camp from our shelter to the others, the situation was the same. The excitement of the early months had given way to fatigue, hunger, and a general depression that hung low, as if suspended in the mist. On the third day, I watched Luciano make his way from his shelter toward the side of the road just outside the gate where men would often go to urinate. He appeared to move in slow motion, barely lifting his feet from the ground to skate-shuffle across the muddy expanse. With a cigarette dangling from his lips and head cocked slightly to the right, Luciano's eyes fixed on a point far in the distance, his face expressionless. I watched from our tent as he moved across a span of 30 meters in a matter of minutes, never touching his cigarette with his hands but slowly inhaling and exhaling smoke that disappeared into the mist.

Those days of rain, mist, and mud underscored the shifting temporalities of resistance and violence that permeate Enxet and Sanapaná struggles. The act of reoccupying Retiro Primero was literally decades in the making, following a series of legal and bureaucratic measures where everything is slow, as one of the eldest members of the community Felix Dermott once told me: "The patrones, the people from the state all go fast. They have trucks and can go here and there. But the Indigenous don't. We walk. We have to wait, but they can go whenever they want. You know. You have money, a truck. You can go. We are poor and everything is slow. When they want land, they can buy it. We have tried for a very long time. It is slow."[19]

Time is central to the biopolitics of neglect, as I suggested in chapter 3. It is used as a tool to erode Indigenous lifeways, to slowly drain people of the will to continue their struggles and eventually acquiesce. Yet Enxet and Sanapaná resistance has endured for generations. In stating this, I do not purport to glorify resistance. The repeated denial of due process, of rights, of land is a source of great pain and indignation for my interlocutors. Yet as Indigenous scholars writing of current-day Canada and the United States insist, we must confront relentless efforts to eradicate Indigenous lifeways by centering endurance and futurity.[20] Without such a focus academic knowledge production can quickly replicate the epistemic erasures inherent in settler logics of elimination. While delaying Indigenous access to justice is a tool of oppression that emanates from state authority, the inverse is also important to denote. Enxet and Sanapaná refusal to relinquish their demands disrupts the temporalities of settler colonialism, which seeks to continually speed processes of dispossession and capital accumulation. Slow resistance has thus become a sort of "weapon of the weak."[21] Enxet and Sanapaná persist despite the grinding slow violence manifested as efforts to erase them, materially and spatially, from the land.

Viewing neglect as a biopolitical calculus pushes the notion of slow violence further by showing that time, particularly bureaucratic processes that delay effective change, is a core element that settler states in Latin America use to govern lives not deemed worthy of protection. The poisoning of Indigenous peoples by the oil industry in Ecuador's Amazon and long-standing efforts to thwart legal demands by Indigenous peoples and their allies that the responsible companies rectify such harms are an emblematic example of how slow violence intersects with legal bureaucratic procedures.[22] On the outskirts of Buenos Aires, Argentina, the periurban poor working class contend with systemic lead poisoning, yet are left without access to necessary medical services despite well-known exposure to such environmental harms.[23] Land dispossession is another form of slow violence. Refusing to reconcile legally enshrined land claims for communities like Xákmok Kásek ensures the prolongation of dispossession and its attendant harms: the erosion of Indigenous cultural practices, the gradual wearing of the will of those who resist, the loss of life by those who succumb to preventable diseases induced by exposure but exacerbated by lack of access to basic medical services, adequate housing, or nutrition.

Neglect is not the product of happenstance behavior; it is an active process of negation that, in this case, intends to diminish the life chances of Enxet and Sanapaná peoples to ensure compliance with the settler political economy. Luciano's passage through the entrance to Retiro Primero and the slow grind of the Xákmok Kásek lucha—from the moment community members launched their efforts to take land back in the 1980s to the fraught restitution-as-development politics—reveal that slow violence is inherently tied to the temporal politics of justice. If justice delayed is justice denied, the arc of Enxet and Sanapaná efforts to reclaim their lands has shown that relying on settler legal orders is tantamount to the very denial of rights on which those claims rest.

REJECTING THE INDIO PERMITIDO

Throughout their generation-long efforts to reoccupy their lands, Xákmok Kásek community members have largely comported themselves within the mandates of Paraguayan law and policy. However, as Coulthard argues, "without conflict and struggle, the terms of recognition tend to remain in the possession of those in power to bestow on their 'inferiors' in ways they deem appropriate."[24] Enxet and Sanapaná peoples of Xákmok Kásek have gained recognition from the state and the Inter-American System in their efforts to reoccupy a portion of their ancestral territory, but the power to define the terms of land control, a key facet of recognition in Paraguay, remained with the state. State recognition of the Xákmok Kásek community in 1986 clearly did little to quell the dispossession of the Sanapaná and Enxet peoples or ensure their full rights of citizenship. The experiences I discussed in chapter 2 illustrate this point, as does the fact that the Xákmok Kásek community engaged the Paraguayan state for more than twenty years by following the law to maintain their claims. Although involvement in the Marandú Project, the use of Law 904, and the case before the IACHR each attempted to disrupt the status quo of patrón-Indigenous relations, state support of settler rancher interests remained unaltered. Trusting that justice would be served through the guarantee of rights established a new status quo, one where the settler state repeatedly denied ensuring the very Indigenous rights it had codified in law. This pattern is not unique to Paraguay. Thus disrupting the patrón requires radical action. For the people of Xákmok Kásek, years of state neglect served as a pedagogy, with the lesson that recognition only comes with one guarantee: rights will never be given but must be taken.

The reoccupation of Retiro Primero defined new terms of recognition based on a rejection of the dictates of the law and charted a new direction in Xákmok Kásek's political strategy. Akin to the Sawhoyamaxa reoccupation, members of Xákmok Kásek sought to challenge the limits of private property rights to see if state officials would enforce the rights of the ranchers or of the community members. It turned out that state officials did little to enforce private property rights or remove community members from the Retiro Primero land. After reoccupying the land, community members learned that financial hardship had fallen on Eaton and Cía and that some partners in the company were in favor of selling the land to the state so it could be returned to Xákmok Kásek. Simultaneous with the reoccupation, the majority partners of ARPA, the company that subsumed Eaton, began to actively lobby the state to purchase the land. Moreover, nearly all pertinent political actors within the Paraguayan government were publicly in favor of resolving the claim: the president of INDI, the vice president of the republic, and the minister of finance, who stated that the necessary funds were available to purchase the land. Despite the confluence of favorable conditions, the state inexplicably failed to take any action on the case until several years later.

During those early months of the reoccupation, I joined community members in negotiations with state officials. We met with the president of INDI, the minister of foreign relations, the minister of finance, and then the vice president, Juan Afara. Each of these actors plays a central role in the implementation of IACHR judgments, from federal budget management and the governance of Indigenous affairs to leadership of the state's special Commission for the Compliance of International Judgments (Comisión Interinstitucional para el Cumplimiento de las Sentencias Internacionales [CICSI]). Although each actor denied direct responsibility for decision making and indicated that we would meet with another state institution and official in this institutional constellation, each state representative shared the same narrative: Horacio Cartes, acting president of the country, would make the final decision about when and if payment for the land would be made. The direct involvement of the president in making such a decision is not required by law; but the words of INDI's former president from the opening vignette of this book resonate: "el patrón manda" (the patrón is in charge). While Law 904/81 and the Agrarian Statute determine the adjudication of Indigenous land restitution, suggesting that the president would make this decision underscores the authoritarian legacies of the state-as-patrón that continue to shape the function of Paraguay's democratic institutions.[25]

With every return to the camp that followed excursions to Asunción for conversations with state officials, community members called a council meeting to discuss and debate. After several such meetings, a new consensus began to crystallize. Nothing would change without more radical action. Although community members had reoccupied the land, there was little public impact beyond the handful of ranchers, Indigenous peoples, or traveling vendors who passed by the entrance to Retiro Primero. Rather than rile the landowners, the reoccupation underscored their need and desire to sell the land to finance the company's debts, ultimately shifting all decision-making power to the state and, in this case, President Cartes. Under a grove of algarrobo trees near the center of the tarp encampment, women and men of the community sat, shared tereré, and debated about the possibility of staging a multiday road closure. Fear of violent state repression was a central concern, as was the prospect that someone would burn their encampment to the ground if they left to protest. The prospect of gaining title to the lands they had reoccupied and long fought to access proved more compelling than the alternatives. As one woman argued, "We have come this far. We cannot turn back."[26]

TEMPORAL POLITICS OF TERRITORY

Building from earlier waves of settler colonization that introduced ranching to the Bajo Chaco, Mennonite settlers established extensive ranching and dairy operations farther north in the central Chaco. Indeed, the Mennonite towns Filadelfia, Loma Plata, and Neuland comprise a constellation of colonies that are logistical and economic hubs for ranching in Paraguay's Chaco, with the region's only major slaughterhouses and dairies. Together the three colonies comprise an agroindustrial enclave and are the only major cities and towns for hundreds of kilometers in every direction.[27] Led by a minority population of German-speaking immigrants who fled violence in Russia, the colonies wield significant political influence within Paraguay.[28] Colony formation in the 1920s through 1940s helped expand the Paraguayan state's presence during the Chaco War against Bolivia. Since that time, Mennonite agroindustrial settlements have not only been essential to Paraguayan state expansion in the region, but they have provided the technical and logistical hub for the ranching industry to develop. If not for Mennonite lobbying of the US government and their labor and technical expertise, the Trans-Chaco Highway constructed between 1954 and 1967 might not have existed.[29]

At the time of my research, the Trans-Chaco Highway was the only paved road that bisected the Paraguayan Chaco and connected Mennonite colonies with national and international markets. The highway is the central conduit for the flow of people and goods to and from the colonies and ranches that lie beyond, while it is also a material manifestation of settler territoriality. The Trans-Chaco is legally encoded as a site where all Paraguayans are constitutionally guaranteed the right to unimpeded travel and discursively coded as racial infrastructure, because non-Indigenous settlers are those who most readily and reliably use the road. Returning to Felix Dermott's words, "The patrones, the people from the state all go fast. They have trucks and can go here and there. But the Indigenous don't. We walk. We have to wait, but they can go whenever they want." As Appel, Anand, and Gupta contend, infrastructures must be understood as "spatiotemporal projects" that not only connect actors in space but also rework, or promise to rework, the temporality of connection and processes that unfold in and through them.[30] The Trans-Chaco provides a site to examine the territorialities of settler colonialism as not only spatial but also temporal: speed as a cornerstone of economic productivity and capital gains.

David Harvey's classic formulation of time-space compression has provided a productive analytic to evaluate geographic processes, particularly uneven development.[31] When considered in the context of settler capitalism, the notion of time-space compression opens new lines of inquiry about territory and territoriality. So often territory is viewed through a spatial frame of reference; a territory is expressed spatially in land, for example. Yet the settler legal frameworks that support Indigenous land restitution foreground a crucial characteristic of territory that demands it be conceived of beyond merely spatial expression, as one with a vital temporal component.[32] On the one hand, this can be viewed as state efforts to govern "the prior" and ossify indigeneity as a non/premodern relation rooted to a specific place.[33]

However, another way of reading the temporality of territory is to return to how settler capitalism operates in specific sites vis-à-vis the ability to control speed, and in that regard, time. For example, Mennonite dairies require road conditions that allow them to transport their perishable milk-based products hundreds of kilometers through the Chaco—a site of extreme heat in the summer—to Paraguay's primary markets in the southeast. The perishability of the product necessitates speed, as does the issue of transportation expenses, which increase with delays. And as Mario recounted to me, "The cattle get stressed on the long trip [to slaughterhouses near Asunción]. They try to move them as fast as possible. The trucks are full. Cows can't lay down. Sometimes they die on the trip if it takes too long."[34] The importance of transportation speed for the Mennonite dairy and cattle industry reveals the central role the Trans-Chaco plays in maintaining settler territoriality in Chaco. It is a state-controlled space intended to facilitate speed and connectivity crucial to the functioning of settler capitalism. The territory of settler capitalism is more than spatial; it hinges on the control of time as related to the speed required for key economic activities.[35] Aware of these factors and the vulnerabilities they pose to ranchers in the northern and central Chaco, the Xákmok Kásek community decided to close the Trans-Chaco to disrupt settler temporalities and assert new territorialities in that time and space.

The timing of such political acts is crucial if they are to have the desired effect. The road closure could have been staged at any point, but community members coordinated their action to take place in the days immediately before Pope Francis's scheduled visit to Paraguay in July 2015. Radio Pa'i Puku reported the pope's visit would be good business for the Mennonite dairies and slaughterhouses. Asunción would need increased shipments of perishable dairy and beef products to satisfy the estimated two million tourists traveling to Paraguay for the papal visit. Closing the Trans-Chaco just before the pope's visit would spur one of two possible outcomes. As I drove a car full of people from Xákmok Kásek to Rio Verde, where the road closure was planned to take place, someone explained, "The ranchers will be mad because their products won't make it to market. They will call their representatives in Congress. They will call their friends the senators and tell them to negotiate with us. The state will listen to the patrones because they are the ones who control the state."[36] The other possibility was that the state would violently repress the action and subsequently draw the attention of international media already present to cover the pope's historic visit.

Paraguay is one of the most Catholic countries in Latin America, and several activist priests and other adherents of liberation theology like Pa'i Oliva Miguel and Chase-Sardi have played an important role in advancing Indigenous rights.[37] In 1988, Pope John Paul II made the only other papal visit to Paraguay, holding mass for Indigenous peoples in the northern Chaco town of Mariscal Estigarribia, and he is often credited with helping remove Stroessner from power.[38] Perhaps harkening to that previous papal visit, several people from Xákmok Kásek speculated that the international media covering the pope would catch wind of the community's actions in the Chaco and bring it to his attention. In the weeks preceding the planned road closure, many of my interlocutors jokingly referred to the pope as the "spiritual patrón of the Paraguayans" and suggested that he would not remain quiet if the state violently suppressed their mobilization.[39] The road closure was thus designed to test the limits of state restraint or direct violence.

"WE BREAK THE LAW TO MAKE YOU RESPECT OUR RIGHTS"

The road closure took place on July 6–9, 2015, with the idea to increase the amount of time traffic would be blocked each day. "We will close it four hours day one, eight hours day two, twelve hours day three, then indefinitely until the state concedes," Serafin reported in an interview with a local radio station before the protest.[40] Each day presented new challenges and strategies to provoke Paraguayan state officials to acquiesce to the community's demands and comply with the IACHR judgment. Aside from palpable apprehension about potential state responses, the first day was calm. Local police were dispatched to ensure that the event was peaceful. Around 125 community members and local allies occupied a small bridge, blocking the road with human barriers and banners that read, "We demand the immediate compliance with the 2010 IACHR judgment." Though it is unconstitutional to close a national highway in Paraguay, the local police did little to stop the protest other than scold the Xákmok Kásek leaders. The lackluster response, gray skies, and constant mist dampened the moods of many participants who had anticipated a dramatic impact. After three hours, Xákmok Kásek lifted the blockade to allow the cattle trucks, buses, and cars to continue on their way.

Most people involved in the road closure slept next to the highway in an old, abandoned building while a few of us slept in tents. Despite the underwhelming outcome of the first day, upon waking, we saw that the road closure had indeed piqued the attention of state officials. Heavily armed and armored riot police had arrived overnight, deployed along the roadside to ensure that the protest did not continue for a second day. More importantly, a handful of state officials arrived to negotiate a resolution to the protest with community members. The former governor of the Presidente Hayes Department first attempted to convince the community to return to Retiro Primero, though his credibility was compromised by the fact that he had been publicly charged with embezzling state funds for school lunches. Later, the camouflage-clad district chief who accompanied the riot police sought to convince community members they should return home and wait for the appropriate state agencies to resolve the legal process. The threat of violence was latent in his discourse, as he repeatedly stated that the riot police would "not allow" the road to be closed again. As the morning wore on and news about the road closure spread on the radio, more allies from nearby Indigenous communities showed up to observe the situation. A crowd of nearly two hundred people massed on the margin of the highway holding banners and flags, while Gerardo, a Xákmok Kásek representative, stood near the edge of the road debating with the district chief over a loudspeaker so the crowd could hear. At one point Gerardo explained, "They say that Pope Francis is going to bring peace and tranquility to Paraguay. . . . Without land there is no peace, no tranquility. . . . We are only here fighting for what is ours, what the national constitution, the law, and the Court [IACHR] says is ours, our ancestral lands. You are breaking the law by not respecting our rights, so we have to break the law to make you respect our rights."[41]

Gerardo's statement indexes two important processes. First, by calculating that nearly all factors necessary for land restitution were aligned—the landholders wanted to sell, the IACHR judgment called for restitution of Retiro Primero, and several state agencies were purportedly ready to initiate the transfer of ownership—community members surmised that the pope's visit was part of a conjuncture, an open moment, where the state might finally resolve the land claim. Second, Gerardo exposed a central contradiction inherent in the politics of recognition. The district chief argued that they would not allow the road closure to proceed because the constitution guarantees free passage on national highways to all citizens of Paraguay. Gerardo retorted by arguing that the constitution guarantees Indigenous peoples rights to their ancestral lands, that state officials effectively break Paraguayan laws by refusing to enforce Indigenous land rights, and that the IACHR judgment reinforces the fact that the state has violated the human rights of community members. He continued, "Unfortunately we must inconvenience the travelers who use this road, but we have been fighting for land for thirty years and the state has done nothing." Gerardo captured the racialized tensions between the rights of some citizens over those of others, both of which the state recognizes but only some of which the state values. Because of such inequalities, Xákmok Kásek community members decided to selectively break specific laws to create situations to which the Paraguayan state must respond.

Having reached a stalemate, Gerardo called out, "Close the road!," and a mass of bodies surged forward, catching the riot police off guard. A tense but brief clash ensued as police lined up to block the protesters from gaining access to the bridge they had used the day before. In blocking the bridge, the police formed a line

FIGURE 15. Day two of the road closure immediately following the skirmish with riot police on the highway whence the police inadvertently helped block the road. Photo by author, July 2015.

face-to-face with the protesters and inadvertently closed the road. The scene was chaotic and the sound intense as the previously calm protest momentarily erupted. Xákmok Kásek leaders began delivering statements about Indigenous rights and the IACHR judgment over portable loudspeakers that crackled and popped under the strain of the volume. The Paraguayan national anthem blasted from a speaker set up in the space between the protesters and police. An elder woman who had been thrown to the ground during the melee screamed that she would die on the road that day if it meant her children could live on their ancestral lands. Shamans from nearby communities began playing rattles and singing, as men joined arms to form a circle surrounding a drummer whose beat and song started a *choqueo* in the middle of the highway that lasted for the duration of the protest.[42] Over the next six hours, Sanapaná and Enxet peoples from communities across the area negotiated with state officials, visited with one another, made and ate a communal lunch on the worn tarmac, and used the choqueo to form new relations. For kilometers to the north and south, semis carrying cattle, beef, and dairy products stopped, along with all other traffic.

Road closures are common protest strategies in Latin America. However, Xákmok Kásek's action draws particular attention to how Enxet and Sanapaná peoples leverage time as a key facet of territoriality. Whereas many scholars suggest that settler states govern Indigenous rights in ways that reify Indigenous temporalities as anachronous to modernity, protests such as these reveal how many

Indigenous movements disrupt settler time as a sovereign act. Instead of being oppressed by settler time, that is, waiting for the state to act, Enxet and Sanapaná endurance uses the temporality of resistance as a tool to disrupt settler life. In this way, by stopping traffic and commerce to create a space whereby new relations can be made and old ones fortified, Enxet and Sanapaná take time from settlers and thereby reterritorialize the site even if only momentarily. The road closure made time and space not just for a call to defend rights, but for the choqueo to draw together peoples across the Bajo Chaco to rekindle lost connections and form new relationships through resistance.

The choqueo is a dance vital to Indigenous peoples in the Maskoy language family, who use the practice to build new kin relations but also to leverage the power of shamans who play the drum at the center of the circle and sing. The choqueo served as a de facto anchor for the road closure, lying at the physical center of the mass of bodies that occupied the tarmac in front of police and a growing line of semis. With each round of the choqueo, new people would step into the circle, laughing and dancing with arms wrapped around waistlines to form embodied and emplaced relations while settlers waited and watched. Enxet and Sanapaná territoriality in these acts of disruption and defiance focus attention on inequities in time that mark differences between settlers and Indigenous peoples insofar as many settlers have access to a different form of time—speed—whereas Enxet and Sanapaná are forced to wait generations for land restitution, hours for scheduled meetings, and at the whim of patrones who so often decide who gets what and when.

Early in the morning on day three, Xákmok Kásek leadership met with police officers. The leaders agreed to comply with the law and only close one lane of the highway as they marched 2 kilometers to the Enxet community of Jerusalén, where they would continue the negotiations with state officials.[43] Shortly after coming to that agreement, everyone marched south with police escorts, who ensured that traffic flowed around the mass of bodies moving down the highway. Upon rounding the bend in the road before Jerusalén, the escorts rushed ahead, startled by the new strategy community members used to close the road. "We knew that the police would be mad that we closed the road yesterday and we didn't want anyone to get hurt. We coordinated with Jerusalén to have them close the road before we arrived so the police wouldn't see," Clemente later explained to me.[44] The plan worked well. Hundreds of Sanapaná and Enxet occupied the road, subverting police efforts to thwart the mobilization. As a result, the top military official for the Presidente Hayes Department arrived to negotiate directly with Xákmok Kásek, while families visited and another large choqueo took place in the middle of the highway, stopping traffic for the rest of the day. The road closure was lifted when the Paraguayan finance minister and INDI president publicly agreed on the popular radio station Pa'i Puku that they would arrive at 9:00 a.m. the next day to negotiate with community leaders and initiate the purchase of the Xákmok Kásek land.

The sound of a helicopter approaching pierced the quiet morning air in Jerusalén just before 9:00 a.m. on the fourth day, bringing with it the promised officials, who publicly negotiated with the Xákmok Kásek leadership and committed to a date that the land-purchase process would begin. After the events, many people from Xákmok Kásek were hopeful that disrupting the cattle ranching patrones and invoking the spiritual patrón of Paraguay—Pope Francis—had resulted in finally breaking the pattern of state neglect. After the protests, we returned to the encampment at the entrance of Retiro Primero and a familiar pattern set in—waiting, with promises of land restitution "soon." The deadline for the land purchase set at the end of the road closure came and went; with it, Xákmok Kásek community members abandoned the tarps they had occupied for the previous six months and moved deep into the land, where each family began to build permanent homes.

TIME, TERRITORIALITY, PATTERNS

Environmental justice must account for the ability of place-based collectives to ensure their well-being in the present and future on their own terms. The ability of Indigenous collectives to maintain self-determination, social resilience, and well-being is necessary for transformative environmental justice.[45] Ecological integrity, understood as the ability of humans and nonhumans to maintain their collective relations and change with time, is central to Whyte's framing of Indigenous environmental justice. In the case of Enxet and Sanapaná peoples, retaking control of ancestral territories is crucial to collective continuance as both decolonial praxis and the ability to live free of environmental harms. Yet land restitution alone does not, in my view, guarantee decolonization or environmental justice because the aftermaths of land titling are uncertain and property as the vehicle for reparations is inherently constrained by colonial logics of exclusion, quantification, and control. For example, the Cofán peoples of Ecuador contend with environmental pollution because of petroleum extraction on lands near their territories.[46] The Dakota Access Pipeline construction and the policing of that project in the United States threatened the water and territories of Lakota peoples.[47] Accumulation of hazardous chemicals in mining effluent deprives Indigenous peoples of the Bolivian Altiplano of access to clean waters and lands.[48] Indeed, in southeastern Paraguay the hard-fought restitution of Aché lands opened a new chapter of social-ecological struggles for community members, who now must defend their territories from invasion and deforestation driven by illegal logging and marijuana plantations.[49] These enduring challenges shed light on the need to link grounded struggles across sites of co-resistance.[50] Further, in thinking with my Enxet and Sanapaná interlocutors, it is clear that land restitution is but one important step in the process whereby communities can begin to reconstitute place-based collectives.

Shortly after the 2015 road closure, community members pooled their resources to rent a tractor and trailer to haul their belongings from the Retiro Primero entrance to the sites where they built permanent homes. Although Clemente's shelter had been closest to the entrance, his home is now one of the farthest away, some 6 kilometers down a narrow dirt road. It was still dark when I heard the creak of the door to Clemente's house opening as it strained against old wire hinges and scraped on the dirt floor. Clemente had just stepped outside to start a fire. Having slept fully clothed to stay warm in the winter night, I rolled out of my bed, slipped on shoes, and headed outside. At 4:30 in the morning, the air was still, and stars shone brilliantly in the sky as if they were shards of ice casting a frigid blanket on us. We sat in blue plastic chairs, watching flames erupt from the emerald-colored palo santo wood Clemente used to start the fire. The wood's highly flammable resin bubbled and burned bright with a sweet scent. As we drank tereré by the fire, Clemente's home was unusually quiet. Clemente's parents, two of his sons, and his sister had also built their homes nearby. Since the move, the area had always been full of life, with sounds of kids running about and lots of daily action. Yet on this visit, things were different. In the year I had been away, his three sons had left to work on different cattle ranches far-flung across the Chaco. His parents were visiting relatives in another community. Nelsie was with their newborn son in Filadelfia, the nearest hospital some 150 kilometers to the north.

With so many of his people gone, Clemente and I had ample time to catch up. We are in regular communication by WhatsApp, but this was the first time we had a long stretch to talk in person about the advances in their case. "They finally paid for the land. That part is good. They haven't given us the title yet or begun negotiations to purchase the rest of the land for us. We are happy with the 7,701 hectares. People live more peacefully now. . . . We are not happy that they think they can forget about the other 3,000 hectares. We want the title." INDI and pertinent state officials had cited a familiar string of reasons to explain that the title was "in process" but not yet ready. In effect, INDI had purchased the land in the name of Xákmok Kásek, yet retained legal guardianship because it had not completed the requisite survey to issue the property title. With his calloused bare feet resting on a small orange brick near the fire, Clemente slowly shook his head from side to side. "It is always like this. The state does nothing. Meanwhile the Indigenous have to wait. But we have seen that when we protest and do things like the road closure, that is when the state takes notice and things happen. . . . We always have to do these kinds of things. No one likes it. Sitting in the road, going to Asunción for meetings. It is hard work. It is dangerous. They clearly don't care about the Indigenous because they always make us wait."[51]

Without doubt, the Xákmok Kásek community has disrupted many long-standing norms of patrón-Indigenous relations in the Chaco. Through place-based embodied acts, community members have learned from the land while simultaneously reterritorializing settler spaces as reemergent Indigenous geographies.

Indeed, the long arc of engaging and refusing the politics of recognition have reworked the racial geographies of spatial dispossession in ways that underscore the uneven terrain of decolonial praxis. Such acts draw together divergent actors and processes into constellations that help chart the direction of my Enxet and Sanapaná interlocutors' actions to realize more just futures. As Daigle and Ramírez state, "Constellations are in formation all around us, re-envisioning and re-embodying a politics of place by interweaving spatial practices of resistance, refusal and liberation."[52] The reoccupation of Retiro Primero not only marked the beginning of "five years of life," but set in motion the creation of new constellations of Sanapaná and Enxet families in "the place of many small parrots"—Xákmok Kásek. Yet despite such an incredible achievement, Clemente's words and the state's failure to issue title or finalize the restitution of all lands to the community underscore the durable temporalities of settler captialism. Returning land facilitates the possibility for decolonial futures, and more environmentally just futures can become a lived experience, not only an aspirational vision that motivates resistance. Yet land alone cannot guarantee this outcome.

Spectacle

"Come Wednesday night. The president is coming Thursday." The WhatsApp message was brief but clear. President Mario Abdo was headed to Sawhoyamaxa to officiate the transfer of 144 houses the Ministry of Urbanism, Housing, and Habitat (MUVH) had recently constructed for the community. Although Sawhoyamaxa did not yet have a land title, the 2014 law of expropriation coupled with community resistance eventually impelled the former landowners to leave the retiro they long resisted relinquishing. Six years after cutting the fence and reoccupying their lands, Sawhoyamaxa families would now have two-bedroom homes with a kitchenette and latrine, all built of brick, wired for electricity, and with glass windows. It was cold when I arrived in Sawhoyamaxa that night in late June 2019, but spirits were high and the mood was festive. A delegation from Kelyenmagategma was there, as were representatives from Amnesty International and Tierraviva and lots of people from Sawhoyamaxa. We gathered around small fires in Eriberto's aldea to share stories, eat dinner, and enjoy time together before the momentous occasion. As the fires waned, all the guests retreated to their sleeping quarters in the retiro.

Early the next morning, we prepared maté, which we drank while sitting on the screened porch of the retiro and talked about the day's planned events. President Abdo would arrive by helicopter, proceed directly to the small stage that had been constructed, officiate the ceremony, then tour one house before leaving. What sounded like a simple plan was quite involved. State officials had trucked in several loads of red earth from Concepción to ensure the path from the helicopter to the stage and back was firm, dry ground, not the muddy clay soil common to this part of the Bajo Chaco. A few of us watched as MOPC functionaries worked to fill in and tamp down a handful of stubborn puddles that had formed in the night. "He will cancel his trip if it is muddy," one man said to me, as we contemplated the expense of creating this temporary path compared to many other necessities that warranted funding but never received support.

The morning warmed with the rising sun as state trucks emblazoned with different agency logos pulled in and parked: MOPC, SEN, MUVH, and the Ministries of Health, Justice, and Foreign Relations, along with an advance team of special forces that arrived to secure the location. A brand-new white Toyota Hilux truck purchased with restitution-as-development funds pulled up shortly after that with an altogether different logo emblazoned on the side: Yakye Axa Comunidad Indígena con Personería Jurídica (Yakye Axa Indigenous Community with Legal Personhood). Out stepped Anivel and Anibal, along with other community members. The event was a sort of reunion, convened on the one hand to celebrate advances in the restitution as development process and on the other for community members to continue pressuring the state to act. Some state functionaries had worked for Tierraviva previously or rotated jobs through different state agencies.[1] Several had been to Sawhoyamaxa, Yakye Axa, or Kelyenmagategma at one point or another in their careers. People shook hands, laughed, shared gossip, and waited for the president.

Sometime midmorning, a deep percussive rhythm could be heard approaching from the east, then the president's helicopter appeared overhead, circling the retiro before landing in a former pasture turned soccer field. A large group waited to greet Abdo and escort him along the freshly laid road of red earth that stretched several hundred yards from the soccer field to the makeshift stage for the event. Abdo, the governor, and a district representative of Presidente Hayes, along with the heads of several key state agencies, took their seats on chairs under the small white tent facing a crowd of perhaps 150 people. Then the president of INDI at the time, Ana María Allen, opened the event with a scant ninety-second statement. She noted the "historic debt" that the Paraguayan state has to the Indigenous peoples who live in the country. A man with a baritone voice who sounded like a skilled radio deejay then took the microphone to emcee the rest of the event. In true state-as-patrón form, he proceeded to announce that the state would give symbolic checks to leaders of Kelyenmagategma and Sawhoyamaxa "in accordance with the Inter-American Court." "Will the leader of Kelyenmagategma, Mr. Celso Benitez, please come forward to receive the symbolic check for 983,333,000 guaranies?" Akin to a game show host, he repeated the amount three more times, emphasizing and drawing out the number in a dramatic voice that reverberated through the loudspeakers. As the president handed over the symbolic check, the emcee announced, "Mr. Benitez will receive 983,333,000 guaranies for Kelyenmagategma!" "Next is Eriberto Ayala, leader of the community . . . " Reading from his cue cards, the emcee's suave voice did not know how to pronounce Sawhoyamaxa. He went silent for a full three seconds without naming the community before continuing, " . . . to receive 1,966,000 guaranies!" Again, he repeated the check amount three times in the span of no fewer than two minutes as Eriberto shook hands with Abdo, then showed the check to the crowd. "Now the president of INDI, Mrs. Ana María Allen, will sign the symbolic checks," which she did, after Celso and Eriberto handed them to her. The emcee then called the leader of each Sawhoyamaxa aldea to the front to receive symbolic keys to their houses from Abdo, after which they sat again among the crowd.

Throughout the ceremony, Abdo said nothing but smiled and nodded, as did the other officials surrounding him. "Now we have a special surprise," announced the emcee, as a man appeared with a bag of about forty soccer balls. "Please form a line and come to get a ball from Mr. President!" Kids cautiously but excitedly lined up to receive the gifts. With that, the ceremony was over ten minutes after it had started. Yet before anyone could move, Eriberto took to the microphone: "Today, Mr. President, the credibility of the state begins again. The Indigenous will have faith in your government, and we are happy in our hearts. All five leaders of Sawhoyamaxa would like to be in a picture with you, the president of INDI, and the minister [of justice]. This will be the only lasting memory of the visit of an authority of such high ranking in our community." Several people in the audience from Sawhoyamaxa shook their heads slightly, seemingly skeptical at the comment, perhaps not agreeing with the statement but understanding its persuasive end; the power of the dialectics of disruption lies in strategically working with and against the patrón, with and against the law. The state dignitaries lined up alongside the leaders of Sawhoyamaxa for a picture. "Thank you," announced Eriberto. "Everyone, please give a strong round of applause before we take the president to show him our new homes." As the crowd clapped, a young man from Sawhoyamaxa approached me with a look of disdain, gesturing toward Abdo as he walked by. "He didn't say anything, just sat there smiling and handing out toys like a poster boy for Coca-Cola." The entire ceremony, from the opening statements to the president's exit, was fourteen minutes long. Yet the photos that remain show images of care, the president smiling with his arm around community members, giving out soccer balls to kids, and handing checks to victims of human rights abuse caused by the state he leads. Indeed, news headlines following the event read, "President Intends to Raise His Image due to Social Pressures."[2]

Predictable unpredictability precipitates the politics of recognition, thus creating spaces and situations of legal liminality that manifest as the slow violence of environmental injustice that Enxet and Sanapaná live with. With Abdo's visit, 144 families from Sawhoyamaxa received new homes, monetary disbursements were made to further restitution as development, and Enxet peoples achieved an important goal in their long struggle to force the state to recognize them on their terms by coming to their land—no less, in the shadow of the retiro once used to surveil the community. On the other hand, the pomp and circumstance of the president's visit embody the optics of care that masks the biopolitics of neglect.

Shortly after the president's helicopter left for Asunción and the crowds left Sawhoyamaxa, I took a couple of people to check out the progress on the Yakye Axa access road that had begun in 2016 but was yet to be completed after three years of "work." The road was impassable just 6 kilometers into the 35-kilometer

FIGURE 16. President Mario Abdo with his arm around a woman from Yakye Axa (center left) arriving in Sawhoyamaxa to inaugurate the SENAVITAT homes. The main retiro is the large building in the background, with a new home visible immediately behind Abdo. Photo by author, June 2019.

route due to a washout that swallowed my 4x4 rental truck in mud at the first creek crossing. MOPC has since restarted road construction, but it remains to be seen if it will provide a road built well enough to resist the seasonal floods. When I returned to Paraguay in February 2020, I encountered Gladys, Celso, Clemente, and several other interlocutors at the Tierraviva offices in Asunción. Gladys was there to launch a complaint against the construction company that had built the homes in her aldea of Sawhoyamaxa. "*ndovalei* [They are no good]. When it rains, the windows leak, and now most don't open. You have to break out the glass for air to enter in the summer." Celso was doing *seguimiento* (follow-up) on the land-titling process for Kelyenmagategma because it had still not been resolved. Clemente had come nearly 400 kilometers to bring his daughter to the doctor. Conversations about issues like these have become commonplace over the years of our relationships—so much that they seem almost natural, expected. Yet they are anything but.

There is nothing natural about environmental racism, persistent discrimination, and the biopolitics of neglect. They are conditions actively produced, often by direct state action or inaction. The Paraguayan state's repeated neglect to ensure the rights of its Indigenous citizens naturalizes daily violence experienced across several registers: the loss of language and the ability to practice vital ceremonies, the uncertainty of living with and without de jure land rights, the forms of material poverty that reproduce vulnerability to labor exploitation, and so much more. Several days after those conversations in Tierraviva, I celebrated five years of life in Xákmok Kásek—a ceremony that was a testament to the endurance of Indigenous resistance and the fact that the state cannot be relied on to ensure environmental justice. Instead, the pursuit of justice requires radical co-resistance that builds from the existing infrastructures of liberation that Enxet and Sanapaná peoples have forged through solidarity with one another and allies in their struggles.[3] Little did we know at the time of the celebration that the specter of a global pandemic would manifest. I left Paraguay six days before the country's borders closed due to COVID-19. Since that time, Enxet and Sanapaná from across the Bajo Chaco mobilized a mass road closure to demand basic state services in response to the pandemic and the issuance of land titles to Yakye Axa, Sawhoyamaxa, Xákmok Kásek, and Kelyenmagategma. With each protest, community members gain new minor concessions from state officials but always lament that they are forced to take such actions. "We do not like to protest. It is dangerous. You never know what will happen, if the kids will get hurt, if someone will raid the community when you are gone. But we have to do it because the state does not see Indigenous people unless we make them," Clemente noted via WhatsApp.

Conclusion

In Pursuit of Environmental Justice

Disrupting the Patrón centers Enxet and Sanapaná futurities and endurance, despite generations of efforts to erase them from the history and present of the Bajo Chaco. This book has traced the interwoven luchas of the Yakye Axa, Sawhoyamaxa, and Xákmok Kásek communities that are working to rebuild relations with their ancestral territories and enacting environmental justice otherwise on Paraguay's cattle-ranching frontier. The Chaco is a site where racialized regimes of resource control produce uneven geographies of power that attempt to reduce biocultural diversity to one basic logic: settler capitalism. Enxet and Sanapaná endurance shows that coloniality is not total and that resistance is not futile but necessary. My analysis weaves hemispheric debates about the politics of recognition, indigeneity, and environmental justice with Enxet and Sanapaná insights to show how the *longue durée* of settler colonial dispossessions conditions contemporary land rights struggles.

That is not to suggest that Paraguay has been outside the reach of neoliberalism and many of its associated reforms. Neoliberal economic reforms have radically shaped the direction of agrarian politics by emphasizing international exports, lowering all trade barriers, and opening Paraguay to world markets by creating an economy with minimal regulations, extremely low export taxes, and attracting foreign investors in all sectors. The effects of these policies reverberate throughout Paraguay, shaping migration dynamics, land-tenure inequality, and formal politics at all levels of governance. Former president Horacio Cartes infamously said, "You have to use and abuse [*usar y abuser*] Paraguay because this is a moment of incredible opportunity," shortly after taking office in 2014.[1] His goal was to encourage Brazilian financiers to invest in the country, capturing the elite class's embrace of neoliberal free-market logics. Simultaneously inflammatory and repugnant, Cartes's discourse was but one utterance in a long history of actions by

Paraguayan agrarian elites who have leveraged populist imaginaries to advance the concentration of resource access along lines of class, gender, and racial difference. Moreover, Cartes followed several recent Paraguayan presidents whose administrations embodied the governance model that the Stroessner dictatorship established. Stroessner cultivated an image of the state-as-patrón whose institutionalized corruption helped establish a generation of leaders who rule not by direct torture and violence but by a biopolitics of neglect that prioritizes other-than-human life over the country's most marginalized.[2]

The politics of Enxet and Sanapaná luchas are not determined by neoliberalism despite the neoliberal imperative that has gripped Paraguay, like many of its neighbors in Latin America. Reducing the lucha to neoliberalism would erase the very historical material, discursive, and epistemic modalities of violence that continue to shape the contemporary conjuncture and the social-environmental challenges that many Enxet and Sanapaná navigate. Without doubt neoliberalism exacerbates already existing forms of racism and oppression. Still, older forms of racial capitalism and their exclusionary logics condition how the politics of recognition play out in Paraguay and their effects on Enxet and Sanapaná justice struggles. This is evident in my excavation of the sedimented histories of settler land appropriations and their expression as racial geographies. State policies that effectively ensure the recurrent dispossession of Indigenous peoples in place reveal how patterns of patrón-Indigenous relations transcend the politics of recognition by reproducing environmental harms. Therefore, I have done more than argue for another approach to studying Indigenous rights struggles in Latin America. *Disrupting the Patrón* expands the conceptual and empirical study of Indigenous environmental justice struggles outside the US and Canadian contexts by centering Enxet and Sanapaná futurities based on rebuilding relations with their lands.

Enxet and Sanapaná dialectics of disruption informed my analysis in many ways, but I want to reiterate two of them here. First, interlocutors like Anivel, Eriberto, Ignacia, Clemente, and others shared stories about the strategies they have developed and adapted to employ a dialectical praxis over the long arc of their luchas that work to unsettle settler territoriality. Leveraging the law as a tool to disrupt settler land control while also seeking to improve the material conditions of life for Enxet and Sanapaná peoples, my interlocutors worked with the politics of recognition to a certain degree. Yet on confronting the limits of recognition within Paraguay, Yakye Axa, Sawhoyamaxa, Xákmok Kásek, and Kelyenmagategma all turned to their legal counsel at Tierraviva to scale up their struggles to the international sphere by petitioning the Inter-American System. The legal victories that each community achieved before the Inter-American Commission and the IACHR cannot be minimized. Each case was a landmark victory for Indigenous rights that has established important jurisprudence, which Indigenous communities have used across the world in their respective efforts to hold states accountable for human rights violations. However, the lack of enforcement of the Inter-American System's decisions in Paraguay has required that Enxet and Sanapaná peoples turn to extralegal actions to compel the state to act. Through this constantly shifting dialectic of working with and against the law, working with and against the patrón, my interlocutors have moved to unsettle racial geographies and overcome legal liminality. The dialectics of disruption entail never totally rejecting the politics of recognition while never fully accepting the terms established by the settler state. Instead, the strategy rejects *and uses* the politics of recognition to erode the power relations and patterns of dispossession inherent in the logics of settler capitalism that shape the Bajo Chaco. With each act of disruption, Enxet and Sanapaná not only exert their sovereignty; they also enact radical forms of futurity that summon visions of a more just future in the present by building new relations.

Second, my rationale for the approach taken in this book is informed by the dialectic tension present in the way many of my interlocutors conceive of justice and express their rationale for the lucha. On the one hand, it is clear that justice as adequate recompense for past harms is impossible, an aporia, as Milciades's reflection presented at the beginning of the book insisted: "We will always be scarred from what they have made us live through. I don't think that land will bring justice, but it will help us find a sense of peace." On the other hand, Enxet and Sanapaná futurity is a politics of the possible that reworks time, territoriality, and social relations through "de facto self-determination" enacted in the dialectics of disruption, showing that faith in a better future animates enduring struggles for justice.[3] Serafin's reiterated framing of the generations-long struggle to reclaim lands and lifeways shows this clearly: "We do this for our children and their children. . . . We fight so that they might have a future." Working with and through this dialectical tension and the many other dialectical relations that permeate this book, I have chosen to focus on the *pursuit* of Indigenous environmental justice because, in my view, justice is simultaneously an aporia and a political horizon that we cannot turn away from. But like the horizon we travel toward, justice always seems just out of reach, propelling the struggle further to other spaces, temporalities, and "yet-to-be possibilities."[4] Forms of justice otherwise are both necessary and are not constrained by the limits of liberal political and legal theory. Environmental justice otherwise is defined by front-line actors fighting against environmental racism and for the environment as freedom.

THINKING WITH AND BEYOND
ENVIRONMENTAL JUSTICE

Enxet and Sanapaná struggles to maintain collective lifeways are shaped by settler capitalism but not determined by it. Here I want to clarify two points—one about the current moment and the other about environmental justice studies within it. First, I opened the book with reference to how cattle ranching in Paraguay's Chaco—both its material form and its political-ecological consequences—resonates with the geographies of extractivism in Latin America. In the chapters that followed, I showed first how missionaries settled the Bajo Chaco to establish

FIGURE 17. Simplifying landscapes for cattle ranching. Recent deforestation (right) lays bare pasturelands just outside the Xákmok Kásek land (left), while two semis full of cattle kick up dust as they travel to local slaughterhouses. Photo by author, February 2020.

cattle ranching, then how the social-spatial relations of power produced through that system persist to the present through the politics of recognition and the ways that state officials govern Indigenous affairs. In so doing, I sought to show how a specific facet of the current conjuncture—the cattle ranch—has reconfigured life. Latin American studies scholars have long examined the role of economies and haciendas in structuring social relations of power and development.[5] Further, the geographer Wendy Wolford queries the contemporary proliferation of plantation systems to suggest that "the long-distance simplification of landscapes; alienation of land and labor; and transportation of genomes, plants, animals, and people" is tied to race-based systems of modernity and coloniality.[6]

Cattle ranches of the Bajo Chaco operate on extractive logics. They are race-based systems that required Indigenous labor, often without monetary remuneration, to become established; they work by altering the preexisting diverse social-ecological systems to create new sites intended to support one genetically enhanced life-form. Instead of palm oil plantations like those in Colombia or soybean plantations like those across the Southern Cone, the Paraguayan Chaco has been made for cattle. The resulting racial geographies are simultaneously sites of Indigenous dispossession and labor exploitation as they are sites of dramatic ecological change. As I recounted earlier, ranching is driving massive land-use change across Paraguay's Chaco and has turned the region into one of the world's greatest deforestation hotspots, with severe implications for Indigenous well-being. The current dynamics stem from the country's deep relationship with agro-export industries, namely, soybeans and cattle, that influence a land politics where Indigenous dispossession and the biopolitics of neglect imbricate. Each industry's specific effects and outcomes are distinct, but taken together they drive land-tenure inequality and work to ossify hierarchies of race and class that have always subjugated Indigenous labor as an enduring organizing principle. Attention must be paid to the environmental outcomes of the politics of recognition in Latin America and their effects on social justice.

Second, I have argued that Indigenous justice struggles for land and political recognition are always about more than rights-based claims. They are also intimately articulated with the long history of extractivism and the racial projects it facilitated in Latin America.[7] Coombes, Johnson, and Howitt argue, "Indigenous motivations in environmental disputes are connected to broader projects of recognition, reclamation of sovereignty and resistance to northern capitalism; they are not mere resource conflicts."[8] Struggles for land and the ability to maintain collective lifeways are social-environmental processes that exceed the limits of liberal legal frameworks that enable some to live well while others are excluded from their most basic rights. Environmental justice otherwise must foreground the social nature of "environmental" harms while attending to justice beyond legal remedies. Rather than reduce justice to monetary remuneration through, for example, indemnity payments that are often a default for reparations, a transformative approach begins with front-line actors defining what justice can be in the context of the harm experienced and works to ensure those harms are not reproduced.[9] Enxet and Sanapaná strategies of resistance demand a more expansive notion of environmental justice than those based primarily on distributional and procedural remedies. This book thus joins a body of scholarship working to advance the conceptual frame of environmental justice studies by considering a wider array of actors, processes, geographies, and forms of justice than those that initially spurred this field of activism and study in the United States.[10] These are not efforts to distort environmental justice but ways to think with and beyond defined concepts in an era of radical planetary change and disruption.

If more just futures are ever to be realized, it is necessary to attend to the specific ways that settler colonialism produces environmental injustice across distinct geographies and the strategies that Indigenous peoples and their allies use to disrupt the persistence of injustice. Such an approach underscores the importance of working with *and moving beyond* the taxonomies of justice that have so informed the core of environmental justice scholarship from the United States to date.[11] While cognizant of critiques that draw attention to the "coloniality of justice" and call for decolonizing environmental justice studies, I employed language and approaches from both critical environmental justice studies written from North America because those approaches operate as intellectual "boundary objects" that translate across intellectual, epistemic, and geographic worlds.[12] In keeping with Native environmental justice scholars, my approach has attended to "the challenges of the ecological crisis as well as the various forms of violence and injustices experienced specifically by Indigenous peoples" by grounding this analysis in Enxet and Sanapaná "philosophies, ontologies, and epistemologies in order to reflect Indigenous conceptions of what constitutes justice."[13] Yet I have intentionally resisted offering a coherent theorization of Enxet or Sanapaná environmental justice because I refuse to speak for my collaborators. Enxet and Sanapaná peoples speak for themselves.

My interlocutors' perspectives populate the pages of this book while showing that the *pursuit* of justice transits the social-environmental politics of place and the histories that shape racial geographies. Shifting environmental justice studies from a strict focus on distributional and procedural issues to one that considers the capabilities of collectives and communities to live well on their own terms is imperative.[14] As many of my interlocutors from Yakye Axa, Sawhoyamaxa, and Xákmok Kásek would say, *roikosé porã* (literally, "we want to live well"). In this regard living well requires land restitution as the basis of life free of the social-environmental harms that dispossession generates.[15] Moving beyond a narrowly defined vision of environmental justice toward what Pellow has called "critical environmental justice," I show how settler capitalism and the politics of recognition threaten Enxet and Sanapaná collective lifeways while my interlocutors nonetheless refuse to abide by the limits of statist law.[16] As a result, I offer an environmental justice otherwise that foregrounds Enxet and Sanapaná experiences through decolonial border thinking with hemispheric analyses of Indigenous politics across the Americas.

LAND IS NOT ENOUGH

How is justice possible given that all the land was stolen? Is justice served by giving back a portion of land, even if the basic conditions to live well on that land have been radically altered by generations of dispossession? What is environmental justice in the context of persistent settler colonialities? For all of the gains my Enxet and Sanapaná interlocutors have made to reclaim their lands and rebuild their relations, Milciades's words haunt. Since I began this research in 2012, Yakye Axa, Sawhoyamaxa, Xákmok Kásek, and Kelyenmagategma have gained land rights from the Paraguayan state after decades of struggle. While returning to the land has brought more peace to members of these communities, life is still marked by uncertainty because land alone is not enough. Demarcation and property titles are still lacking. State officials have refused to guarantee the basic conditions to live safely: due process, clean water, support for education, medical services, other forms of vital infrastructure, or respect for Indigenous self-determination without being forced to do so. Yakye Axa has had land since 2012 but no viable road to access it at the time of this writing. These are some of the recurrent dispossessions and forms of slow environmental violence that legal liminality produces, and they threaten collective life even after land restitution has been achieved.

Further still, what of the veritable prison that Belfio spoke of when reflecting on his twenty-five years of life living on the margin of Ruta 5? Life dispossessed of land and decades on the side of Ruta 5 are a form of carcerality that is not inherently different from having to live and work on the ranches built on the lands taken from one's community for little to no pay because no other options exist.[17] Unfreedoms such as these perpetuate environmental injustice because the incarcerated are denied the ability to live free of environmental harms. Stock pond water that people must drink is often polluted with animal feces and makes them sick. Passing traffic kicks up dust that people living in roadside communities inhale, to say nothing of the threat of being struck or the constant sound that interrupts daily life. Land reoccupations, road closures, and other forms of protest place community members in harm's way but have become necessary to make state officials act on Indigenous demands.

Environmental justice is more than a line of academic inquiry, government policy, or direct action and mobilization. Environmental justice is also an act of storytelling. Julie Sze reminds us, "Stories and how they are told matter. Storytelling is a deeply political act that brings a radical democratic vision to an issue often seen as largely scientific, based in engineering or the realm of policy-making."[18] I have tried to tell this story with care and respect for my interlocutors, their struggles, and the futurities they are enacting. If we are to understand the "environment as freedom," as Malini Ranganathan has beautifully envisioned, it is necessary to abolish the conditions that produce the unfreedoms of everyday forms of carcerality produced by the racialized distribution of social-environmental harms.[19] Another world is possible. Many already exist. Through solidarity, relationality, and stories perhaps we can bring them more fully into the light. This is the work of critical environmental justice and the challenge of enacting justice otherwise.

Postscript

The final revisions to *Disrupting the Patrón* were written in the Paraguayan Chaco. I was fortunate to return in May 2022 after more than two years away due to the COVID-19 pandemic. The uncertainty that precipitated during the months and years immediately following my previous trip in February 2020, just days before border closures and flight cancellations, took its toll. Although I remained in contact with colleagues, collaborators, and friends (often one and the same) through virtual communication, a new form of uncertainty was omnipresent. At the peak of COVID's ravage through Paraguay, one colleague who lives in a suburb of Asunción commented, "Everybody knows at least one or two people who have died." Fortunately, COVID has had less of an impact in the Chaco. But there are still many who have perished. With every new message that arrived, there was always a latent fear that it would bear bad news. I did not know what to expect on my return in the midst of the pandemic. It is difficult to express in words the feeling of being present in relation with people and place again, but it did bring a sense of peace and joy. *Che py'aguapy.*

Place matters. As a geographer, this is a key point in our field of study and analysis. While different facets of this book were written at different times and in different places, I wrote it during the pandemic. It was odd to focus on this work without the opportunity to return physically to the places that shape its pages. I spent countless hours poring over photographs, reading fieldnotes, and listening to interviews, during which time I heard more than the words of my interlocutors but took note of the ambient sounds that helped provide the texture of place—the shrill call of locusts, the wind in the leaves of an algarrobo tree, the echo of a state functionary's voice in a scantily outfitted office, the rumble of a truck passing on the road, the sound of children playing. In this way and through the act of writing, I spent much time thinking of places and experiencing them in memory. Yet as the book came closer to conclusion, I feared that geographic distance from the Chaco would abstract the work from its place-based analysis.

Returning to the Chaco with the task of completing the revisions was simultaneously onerous and generative. I returned to Paraguay to research the new Bi-oceanic Highway construction project and its social-ecological impacts. However, a looming deadline meant book revisions had to be completed at the same time that I was in Filadelfia—the heart of Paraguayan Chaco Mennonite colonies and the booming agro-industrial complex. As I made the final revisions, I also traveled to meet with Enxet and Sanapaná friends, colleagues, and interlocutors who inform this work. Drinking tereré with folks in the Chaco and having time to return to places in the pages of this book made abundantly clear that agro-extractivism and state neglect are not going away anytime soon. With the suite of new roads being built across the Chaco, the challenges may increase as the development projects have one primary aim: to facilitate export commodities and the spread of agrarian capital.

The pandemic disrupted everything. Some things remained the same. The five-year anniversary of Xákmok Kásek's return to the land discussed in chapter 5 was a celebration of "five years of life." On the community's seventh anniversary in 2022, they returned to the Trans-Chaco Highway to close the road and demand the state issue land title and conduct a legal demarcation for the 7,701-hectare parcel returned to the community. The Xákmok Kásek community received title on June 21, 2022, and the process to demarcate the land began later that month. The community is still demanding that the state return the 2,999 hectares that they claim and that the IACHR included in its 2010 ruling against the Paraguayan state. To date, the land is owned by a Mennonite cooperative, and precautionary measures that prohibit innovations have been ignored or unenforced since 2008. The Yakye Axa community continues to demand that the Paraguayan state finish the access road to the community's "alternative land." The road now nearly reaches the returned lands, but it is of a very poor quality and impassable for many months of the year due to flooding. Some community members left the roadside and moved onto the land in 2021, yet have no ability to leave in times of flood. It is unclear when MOPC will finish building the road per the IACHR requirements. The Sawhoyamaxa community still awaits issuance of their land title and legal demarcation of their lands, though nearly every family now has a permanent home and many new buildings (schoolhouses, churches, small stores) have been constructed. According to the National Cadastral Service, the land is still technically owned by the Kansol and Roswell Companies. When the 2014 law of expropriation will be fully enforced is unknown.

INTRODUCTION: ENVIRONMENTAL JUSTICE OTHERWISE

1. Garay Caballero 2015.

2. *Retiro* is a Spanish word commonly used in Paraguay to denote a house for ranch personnel or a patrón.

3. In November 2015, a group of Avá Guaraní protested the proposed criminalization of land-renting laws in front of INDI, when the acting INDI president was caught on film kicking a woman in the stomach as he tried to enter the building.

4. See MIT (n.d.), Observatory for Economic Complexity, for global commodity trade dynamics.

5. Huang et al. 2007.

6. Several works show this, including Correia 2019b; Ezquerro-Cañete 2020; and Hetherington 2020. Moreover, the last agrarian census conducted in 2008 clearly demonstrates that unequal land tenure helps facilitate such rapid and radical change, with 80 percent of arable land in Paraguay being held by approximately 2 percent of the population.

7. State officials have made this claim repeatedly in media interviews promoting the Bi-oceanic Highway since its inception in 2019.

8. Cattle production dominates the Paraguayan Chaco landscape, but it is also important to note that Mennonite colonists have highly diversified agricultural production in the central Chaco that includes sesame, sorghum, cotton, corn, peanuts, soybeans, and other crops. Soybean production is minimal though emergent in recent years, with less than 50,000 hectares in production in 2022. The total land area dedicated to agriculture pales in comparison to that dedicated to cattle ranching at the time of this writing.

9. See Vázquez 2010.

10. Baumann et al. 2022.

11. MIT n.d.

12. According to the 2012 Indigenous census, approximately 117,000 Indigenous lived in Paraguay, with 48 percent residing in the Chaco (DEEGC 2012).

13. As of September 2021, there were 6,734,400 cattle registered across the Paraguayan Chaco, whereas the human population was roughly 135,186; approximately 40,300 people identified as Indigenous. Data from the Ministerio de Agricultura y Ganadería (2019), the US Department of Agriculture (2021), and the Dirección General de Estadística, Encuestas y Censos (2018).

14. See Córdoba, Bosert, and Richard 2015; Bhoola 2017; and Canova 2020 on contemporary Indigenous enclaves in the Chaco.

15. Studies by Paraguayan human rights lawyers, civil society organizations, and anthropologists show these phenomena in detail (Ayala-Amarilla 2014; Barrio-Cáceres 2018; Bogado, Portillo, and Villagra 2016; Coordinadora de Derechos Humanos del Paraguay 2013; Quiroga and Ayala-Amarilla 2014).

16. See Offen 2003 and Bryan 2012 on the territorial turn.

17. Details of the cases and the IACHR judgments are discussed in chapter 4.

18. Ranganathan's (2017) "environment as freedom" is helpful here; violent environments, broadly construed, create unfreedoms in the form of human suffering that derives from preventable disease and untimely death due to hazards exposure. Carruthers (2008) and Whyte (2018) each offer distinct insights on environmental justice and "capabilities" that resonate with Ranganathan's approach and the notion of freedom in this context.

19. Commission for Racial Justice 1987; Bullard 1990; Mohai, Pellow, and Roberts 2009.

20. Bullard 1990; Capek 1993; Castellón 2021.

21. On thinking justice otherwise, see Sundberg 2008; Álvarez and Coolsaet 2020; Whyte 2020; Newell 2021.

22. See Blaser 2010; Büscher and Fletcher 2020; Rahder 2020.

23. LaDuke 1999; Voyles 2015; Whyte 2016; Gilio-Whitaker 2019; Jarratt-Snider and Nielsen 2020.

24. See Carruthers 2008 on popular environmentalism and social movements in Latin America. Astrid Ulloa's work (2016, 2017) provides an example of emergent scholarship from Latin America that specifically theorizes environmental justice vis-à-vis Indigenous struggles.

25. My conception "politics of recognition" draws from Taylor 1991; Chakrabarty 2007; and Coulthard 2014.

26. See, e.g., Bullard 1990 and 1993; Mohai, Pellow, and Roberts 2009; Murdock 2020.

27. Robert D. Bullard has been instrumental in driving environmental justice scholarship and activism in the United States with great attention to environmental harms against Black communities in the South. See Bullard 1993, 2000. Also see McGurty 2010 for a helpful overview of the Warren County case. On environmental justice beyond the United States., see Carruthers 2008; Martínez-Alier 1997; Matínez-Alier et al. 2016; Coolsaet 2020; Pellow 2017; and Sze 2020 for helpful analyses.

28. "The Principles of Environmental Justice" 1991, n.p.

29. I am not the first person to state this. Rather, I join Voyles 2015; Whyte 2016; Ulloa 2017; Pellow 2018; Gilio-Whitaker 2019; McGregor 2020; and Álvarez and Coolsaet 2020, among others.

30. Derrida's ([1992] 2002) discussion of the law-justice relation as aporia, as a nonpassage, as an ideal that is lauded and strived for but impossible given the ontological limits of

liberal law and the power structures upheld by such law informs my analysis because the statist legal frameworks Enxet and Sanapaná peoples engage throughout their land struggles are rooted in liberal humanism. See also Wainwright and Bryan (2009) on their use of aporia to assess the limits of Indigenous land rights in Central America.

31. Engle (2010), Povinelli (2002), and Ybarra (2018) each provide distinct analysis of this dynamic in different settler contexts, from a comprehensive multisited study to in-depth critiques of Australia and Guatemala, respectively.

32. Whyte 2018, 126–31.

33. E.g., Ulloa (2017, 178) outlines a relational Indigenous environmental justice "based on the positioning of the relationships between the territory and the nonhuman" in the context of Latin America that resonates with Whyte's framing of collective continuance.

34. Ulloa 2017. On Native Nations and the US federal government, see LaDuke 1999; Voyles 2015; Whyte 2016; Estes 2019; Gilio-Whitaker 2019. On Canadian state policies, see Westra 2008; Olive and Rabe 2016; McGregor 2018; Casey 2020; McGregor, Whitaker, and Sritharan 2020.

35. Jarratt-Snider and Nielsen 2020, 9–10. The edited volume this chapter introduces is a vital resource to understand approaches to Indigenous environmental justice in the United States and Canada, countries that have significantly different juridical frameworks established to enumerate actions for environmental justice as state policy than many countries in Latin America. Significant differences in experiences with colonization, settler colonization, and state-Indigenous relations also shape the distinct contours of Indigenous environmental justice actions across these geographies.

36. Whyte 2016, 2.

37. Voyles 2015.

38. Estes 2019; Gilio-Whitaker 2019.

39. For Speed (2017), settler capitalism is the conjoined process of Indigenous land dispossession and labor exploitation that drives extractive development in Latin America.

40. Here I draw from Sze (2020, 51), who suggests that every environmental justice struggle is both singular and not unique.

41. See Álvarez and Coolsaet 2020; Sundberg 2008; Martínez-Alier 2008.

42. See Berger and Sineiro 2012; Ulloa 2017; Zaragocín 2019; Caretta et al. 2020; Álvarez and Coolsaet 2020.

43. See Rodríguez 2020; Cruz-Rodríguez 2017; Ulloa 2016, 2017; Leguizamón 2020.

44. See Álvarez and Coolsaet 2020; Gilio-Whitaker 2019; Dhillon 2018; Cruz-Rodríguez 2017; Berger and Sineiro 2012.

45. Harjo 2019, 30.

46. See Simpson 2014; Simpson 2017; and Estes 2019.

47. Handwritten notes from January 20, 2016. Indigenous peoples across the Bajo Chaco endured similar histories of labor exploitation and dispossession due to cattle ranching. See Chase-Sardi, Brun, and Enciso 1990; Kidd 1997; and Villagra-Carrón 2014.

48. For other perspectives on this phenomenon, see Speed 2017. Pasternak 2020 and Englert 2020 also provide helpful analyses in the US and Canadian context.

49. Here I draw from Saldaña-Portillo's (2016, 17) framing: "Racial geography is a technology of power, and when used as an analytic and the theory of spatial production, it indexes the series of techniques used to produce space in racial terms."

50. See also Blaser, Feit, and McRae 2004; Gordillo 2004.

51. Casanova 1965, 27; my emphasis. *Note to Readers*: The language in all quotations appears as written; no attempt has been made to change to current preferred usage, for example, *Indigenous* instead of *indigenous*.

52. See Wolford 2007.

53. Wolfe 1999, 3.

54. See Coulthard 2014; Moreton-Robinson 2015; and Nichols 2020; Bhandar 2018; and Estes 2019; and Pasternak 2020; Wolfe 2016; and Rifkin 2019.

55. On this point, I build from the pathbreaking work by Saldaña-Portillo (2016), Speed (2017), and Ybarra (2018).

56. Speed 2017.

57. Sousa-Santos 2007, 6.

58. See also Coulthard (2007, 440–43) on recognition and the intersubjective nature of identity formation.

59. My use and translation of the word *indigenista* is based on Paraguayan usage of the term that is distinct from the broader concept "indigenismo" used in other parts of Latin America. Whereas indigenismo refers to a broad suite of actions and activities regarding Indigenous affairs by non-Indigenous peoples, indigenista explicitly denotes a non-Indigenous person who advocates for Indigenous rights. Blaser (2010, 81–84) provides an excellent explanation that I do not repeat. Outside of the Paraguayan context, Rappaport (2005) provides a formative assessment of interethnic alliances used to advance Indigenous rights.

60. See Foucault [2004] 2007; Li 2010.

61. See Correia 2018b.

62. See, e.g., Auyero 2012; Gupta 2012; and Hetherington 2011.

63. Ryburn 2018, 4.

64. See, e.g., Turner 1969.

65. Relying solely on legal remedies reasserts state and settler colonial power, akin to what Hale (2004, 17), drawing from Silvia Rivera Cusicanqui, calls the "indio permitido," the acceptable indian. The dynamics of Povinelli's (2002) "cunning of recognition" also resonate with this condition of limited acceptable difference that does not alter settler power.

66. See Coulthard's (2014, 6–15) discussion of structured dispossession.

67. A. Simpson 2014.

68. Coulthard 2014.

69. Restrepo 2018; Martínez-Novo 2021; Paschel 2016; Hale 2005.

70. I understand this strategy is akin to, as Ybarra (2018, 17) suggests, "a both/and politics that engages within and beyond settler-state subjections.".

71. *Patrón* is a gendered noun in the Spanish language that refers to a man. *Patrona* is the female gendered version of the noun but was much less frequently used.

72. See, e.g., Blaser 2010, 173–74; Bobrow-Strain 2007.

73. Guerrero (1991) and Lyons (2006) provide helpful analyses of shifting reciprocities on haciendas.

74. In addition to selling land, the Paraguayan state incentivized settler colonization in the central Chaco by granting homesteading rights to German-speaking Mennonite farmers from Canada in the 1920s (Kleinpenning 2003). See also Powell 2007 on Anglican missionary history.

75. See Correia 2022.

76. Following Spanish-language conventions, *patrón* is the singular form of the word, whereas *patrones* is the plural form.

77. Several studies document this phenomenon in Paraguay; see, e.g., Kidd 1997; and Renshaw 2002. It is also widely documented in other sites in Latin America; see, e.g., Guerrero 1991; Peloso 1999; Gordillo and Hirsch 2003; Gibbings 2016.

78. Bobrow-Strain 2007, 72.

79. On dynamic reciprocities, see also Guerrero 1991; Lyons 2006; Bobrow-Strain 2007.

80. See Lambert 1996; Nagel 1999; Hetherington 2018.

81. I have written on this phenomenon in Correia 2019b.

82. This is a well-trodden point for those familiar with Paraguayan politics. See Palau et al. 2015 for an overview.

83. On Cartes, see Martin and Spinetto 2016. On Abdo, see Costa 2019.

84. Here I draw inspiration from Daigle and Ramírez's work on "spatial weaving" (2018, 79) and constellations of co-resistance, which builds on the Mississauga Nishnaabeg writer Leanne Betasamosake Simpson, who avers, "Constellations exist only in the context of relationships; otherwise they are just individual stars" (2017, 215).

85. Lund's (2016) work informs my approach, wherein I employ ethnographic vignettes to highlight political, epistemic, social, and juridical changes that rework power and rule in specific instances to open moments for critical analysis and reflection.

86. Research trips were conducted at least once per year before the COVID-19 pandemic.

87. Blaser (2010) and Villagra-Carrón (2010) discuss the rich oral culture in the Paraguayan Chaco and its centrality to Indigenous social relations.

88. L. B. Simpson 2014.

89. Kovach 2010, 44. I want to stress that this approach does not suggest the casualization of research; it is not just a matter of talking to people. The method is founded on intentionality, time, trust, and ethical relations. Students and other researchers interested in employing similar methods can turn to a robust body of scholarship by Indigenous and non-Indigenous scholars to learn more. For excellent starting points, see Kovach 2021; Tuhiwai-Smith 2012; Liboiron 2021.

90. Medina 2016; Correia 2021a.

91. I conducted this research independently of Tierraviva, but my relationship with members of the organization was central to this study.

92. The interviewees include people from the following communities and organizations: Xákmok Kásek, Sawhoyamaxa, Yakye Axa, Kelyenmagategma, Tierraviva, Paraguayan senators and congressional representatives, present or former INDI employees, present or former Ministry of Health employees, Ministry of Justice officials, directors of the Commissions on Indigenous Peoples, Supreme Court of Human Rights officials, Ministry of Exterior Relations officials, Comisión Interinstitucional para el Cumplimiento de las Sentencias Internacionales officials, Secretaría de Emergencia Nacional official, Instituto Nacional de Desarrollo Rural y de la Tierra officials, police officers, NGO actors (Coordinadora de Líderes Indígenas del Bajo Chaco, Federación por la Autodeterminación de Pueblos Indígenas, Tierra Libre—Instituto Social y Ambiental, Gente Ambiente y Territorio, Iniciativa Amotocodie), Paraguayan academics, media reporters, ranchers, non-Indigenous ranch hands, Indigenous peoples from other communities, and several others, from storekeepers to taxi drivers.

93. Most research participants did not wish to review the interview transcripts, though a handful provided their feedback.

94. On geography's coloniality, see Louis 2007; Shaw, Herman, and Dobbs 2008; and Sundberg 2015. On research as resistance, see Kovach 2009; and Brown and Strega 2015. In the vein of activist scholarship, I am also driven by scholars who have come before me who asked what is to be done in the face of injustice and the ability to use academic research to seek more just futures (Gilmore 2011).

95. See Wainwright 2008; Liboiron 2021.

96. See, e.g., Spivak 1998; and Martínez-Novo 2018.

97. Tuhiwai-Smith 2012, 37.

98. Chapter 2 and chapter 5 include material reprinted from *Geoforum*, Vol. 119, Joel E. Correia, "Reworking Recognition: Indigeneity, Land Rights, and the Dialectics of Disruption in Paraguay's Chaco," pp. 227–37, Copyright 2021, with permission from Elsevier.

99. Chapter 3 and chapter 4 include material reprinted from *Geoforum*, Vol. 97, Joel E. Correia, "Indigenous Rights at a Crossroads: Territorial Struggles, the Inter-American Court of Human Rights, and Liminal Legal Geographies," pp. 73–83, CC BY-NC-ND 4.0 2018, with permission from Elsevier. Chapter 3 also includes excerpts reprinted with permission from University Press of Florida from "Infrastructures of Settler Colonialism: Geographies of Violence, Indigenous Labor, and Marginal Resistance in Paraguay's Chaco," by Joel E. Correia, in *Reimagining the Gran Chaco: Identities, Politics, and the Environment in South America*, edited by Silvia Hirsch, Paola Canova, and Mercedes Biocca (Gainesville: University Press of Florida, 2021), 166–85.

100. The conclusion of chapter 4 includes an excerpt reprinted from *Roadsides*, Vol. 2, Joel E. Correia, "Arrested Infrastructure: Roadwork, Rights, and Racialized Geographies," pp. 14–24, CC BY-NC-SA 4.0 2019, with permission from Roadsides.

RUPTURE 1: OPEN/CLOSED

1. Interview, June 1, 2015.

CHAPTER 1: "A LAND IN THE MAKING"

1. Kleinpenning 2003, 31–42.

2. See Vázquez 2010.

3. Villagra-Carrón 2014, 27. Also note that Carlos Antonio López issued the October 7 decree of 1848 that formally declared all Indigenous lands *tierra fiscal*—state land.

4. Grubb 1914, 20–21.

5. Bonifacio (2017) details the history and evolution of the tannin industry, which was housed in seven riverport towns with a total population of nearly 30,000 people among them at the peak of operations. Though operating north of Enxet and Sanapaná territories, the tannin industry did induce significant colonization of the Chaco that eventually impacted Sanapaná and some Enxet groups (Villagra-Carrón 2014). The collapse of the tannin industry in the early 1950s spurred land subdivision and sale to investors primarily interested in establishing cattle ranches. With the expansion of ranching, many Indigenous communities moved to area cattle ranches in search of work. Versions of this history are recounted in Villagra-Carrón 2014; Renshaw 2002; Bonifacio 2017.

6. Casanova 1965.

7. See, e.g., Martinez-Novo 2021; Saldaña-Portillo 2015; Mollett 2016; Gordillo 2014; Nichols 2020; Bhandar 2018.

8. Every 1915, 53; my emphasis.

9. Such acts of discursively emplacing settler labor work to erase the labor of Indigenous peoples and thereby advances logics of elimination (Morgensen 2009). See Powell (2007) for narrative accounts of Anglican missionaries as protagonists of change and Friesen (2016) for accounts of Mennonite settlers. On radical alterity and its relation to this dynamic in Paraguay, see Blaser 2010; Bessire 2014; Canova 2020.

10. Gordillo and Hirsch (2003) detail the assimilation policy of the Argentine government that sought to erase Indigenous peoples from the nation-state, while Gordillo's *Landscape of Devils* brilliantly details the simultaneous centrality and marginalization of Toba labor in the Chaco.

11. Saldaña-Portillo 2016, 20.

12. Kidd (1992, 2000), Leake (1998), and Villagra-Carrón (2010) each provide detailed accounts of Anglican missionary work in Paraguay's Bajo Chaco that I do not rehearse.

13. Leanne Betasamosake Simpson's work on this point has deeply enriched my understanding: "I understand settler colonialism's structure as one that is formed and maintained by a series of *processes*. . . . I experience it as a gendered structure and a *series of complex and overlapping process* that work together as a cohort to maintain the structure" (2017, 45; original emphasis).

14. The concept "internal colonialism" traces to Latin American scholarship from the 1960s that influenced some Marxist theorizations of similar processes in the United States around the 1970s. Pablo González Casanova's classic article, "Internal colonialism and national development" (1965), and Gonzalo Aguirre Beltrán's *Regiones de Refugio* (1991) have been particularly influential. See also Chávez 2011 for a more recent review.

15. See Asociación Rural del Paraguay n.d.

16. Here I am indebted to Cari Tusing for the idea of cattle as a companion species to settler colonialism.

17. Every year ARP and Paraguay Industrial Union host a weeks-long expo that draws thousands of attendees, serving as both the national fair and the place where ranchers can showcase their cattle and the latest ranching technologies. See http://expo.org.py/.

18. The organization was founded in 1885 under the name Ranching Society of Paraguay (Sociedad Ganadera del Paraguay), though it changed to the Asociación Rural del Paraguay in 1938.

19. Kleinpenning (2003, 463–548) provides a robust history of ranching dynamics from the late 1800s to the 1930s.

20. Ávila and Portillo 2018.

21. Lovera and Franceschelli 2019, 2.

22. The majority of the Gran Chaco is a dry scrub forest, though the "Bajo Chaco" is distinguished from the rest of the region for having higher rainfall, seasonal flooding events, and proximity to the Paraguay River.

23. Pasternak 2020, 303.

24. Per Spanish naming norms, Chaqueño denotes someone/thing of or from the Chaco.

25. See Strong 2007 for a detailed analysis of British imperialism and the Church of England.

26. Gordillo's *Landscape of Devils* (2004) provides a helpful analysis of the Anglican Mission in Argentina's Chaco.

27. For example, Sir Herbert Gibson, a central member of SAMS, owned 270,654 hectares in Enxet territory and was also responsible for administering lands for two private ranching companies with holdings totaling 288,750 hectares in the same region. See Kidd 1992, 61.

28. Daniels 1916, 240.

29. Grubb 1911, 293.

30. Chesterton 2013, 83.

31. Foucault 1991.

32. As quoted in Kidd 1992, 64; my emphasis.

33. Grubb 1911, 21–22; my emphasis.

34. Grubb 1914, 218.

35. These methods were not unique to SAMS in Paraguay but broadly practiced in Latin America. See Gordillo (2004) on Toba experiences Argentina, Bessire (2014) and Canova (2020) on Ayoreo in Paraguay and Bolivia, and Ybarra (2018) on Maya in Guatemala.

36. Enxet peoples who live in this region historically identified as the Chanawatsan Enxet, which is indicative of those who lived near the Paraguay River (Villagra-Carrón 2010). Aside from academic texts, Chanawatsan is not used today, and no one from Yakye Axa, Sawhoyamaxa, Xákmok Kásek, or Kelyenmagategma identified as such.

37. Sanderson 1942, 56.

38. Blomley 2013, 26.

39. Hunt 1933, 229.

40. Nichols 2020, 31.

41. Stuart Hall's essay "The West and the Rest: Discourse and Power" ([1992] 2019) discusses the binary logic of racialization processes vis-à-vis colonialism and its manifestations, while Nichols (2020) and Bhandar (2018) detail the specific legal and discursive mechanisms through which property produces racial difference.

42. Bhandar 2018, 7.

43. Saldaña-Portillo's *Indian Given* (2015) masterfully analyzes the discursive formations that yield to racist tropes such as the "indio bárbaro" and their lasting material effects on Indigenous life in the Mexico-US borderlands. Such racist tropes are common throughout the Americas, serving to normalize the dehumanization of Indigenous peoples by settlers while justifying land appropriation and abuse.

44. Deloria 1988, 30.

45. See, e.g., Guerrero 1998; Peloso 1999; Gordillo and Hirsch 2003; Gordillo 2004; Gibbings 2016; Speed 2017; Kalisch and Unruh 2018.

46. Kidd 1992, 63–64.

47. Grubb 1911, 140.

48. Foucault 1991, 93.

49. Kidd (2021) provides a deep analysis of Enxet moral economies with particular attention to the notions of private property introduced by missionaries and ranchers.

50. See Villagra-Carrón 2014, 255.

51. See Villagra-Carrón 2014, 140.

52. Kidd 1992, 63.

53. Kidd 2000, 23.

54. See Anglican Church 1979.

55. Kidd 1992, 63.

56. Pride 1930, 75, cited in Kidd 1995, 48.

57. Sanderson 1944, 56. Several studies also corroborate the direct relationship between the Anglican Mission and the specific places where ranching first took hold in Paraguay's Chaco; see, e.g., Kidd 1992, 1995; Leake 1998; Renshaw 2002; and Villagra-Carrón 2010.

58. Gustafson's *Bolivia in the Age of Gas* (2020) provides a helpful analysis of the role that foreign petroleum companies played in Bolivia and Paraguay in the years leading to the war.

59. See Richard 2008; Villagra-Carrón 2014; and Kalisch and Unruh 2018 for detailed histories.

60. See Vázquez 2010, 56; see also Dalla-Corte Caballero 2012.

61. See Farcau 1996; Chesterson 2013 for in-depth accounting.

62. Recorded interview, October 21, 2015.

63. Renshaw 2002.

64. Chase-Sardi (1972) and Renshaw (2002) documented the prevalence of Enxet and Sanapana labor on area cattle ranches, noting the widespread use of debt peonage, script, and labor abuse normalized across the Bajo Chaco. The United Nations Special Rapporteur on the Rights of Indigenous peoples reported the prevalence of these issues in a 2015 report (United Nations 2015).

65. Kidd 1992, 67.

66. IACHR 2010, 24.

67. Powell 2007.

68. Kidd 1995, 53.

69. La Herencia acquired 9,500 hectares in 1980 for Sombrero Piri, 22,500 hectares in 1983 for La Patria, and 9,374 hectares in 1985 for El Estribo (Anglican Church 1977). To their credit, Anglican missionaries made extensive efforts to identify high-quality land and engaged in a significant consultation process with Enxet, Sanapaná, and Angaité peoples who would come to occupy the land (Villagra-Carron 2015). Leake (1998) provides an extensive discussion on the methods of identifying and purchasing the lands for La Herencia.

70. Anglican Church 1977, 3–4.

71 At the time of writing, rice farming is the only large-scale agriculture in the Bajo Chaco. The practice is located close to the Paraguay River in sites where producers can regulate water flows with large pumps. It bears noting that rice production is incipient in the region, starting in earnest around the year 2019.

72. See Renshaw 2002.

73. Recorded interview, March 1, 2016.

74. Wolfe 1996.

75. Gordillo (2004) provides an important and in-depth analysis based on research in Argentina's Chaco.

76. Razack 2020, n.p.

77. McKittrick (2013, 3; my emphasis), inspires my analysis of the long-standing links between indigeneity and racial geographies because "it brings into focus the ways in which racial violences (concrete and epistemic actions and structural patterns intended to harm,

kill, or coerce a particular grouping of people) shape, *but do not wholly define,*" Enxet and Sanapaná worlds.

78. See, e.g., Córdoba, Bossert, and Richards 2015; Gordillo and Hirsch 2010; Kidd 2000; Villagra-Carrón 2010.

79. Speed 2017, 784.

80. King 2020, 68–70.

81. See Bobrow-Strain 2006; Peloso 1999; De la Cadena 2000, respectively. Racial capitalism across the Gran Chaco hinges on Indigenous labor, from Bolivian gas fields (Anthias 2018) and soybean plantations in Argentina (Gordillo 2014) to estancias in Paraguay.

82. See also Martinez-Novo (2005) for a related argument regarding the Mixtec of northern Mexico. Yeh and Bryan (2015) provide a broader assessment of the linkages between indigeneity and labor vis-à-vis the International Labor Organization.

RUPTURE 2: BOUNDARIES

1. I am using pseudonyms for the two state functionaries at their request.

2. Here I draw from Joe Bryan's (2011) brilliant analysis of the power and politics of mapping and its role in legal recognition processes for many Indigenous communities in Latin America, where mapping often does not resolve conflict but does open spaces to "critically [assess] the potential of legal recognition, creating an awareness of other configurations of territory that help understand relations of power and influence" (49).

3. It is customary for the youngest person in the group to serve tereré.

4. Inter-American Commission on Human Rights 2007, n.p.

CHAPTER 2: NOT-QUITE-NEOLIBERAL MULTICULTURALISM

1. Donald Moore's *Suffering for Territory* (2005) draws attention to the sedimented histories of colonial land control and racial struggles that entangle people in place-making processes. Here I draw from Moore's idea that "geographies of violence [are] historically sedimented in landscapes of racialized dispossession."

2. My article "Soy States" (2019b) traces some of these violent encounters across the country. For other in-depth reporting, see the annual reports of Coordinadora Derechos Humanos Paraguay (www.codehupy.org.py/category/informes-anuales/).

3. See also Postero 2007, 13; Jackson 2020, 13–14.

4. Throughout his work in this area, Hale's framing of neoliberal multiculturalism has hinged on two primary axes: (1) that it is "a project" of governance; and (2) that a Gramscian-inspired analysis of hegemony/counterhegemony explains how and why Indigenous actors ascribe to the limited political arena permitted by multicultural rights, which in turn often uphold long-standing racial hierarchies. This framing has inspired an important body of research too vast to thoroughly engage here but has been particularly productive for scholars focusing on the alignment of environmental governance and state-legitimated imaginaries of indigeneity and ethnic difference in Panama (Velásquez-Runk 2012), Colombia (Offen 2003; Asher 2009; Cárdenas 2012; Jackson 2020), Mexico (Martínez-Novo 2005; Muehlmann 2013), Nicaragua (Wainwright and Bryan 2009; Bryan 2011), and Honduras (Mollett 2013; Loperena 2016; Galeana 2020). See also Martínez-Novo and

Shlossberg (2018) and the special issue they coedited for *Cultural Studies*, in which many articles address facets of neo-extractivism and multicultural rights across Latin America.

5. For analyses that focus on this dynamic in different contexts across the Americas, see, e.g., Hale 2005, 2006; Engle 2010; Byrd 2011; Coulthard 2014; Martínez-Novo and Shlossberg 2018; Restrepo 2018; Jackson 2020; Martínez-Novo 2021.

6. See Povinelli (2002) on liberalism and multicultural rights, as well as Bessire (2014).

7. Melamed 2015; Restrepo 2018; Razack 2020.

8. Recorded interview, October 21, 2015.

9. Recorded interview, July 27, 2016.

10. See Kidd 1997 and Renshaw 2002 for detailed accounts. Tauli-Corpuz (2015) and Bhoola (2017) have documented the extreme Indigenous labor exploitation found across the Paraguayan Chaco in the present.

11. Tierraviva a los Pueblos Indígenas del Chaco n.d., 16–17.

12. Renshaw 2002, 138.

13. Chase-Sardi, Brun, and Enciso 1990, 77.

14. Handwritten interview, January 13, 2016.

15. Recorded interview, July 27, 2016.

16. See Chase-Sardi and Colombres 1975.

17. IWGIA 1971.

18. See Harder-Horst 2007; Blaser 2010; Bonifacio 2013 for detailed histories of the Marandú Project.

19. *Tavy* has various connotations in Guaraní but is generally used to mean "crazy" or "stupid."

20. Marcelino was not suggesting that Sanapaná peoples had no connections to territory but that before such workshops no one in the communities used the concept in the contemporary normative juridical or geographic manner that is now common.

21. Recorded interview, November 21, 2015.

22. Gustafson 2009.

23. In attempts to discredit Chase-Sardi and justify his torture and imprisonment, the Stroessner administration accused him of being both a communist and an informant for the CIA (Harder-Horst 2010, 97). When I interviewed one of the co-owners of Estanica Salazar in 2015 he said that Chase-Sardi "was a communist." The narrative thus persists, though no evidence exists to corroborate the claim other than Chase-Sardi's affinity to liberation theology.

24. See Münzel 1973; Reed and Renshaw 2012.

25. Harder-Horst 2010, 40–48.

26. Harder-Horst 2010.

27. Chase-Sardi, Brun, and Enciso 1990, 79–80.

28. Engle 2010, 36.

29. See Eide 2009, 33.

30. Grandin (2006) and McSherry (2005) provide two helpful overviews, though the literature on this topic is vast.

31. See Harder-Horst 2010; and Grandin 2011.

32. Harder-Horst 2010, 39.

33. Mollett 2016.

34. Graham and Weissner 2011.

35. Jackson (2020, 14) argues, "The multicultural movement and its ideology are typically identified with democratic, liberal societies, polities with a developed civil society or at least a commitment to promote one." See also Povinelli 1998; Lennox and Short 2016.

36. Benhabib (2002) examines the purported claims of multiculturalism and its relations with liberal ideologies of inclusion, something that Povinelli (2002) forcefully exposes for its contradictory and inherently violent nature. Numerous Indigenous scholars from Canada and the United States also inform my thinking on the limits of settler law, e.g., A. Simpson 2014; Coulthard 2014; L. B. Simpson 2017; Whyte 2016; Jarratt-Snider and Nielson 2020. Anthias 2017; Radcliffe 2015; Bessire 2014; and Engle 2010 provide especially helpful critiques regarding Latin America.

37. See Sieder 2002; Engle 2010; Martínez-Novo and Shlossberg 2018.

38. On constitutional reforms, see Van Cott 2005; Jackson and Warren 2012. On Law 70 in Colombia, see Ng'weno 2007; Escobar 2008; Asher 2009.

39. Coulthard 2014, 3.

40. Radcliffe 2015, 22.

41. We see this familiar trend in sites across the world (Ramos 1998; Povinelli 2002; Hale 2005; Coulthard 2014; Wolfe 2016). Anthias's *Limits to Decolonization* (2018) provides a helpful demonstration of this point through a critique of mapping and territoriality in Bolivia.

42. Engle 2010; Gonzales and González 2015; Gilbert 2016.

43. See Povinelli 1998 and Radcliffe 2010 for an extended discussion and critique.

44. Niezen 2003.

45. Correia 2021a; see also Reyes and Kauffman 2011 for a related argument regarding the limits of Indigenous autonomies within the state system.

46. Jackson and Warren 2005, Antkowiak 2014.

47. See Article 2 of Law 904/81, available at Biblioteca y Archivo Central del Congreso de la Nación, https://www.bacn.gov.py/leyes-paraguayas/2400/ley-n-904-estatuto-de-las -comunidades-indigenas.

48. See Glauser and Villagra-Carrón 2021.

49. Sawhoyamaxa is one community identity and common name that references a specific geographic location. However, Sawhoyamaxa comprises several smaller communities— aldeas—formed along kinship lines as well as histories of living on different cattle ranches. At the time of my research, there were three primary aldeas in Sawhoyamaxa: Santa Elisa, 16 de agosto (Kilometro 16), and Sawhoyamaxa Central. Since that time, at least two new aldeas have formed along political and familial lines as community dynamics change.

50. Recognition requires a census to document the number of distinct households and individuals who comprise the community, something challenged by the fact that many Indigenous people in the Chaco still do not have formal identity documents. Exceedingly few Indigenous peoples had state-issued birth certificates or identity cards in the 1980s and 1990s because state services to render such documents are nonexistent in this area. Thus proving one's existence often required a site visit by one of few INDI officials who could verify community censuses in person.

51. See also Gustafson 2009.

52. Recorded interview, July 28, 2016.

53. See Article 10 of Law 904/81, https://www.bacn.gov.py/leyes-paraguayas/2400/ley-n
-904-estatuto-de-las-comunidades-indigenas.

54. Nichols 2020.

55. The Paraguayan state also declared Xákmok Kásek in a state of emergency in 2009, while its case was being adjudicated by the Inter-American Court.

56. See IACHR 2005, 49.

57. Recorded interview, July 24, 2016.

58. Throughout the course of my field research I was surprised that none of my Enxet or Sanapaná interlocutors explicitly employed language about decolonization. Whereas political discourse in many other Indigenous struggles, for example, among many Guaraní of Bolivia (Anthias 2018) and the Zapatistas of Mexico (Mora 2018), often articulate decolonization as an organizing principle, my interlocutors squarely focused on the discourse of human rights. Here it is important to also note a salient difference with many Indigenous struggles in Canada and the United States that have a juridical relationship with the respective settler states. Though there is a history of violation, tribes in the United States and Canada have strong, nationally based sovereign rights that enable them to negotiate different relationships with the settler state and advance development initiatives in ways that Indigenous peoples in Paraguay cannot. Finally, this difference is underscored by the legal definition of Indigenous "communities" in Paraguay—not peoples or sovereign entities—something that truncates their political power in many ways.

59. Guaraní is widely spoken in Paraguay and several sites across the Southern Cone. However, it bears noting that there are many nuances in how people actually speak the language, which creates dialects that are difficult to follow even for native speakers. For example, the Guaraní of Bolivia speak a distinctly different dialect from that of the Avá Guaraní of southeastern Paraguay; and the official Guaraní language spoken by the majority of Paraguayans is distinct from the other two.

60. On Indigenous refusal as resistance and political praxis, see A. Simpson 2014.

61. Handwritten notes, July 6, 2013.

62. Recorded interview, February 10, 2016.

63. Trouillot 2003.

64. For expanded discussions on the role of religion and capitalism in Indigenous dispossession, see Moreton-Robinson 2015; Bhandar 2018.

65. See Pasternak 2020 on the notion of partition that I draw from here.

66. Hale 2005, 2006.

67. Hale 2006, 75.

68. See, e.g., Hale 2006, 2020.

69. I discuss the notion of "rational exploitation" in chapter 5, but suffice to say here that the agrarian reforms clearly frame favorable land use for economic production.

70. Anthias 2018, 10.

71. See Harder-Horst 2010 and Blaser 2010 for analyses of the creation of Law 904/81.

72. Reiterated acts by state officials working in the service of settler extractivists show this to be true, from what happened in Kelyenmagategma to the decimation of Ayoreo Totobeigosodie territories in the northern Chaco (Bessire 2014; Canova 2020) to the recent violent assaults on Avá Guaraní who live "in the way" of soybean expansion in southeastern Paraguay (Correia 2019; Hetherington 2020; Glauser and Villagra-Carrón 2021).

RUPTURE 3: IN/VISIBLE

1. An estancionero works on horseback, a prestigious but dangerous position.

2. Handwritten fieldnotes, October 22, 2015.

3. Amnesty International 2017.

CHAPTER 3: BIOPOLITICS OF NEGLECT

1. As part of a slate of new road construction projects initiated with the Bi-oceanic Highway in 2019, the Paraguayan Ministry of Public Works and Communications started repaving Ruta 5 in late 2021.

2. Literally, "Indigenous culture." Throughout the course of my research, this phrase was often used by both Indigenous and non-Indigenous peoples to refer to traditional Indigenous practices, from spirituality to art, and was considered at odds with evangelical Christian religions.

3. Chapter 4 discusses this history in greater detail.

4. See, e.g., Farmer 1996; Watts [1983] 2013; Nixon 2011.

5. I use "social groups" here to flag populations that are both human and other-than-human (like cows).

6. Throughout my field research, many non-Indigenous Paraguayans would explain the material poverty found in many Indigenous communities as the result of "cultura indígena" (Indigenous culture). The discourse obfuscates the structural factors that produce the material poverty common to many Indigenous communities in Paraguay and places blame for such conditions on Indigenous peoples rather than the processes that ensure dispossession.

7. See Foucault [2004] 2007.

8. See Scott 1999.

9. Doing so advances critical environmental justice approaches to the interdependent indispensability of human and nonhuman populations living in relation (Pellow 2018, 151–52).

10. Walker (2012) and Pellow (2018) provide helpful overviews of the evolution of environmental justice approaches.

11. I am indebted to Stuart Hall's (1986) articulation of Marxism without guarantees.

12. The literature is vast, with many sources cited in the pages of this book. For comprehensive analyses, see Correia 2019a; Hetherington 2020; and the Paraguayan organization BASE Investigaciones Sociales website that offers a compendium of research; see https://www.baseis.org.py/.

13. See Correia 2019b. Lund's (2016) article is a vital resource to think with rupture as an analytic to assess shifting forms of rule.

14. Recent studies show that over 90 percent of cattle raised in Paraguay are for beef production, that approximately 99 percent of that beef is exported, and that Chile, Russia, Taiwan, and Brazil are the primary export destinations (Ávila and Portillo 2017, 18–22).

15. SENACSA 2020b.

16. SENACSA 2020a.

17. See, e.g., Shukin 2009; Nally 2010; Holloway and Wilkinson 2014.

18. By way of comparison, the 2022 operating budget for INDI was 67,310,000 guaranies, whereas the Ministry of Agriculture had 413,577,562,839 guaranies at its disposal.

19. The intensive feedlot model is most commonly used in highly industrialized economies, though it is increasing in Brazil due to deforestation pressures (Vale et al. 2019). It should be noted that while nearly all cattle in Paraguay is pasture raised, producers are increasingly finishing their cattle with forage based on blends of soybean, corn, and other seeds.

20. Li 2010, 66.

21. Foucault's attention to modes of classification, measurement, and scientific practices used to render bodies, populations, and conditions legible for intervention and the exercise of power privileged the human subject as the site of biopolitical action. Further, Agamben's (1995) work on the juridical separation of zoe from bios shows how states of exception legitimate the killing of certain (human) bodies over others. It has been one of the more prescient and productive analyses of biopower in the twenty-first century, though it invites theorizations about how the human/animal binary maps onto entwined processes of racialization and speciation. Recent scholarship thus advances theories of biopower beyond the human. On this point, Pugliese (2020, 6) contends that Foucault's biopolitics is species-centric: "The question of the animal effectively establishes the onto-epistemological ground that determines the cultural intelligibility of the human/animal binary and that, moreover, establishes what can be executed on the body of the animal other (and, concomitantly, those humans designated as 'mere animals') as lawful practice." Other related literatures expand biopolitical inquiry to examinations of livestock and their slaughter for human consumption (Lorimer and Driessen 2013; Grossberg 2016; Asdal, Druglitrø, and Hinchliffe 2017), environmental conservation practice and the valuation of certain life-forms over others (Biermann and Mansfield 2014; Biermann and Anderson 2017; Srinivasan 2017), and the "lively legalities" employed to manage life, broadly construed (Braverman's 2016 edited volume, *Animals, Biopolitics, Law*). Here I also note the biopolitics of plant-human relations. Hetherington (2020, 173) assesses genetically modified soybean production to argue that governance of human populations and well-being in the contemporary era cannot be divorced from the governance of new forms of plant life through agribiopolitics: "new genealogies of life that seek to explain the increasing segregation between diverse communities of humans and increasingly uniform populations of plants." My attention to the governance of cattle life thus shows how other than human biopolitics are invariably linked to the de facto state policies of governing "surplus" Indigenous populations through neglect.

22. Correia 2019b; see also Hetherington 2011, 2020.

23. See Borras et al. 2012; Borras et al. 2016; Galeano 2012; Rodríguez 2001.

24. See Li 2014 on the fungibility of land and its allure to investors during the most recent global land rush.

25. Although Paraguay exports more than 99 percent of all beef produced in the country, Paraguayans have among the highest rates of beef consumption per capita in the Americas.

26. Miró Ibars 2004.

27. See Nickson 1988; Hetherington 2011.

28. Several analyses show this. See Ezquerro-Cañete 2016; Correia 2019b; Hetherington 2020.

29. Oliva 2011.

30. My article "Soy States" (2019b) provides a comprehensive analysis of this process as it pertains to southeastern Paraguay. Canova (2020) and Bessire (2014) each provide

excellent assessments of Mennonite enclaves and their effects on Ayoreo life in the Central Chaco.

31. Asociación Rural del Paraguay n.d.

32. Tauli-Corpuz 2015.

33. See Hetherington's (2020) discussion of agribiopolitics.

34. Recorded interview, February 21, 2016.

35. See "emergency." Merriam-Webster.com, 2021 online edition.

36. Mbembe 2003, 27; original emphasis.

37. Agamben 1995, 2005.

38. Saldaña-Portillo 2016.

39. See also Mbembe 2003, 26.

40. Li 2010, 67.

41. SEN 2017.

42. In the eyes of early Anglican missionaries, settler cattle ranchers, and state officials, the original inhabitants of the Bajo Chaco were "indios"—Indians. Specific names for different Indigenous peoples were also used, like Lengua (Enxet), Morros (Ayoreo), and Chulupi (Nivacle); but the racial stamp "indio" was the generic, normative form to describe those who were not white. The "indio" discourse is loaded with meaning beyond that of merely a nonwhite person. As Saldaña-Portillo (2015) has argued in similar ways, the indio was the "savage" type that connotes a spatial and racialized order that distinguishes human from nonhuman by equating the notion of savagery with other-than-human natures. The indio is thus a liminal being that transited a terrain between human and nonhuman form and thus was denied protections under the law, to say nothing of citizenship. Historical narratives from early settlers are rife with such racist stereotypes and depictions, as the previous chapter clearly showed. Indeed, the contemporary use of the term "indio" in Paraguay marks racist discourse. Since I began working in Paraguay in 2006, I have never met an Indigenous person who refers to herself as an *india*. To call someone an indio, or "avá" in Guaraní, remains a serious insult intended to equate the interpellated subject as filthy or savage; this is particularly true for non-Indigenous Paraguayans. The exception to this lies with the Avá Guaraní, a specific Indigenous people.

43. See Blaser 2010, 80–103 for a related discussion.

44. See also Renshaw 2002, 132–43.

45. *Makatero* is the colloquial name for mobile vendors who sell items across the Chaco, driving from community to community to peddle their wares. A variant of this response was reported by people across all three communities during twenty-two interviews.

46. Handwritten fieldnotes, September 20, 2015.

47. On strategic essentialism, see Grosz's (1985) interview with Gayatri Spivak.

48. Blaser (2010, 162) calls a similar dynamic used by Indigenista organizations in the 1990s the "hunter-gatherer paradigm."

49. Recorded interview with person who wished to remain anonymous, January 30, 2016.

50. Povinelli 2002, 2011; Melamed 2015.

51. In October 2015 and again in January 2016.

52. Handwritten fieldnotes, October 7, 2015.

53. Recorded interview, June 18, 2017.

54. When I refer to "the state," I do so in recognition that it is not a singular entity with a unified logic but a constellation of institutions with many functionaries who are working to improve their country and the everyday lives of its citizens. However, as this interview demonstrates, there are significant structural factors that limit the ability of many functionaries to achieve their goals and thus manifest as neglect that my interlocutors experience. There is a difference between the decision-making power of elites who influence state actions and the everyday work that many functionaries are tasked with completing. See Gupta 2012 for a helpful analysis that informs my thinking here.

55. Morgensen 2011.

56. Mbembe 2003, 39.

57. See also Membe 2019 for a much expanded analysis.

58. See Nixon (2011) on "slow violence" and Galtung (1969) on "structural violence," among others.

59. Pratt 2005, 1054.

RUPTURE 4: PRISON

1. Open Society Justice Initiative 2017.

2. My translation maintains both the literal words Belfio used and the figurative meaning of his responses while maintaining the cadence and repetitions of his speech. This is an excerpt from an interview on July 28, 2016.

CHAPTER 4: RESTITUTION AS DEVELOPMENT?

1. Fieldnotes, February 27, 2016.

2. Using violent land dispossessions to uphold the private property rights of large-scale landholders is common in Paraguay's soybean territories (see, e.g., Ezquerro-Cañete 2016; Correia 2019a; Hetherington 2020). The Paraguayan NGO Coordinadora de Derechos Humanos Paraguay (Paraguayan Human Rights Coordinator) publishes an annual assessment of human rights in the country, and violent land dispossessions are regular features in each year's edition; see https://codehupy.org.py/category/informes-anuales/.

3. See also Galemba 2013.

4. *Merriam-Webster*, 2021 online ed., s.v. "liminality."

5. Immigration scholars have provided novel theorizations of legal liminality with regard to worker's visas and threats of deportation in the United States (Menjívar 2006; Chacón 2015; Abrego and Lakhani 2015).

6. Povinelli (2011, 75–79) outlines a similar dynamic, "brackets of recognition," whereas Simpson (2014, 12) shows that liminal legality intends to thwart Indigenous sovereignty, arguing that "under the conditions of settler colonialism, multiple sovereignties cannot proliferate robustly or equally."

7. Hetherington (2011), Auyero (2012), and Gupta (2013), respectively, show that what at first glance might seem like state inefficiency or malfunction is actually a powerful form of governance whereby the politics of waiting become a de facto means of governing marginalized populations by ensnaring them in banal technocratic processes that deflect attention from concerns that drive people to seek state services. As I argued in chapter 3,

such protracted bureaucratic processes function hand in glove with the biopolitics of neglect.

8. On the Mayagna (Sumo) Awas Tingni case, see Grossman 2001. For excellent critical analyses, see Bryan 2009, 2011; Engle 2010; Gilbert 2016.

9. Anaya and Grossman 2002, 12.

10. The subsequent cases at the time of this writing are *Yakye Axa v. Paraguay* (2005); *Moiwana Community v. Suriname* (2005); *Sawhoyamaxa v. Paraguay* (2006); *Saramaka v. Suriname* (2007); *Xákmok Kásek v. Paraguay* (2010); *Sarayaku v. Ecuador* (2012); *Kaliña and Lokono Peoples v. Surname* (2015); *Garífuna Punta Piedra Community v. Honduras* (2015); *Garífuna Triunfo de la Cruz Community and Its Members v. Honduras* (2015); *Xucuru Indigenous Community and Its Members v. Brazil* (2018); *Indigenous members of the Lhaka Honhat Association v. Argentina* (2020).

11. See International Justice Resource Center 2014.

12. Garavito and Kauffman (2015, 277) argue that the gap between Inter-American System decisions and state compliance "has grown as the system has devoted itself to tackling generalized rights violations that stem from structural injustices of an economic, social, or cultural nature." Similarly, Hillebrecht (2012) notes that the IACHR has limited ability to enforce its judgments in situ because although compliance is legally mandated when a country accepts IACHR's jurisdictional authority, compliance is voluntary in practice.

13. See also Bryan 2019 on the challenges that emerged following the Awas Tingni case in Nicaragua.

14. Paraguay ratified the Inter-American Convention on Human Rights in 1978.

15. The very notion of being human has been tied to liberal philosophies of universal human rights, whereby rights themselves can be understood as a form of inalienable property (Asad 2000). Studies evaluating the exclusionary regime of property and its intimate relations with citizenship have argued that private property in land functions as the mechanism that enables settler colonial power and mechanisms of elimination (Moreton-Robinson 2015; Bhandar 2018; King 2019; Rifkin 2019; Nichols 2020). Regarding the IACHR specifically, Engle (2010, 126) suggests that "the inter-American system settled on its own rubric for protecting [Indigenous] culture: "the right to property," whereby in this context "culture" can be understood as mapping onto Indigenous personhood before the law.

16. Engle (2010, 123–32) provides a helpful interpretation of this approach by assessing links between property and culture in IACHR decisions.

17. See Nelson and Dorsey 2018.

18. Menton, Larrea, and Martinez-Alier et al. (2020) argue that contradictions inherent in the SGDs with regard to maintaining focus on economic growth ensures they will not meet their goals and, by extension, undermine the principles of the human rights-development nexus.

19. See Engle 2010.

20. See Blaser 2010, 96–97, for a discussion of the "hunter-gatherer paradigm."

21. Blaser (2010, 97–99) discusses the ARP efforts vis-à-vis sustainable development agendas and provides a provocative analysis of this period. Kidd (1995, 71–74) also discusses the ARP efforts, noting that its membership included landowners, lawyers, and high-level politicians who circulated documents stating, "Non-Indians are asking openly why is it that preferential treatment is given to Indians" (72).

22. In addition to the presentation discussed here, this rancher also lent me documents that he provided to the IACHR in defense of his refusal to cede land at Retiro Primero during an extended interview at his home in October 2015. The documents are also publicly available in the Museo Etnográfico Andrés Barbero archives located in Asunción, Paraguay.

23. "Lengua" is a colonial name for Enxet peoples that is widely viewed today as derogatory.

24. IACHR 2006, 70.

25. See my discussion of "wandering instincts" and private property in chapter 1.

26. IACHR 2006, 76.

27. Fieldnotes, December 10, 2015.

28. Fieldnotes, July 9, 2015.

29. See, e.g., ESCR-Net 2016.

30. Such "improvements" are common in staking claims to property rights in different sites in South America (see, e.g., Hetherington 2011; Campbell 2015). Paraguay's 1964 Agrarian Reform cemented the importance of so-called improvements in land law to usurp mere occupancy rights, ensuring that practices legible to economic production were valued over all other forms of land use (Hetherington 2011, 105–6).

31. I am drawing from Nichols's (2020) notion of recursive dispossession.

32. Recorded interview, July 29, 2016.

33. IACHR 2006, 76.

34. Whereas the notion of *terra nullius* can be traced to the British colonization of Australia, the discourse of *tierras baldías* (wastelands) has long been used to justify land dispossession in Latin America. Indigenous practices and occupancy have been framed as useless with regard to capitalist political economy (Sundberg 2008; Wainwright 2008; Mollett 2016; Sletto 2016).

35. Povinelli (2011, 34–39) refers to a similar dynamic as "the governance of the prior," to which I am indebted: "Although originating in settler nationalism and concentrated there, the governance of the prior provides an essential formation of tense and event to the governance of difference in late liberalism" (34).

36. Stocks 2005, 97.

37. For a photograph depicting this moment, see Correia 2018b, 80.

38. This logic is not unique to Paraguay. Indeed, the notion of rational exploitation has been used as a premise of agrarian reforms in several Latin American countries. As in the Paraguayan Chaco, such reforms intended to break up large latifundia, often owned by absentee landowners who controlled but did not use their lands for economic activities or "improve" them through investments. US president John F. Kennedy's program Alliance for Progress aggressively promoted agrarian reforms across Latin America in an attempt to thwart the spread of communism, the logic being that smaller private properties used for commodity production would undermine the potential for collective organizing. The strategy had an impact on Indigenous peoples across the region, however, by forcing many to maintain sedentary livelihoods as a means to gain property rights under the banner of campesino politics in the decades before Indigenous rights law or the multicultural turn.

39. My interviews with an assistant to the Paraguayan vice president, the president of the National Institute for Indigenous Affairs, and representatives of the Ministry of Justice from 2015 to 2017 substantiate this point.

40. See IACHR 2005, 17.

41. Recorded interview, July 27, 2016.

42. The tuyuyú (*Jabiru mycteria*) is a stork often seen in the Bajo Chaco.

43. Interview, July 1, 2016.

44. The living conditions on the side of the road created the premise for the Yakye Axa petition to the Inter-American Commission on Human Rights and eventual hearing before the IACHR. While the reporting and documentation of these living conditions and challenges are too great to comprehensively detail here, the following reports from Paraguayan state agencies, NGOs, and the IACHR demonstrate the breadth of knowledge about this situation: SIMORE n.d.; IACHR 2005, 2006, 2017; Tierraviva 2014; Amnesty International 2017; Open Society Justice Initiative 2017; OAS 2017.

45. IACHR 2005, 90; my emphasis.

46. Interview with Veronica, July 9, 2016.

47. I received copies of some of these reports from functionaries working for the Ministry of Justice, the Office of the Vice President of Paraguay, and Tierraviva.

48. Handwritten fieldnotes from visit to the alternative land, March 25, 2015.

49. The state officials included two police officers, two Ministry of Public Works and Communications functionaries, and one Institute for the Indigenous functionary.

50. Pratt 2005, 1068.

51. We see this in the boarding schools of Canada and the United States and the continued appropriation of Indigenous lands for extractive development. We see the suspension of legal protections for human rights and environmental rights defenders across Latin America, which has made the region one of the deadliest in the world since 2010 (Global Witness 2021; Middledorp and Le Billon 2019).

52. Over the course of my research that informs this book, it became clear that some people from affected communities prefer group conversations rather than private interviews. Small groups often provide a sense of security and familiarity for survivors of collective trauma to process and discuss the hardships they have endured and continue to endure.

53. Recorded group interview, July 6, 2016.

54. Recorded group interview, July 6, 2016.

55. Fanon 1963, 3.

56. Bessire 2014, 170.

57. See, e.g., Pratt and Hanson 2007; Mollett 2018; Radcliffe 2018; Sultana 2020.

58. Chaco Sin Fronteras 2019.

59. See Haglund and Stryker 2015.

60. Radcliffe 2015, 125–28; see also Perreault 2015.

61. Fieldnotes, July 6, 2016.

RUPTURE 5: HEART

1. Ignacia was talking about Roberto Eaton Sr.

CHAPTER 5: FIVE YEARS OF LIFE

1. As discussed in chapter 2, many scholars of neoliberal multiculturalism in Latin America refer to this relation as the indio permitido, the acceptable or permissible indian who is granted rights insofar as they do not disrupt the order of settler life.

2. See Ybarra's *Green Wars* (2018) for a helpful discussion of the both/and dynamic that I think with here.

3. Recorded interview, July 29, 2016. The Guaraní word ári approximately translates to the English concepts above, on top of, in addition to.

4. See A. Simpson 2014 on Indigenous refusal as political action.

5. There are too many excellent sources to adequately cite here. But I want to highlight some that I have found especially powerful: Gordillo 2004; L. B. Simpson 2014; Escobar 2008; Larsen and Johnson 2017; Whyte 2016; Sletto et al. 2020; Kalisch and Unruh 2018; Liboiron 2021; Tuhiwai Smith 2012; Byrd 2011; Corntassel 2012; Estes 2019; Risling Baldy 2018. Gordillo's (2011) critique of "stable spatiality" is also helpful.

6. Povinelli's (2002) notion of the "invisible asterisk" has been highly influential, particularly as employed in Engle 2010; and Radcliffe 2015. Debates about neoliberal multiculturalism (Hale 2005) have also shown this process in practice in several studies in the Americas, with Martínez-Novo (2005), Muehlmann (2009), Seider and Barrera-Vivero (2017), and Martínez-Novo and Shlossberg (2018) providing vital critiques. Finally, Indigenous studies scholars of Canada and the United States such as Coulthard (2014), A. Simpson (2014), Melamed (2015), Byrd et al. (2018), and Pasternak (2014, 2020) have also made similar arguments with regard to Indigenous and Native sovereignties.

7. See, e.g., Chapin et al. 2005; Sletto 2009; Wainwright and Bryan 2009; Hale 2011; Mollett 2013; Bryan and Woods 2015; Anthias 2019.

8. Two helpful exceptions are Sletto et al. 2020; and Anthias 2017.

9. Whyte 2016, 2018.

10. Whereas other countries in South America, such as Bolivia, have had closer diplomatic relations with China that have resulted in major development investments, Paraguay's close alignment with the United States has resulted in relations with Taiwan. As a result, the Taiwanese government often funds development projects in Paraguay to maintain strong geopolitical relations.

11. See chapter 1 for Eulalio's account about this retiro.

12. Stone 1998. Joe Bryan was the first person to introduce me to this idea (it also happens to be part of his dissertation title).

13. See Anthias 2014, 175, on precolonial notions of territory as animating contemporary struggles.

14. There is an important body of Indigenous literature on land as pedagogy too vast to adequately survey here, though I want to flag a few works that have influenced my thinking: Tuck, McKenzie, and McCoy 2014 (this article appears in the special issue of *Environmental Education Research* they edited); L. B. Simpson 2014; Risling Baldy 2018.

15. L. B. Simpson 2014, 10; Whyte 2018.

16. Saldaña-Portillo 2015, 19.

17. Fieldnotes, March 30, 2015.

18. President Horacio Cartes, who served from 2013 to 2018, has owned several banks, including Banco Amambay (International Consortium of Investigative Journalists 2013) and Banco Basa (EFE 2019).

19. Fieldnotes, July 13, 2015.

20. For excellent critiques, see Byrd 2011; Tuck and Yang 2012; De Leeuw and Hunt 2018. On Indigenous futurity, I also draw from Harjo 2019; Estes 2018; Aikau and Aikau 2015, 659. In addition, see Tuck, McKenzie, and McCoy (2014, 8), who argue for dislocating settler

futurities "as the central referent for the effectiveness of an interpretation, the viability of a theory, or the possibility of reinvisionings or reimaginations."

21. See Scott 1987 on the weapons of the weak.

22. See Sawyer 2004; Lu, Valdivia, and Silva 2016; Cepek 2018 for comprehensive accounts.

23. Auyero and Swistun 2009.

24. Coulthard 2007, 449.

25. Whereas it could be suggested that President Cartes would comply with the IACHR judgment to gain political advantage with Indigenous peoples or international actors, I refute such a claim. The repeated narrative by state officials in several top ministries and institutes that placed sole decision-making power in the president's hands and repeatedly delayed the process despite available resources suggests a more arbitrary process.

26. Fieldnotes, June 16, 2015.

27. Canova 2015.

28. Paola Canova's *Frontier Intimacies* (2020) is a powerful ethnography that reveals many nuances of Mennonite political influence in Paraguay's Chaco.

29. Ratzlaff 1999.

30. Appel, Anand, and Gupta 2018, 17.

31. Harvey 1990.

32. On the relationship between territory and temporality, see Radcliffe 1996; Sassen 2006; Smith 2013; Gordillo 2004, 2014; Anthias 2017; Li 2017; Smith and Vasudevan 2017; Lazala 2020; Gergan and McCreary 2022.

33. Povinelli 2011; Gordillo 2011.

34. Fieldnotes, July 7 2015.

35. Mezzadra and Neilson 2019.

36. Fieldnotes, July 6, 2015.

37. Nearly 90 percent of Paraguayans identify as Catholic (Latinobarometro 2018). See also Harder-Horst's *The Stroessner Regime and Indigenous Resistance in Paraguay* (2010) for a comprehensive analysis of the Catholic church and Indigenous rights movements in the country.

38. Harder-Horst 2010, 136–43.

39. "Papa ha'e paraguayo ijespíritu jara."

40. Fieldnotes, July 2, 2015.

41. Excerpt from a video recording, July 7, 2015.

42. The choqueo is an important an important dance many Indigenous peoples of the Maskoy language family practice. Men and women interlock arms to form a circle that surrounds a drummer who sings as the group dances in a slow rotation around him (the drummer and singer is always male).

43. Paraguayan law ensures the right to protest and will tolerate the preapproved closure of one lane of traffic.

44. Fieldnotes, July 10, 2015.

45. See Whyte 2018 on Indigenous environmental justice and Newell et al. 2021 on transformative justice.

46. Lu, Valdivia, and Da Silva 2017.

47. Gilio-Whitaker 2019; Estes 2019.

48. Perreault 2012.

49. Correia 2019c.

50. Drawing from L. B. Simpson's *As We Have Always Done* (2017), Daigle and Ramírez "theorize decolonial geographies as constellations in formation," highlighting the spatio-temporal and social heterogeneity of "the decolonial" (2019, 79).

51. Fieldnotes, July 8, 2017.

52. Daigle and Ramírez 2019, 82.

RUPTURE 6: SPECTACLE

1. Though a small organization, Tierraviva has played an outsized role in the area of Indigenous human rights advocacy in Paraguay. Several young lawyers and Indigenous advocates began their professional careers with Tierraviva to later transfer to positions within different NGOs working to advance human rights and social justice or to state agencies.

2. UltimaHora 2019.

3. Pellow (2018) and Pulido and De Lara (2018) both argue that critical environmental justice approaches must move beyond engaging the state as a site for justice but as a perpetrator of violence.

CONCLUSION: IN PURSUIT OF ENVIRONMENTAL JUSTICE

1. The statement was widely reported in Paraguayan and Brazilian media. An online article in UltimaHora (2014) contains a recording of the statement: "Usen y abusen del Paraguay porque es un momento importante de oportunidades."

2. The election of former Catholic bishop, Fernando Lugo, as president of Paraguay in 2008 was a historic rupture in the previous decades of Colorado Party political rule. Having campaigned on a platform with a strong focus on supporting Indigenous rights and addressing land reforms, Lugo garnered broad popular support and generated hope in lasting change. However, he immediately confronted structural challenges that limited his ability to enact his policy proposals. The Paraguayan Congress remained under Colorado Party control, something Lugo was never able to overcome to advance his agenda. Ultimately, Lugo's opposition curtailed any major changes to Indigenous affairs, and it is notable that the IACHR judgment on the Xákmok Kásek case was made during his administration, though no actions were taken to advance land restitution. Lugo was deposed by a coup in 2012, to be replaced in the following election by Horacio Cartes.

3. Jarratt-Snider and Nielson's (2020, 12) analysis of Indigenous and Native environmental justice in the United States informs my use of the phrase "de facto self-determination. "

4. As stated in the introduction, Harjo (2019, 30), whose work inspires my thinking on this point, defines futurity as "space, place, and temporality produced socially [that] invokes many other temporalities, other spaces, and yet-to-be possibilities."

5. See Guerrero 1991; De la Cadena 2000; Lyons 2006; Bobrow-Strain 2007; among others.

6. Wolford 2021. McKittrick's (2013) work has been pathbreaking in this area.

7. Galeano 1971; Mollett 2016; Speed 2017; Correia 2021a.

8. Coombes, Johnson, and Howitt 2012, 818.

9. I am not arguing against monetary reparations. Monetary reparations can be vitally important. But there is a risk that cash payments can be used to paper over deeper responsibilities for lasting justice processes. Monetary payments are often insufficient or create more harm after distribution within communities. The process matters. In the Yakye Axa, Sawhoyamaxa, and Xákmok Kásek cases, the IACHR recommended indemnity payments for undue loss of life. The process for determining what lives counted and what lives did not for such payment created anguish among each community. When payments were made, they were done to individuals, not the community. This created further pain and division in some cases because many people argued that the loss of life was not from one family but from the entire community. Yet the logic for indemnity in this context applied to a singular family. Finally, people in each community recounted stories that state officials arrived with huge sums of cash to pay victims' families with no support for how to manage such large sums of money. Only in Xákmok Kásek did the community devise a plan to use some of the funds for a collective good, whereas recipients in other communities reported to me that all the funds were quickly spent, leaving little in their wake beside greater inequities.

10. Some of the work that has influenced my approach in this arena is Carruthers 2008; Nixon 2011; Corntassel 2021; Tuck, McKenzie, and McCoy 2014; Martínez-Alier et al. 2016; Pellow 2018; Pulido and De Lara 2018; Whyte 2018; Álvarez and Coolsaet 2020; Coolsaet 2020; Sze 2020.

11. Kuehn 2000.

12. Star 2010. On decolonizing environmental justice studies, see Álvarez and Coolsaet 2020, 55.

13. McGregor, Whitaker, and Sritharan. 2020, 35.

14. See Carruthers 2008; Ranganathan 2017; Pulido and De Lara 2018; Whyte 2018, 2020; Newell et al. 2021; Sze 2020.

15. Schlosberg and Carruthers 2010.

16. Pellow 2018.

17. Here I think with Pellow's (2018) analysis of the prison, and life within it, as a site of environmental injustice as well as Gilmore's (2007) critique of ways that carcerality dehumanizes.

18. Ranganathan 2017.

19. Sze 2020, 68.

Abrego, L. J., and S. M. Lakhani. 2015. Incomplete inclusion: Legal violence and immigrants in liminal legal statues. *Law and Policy* 37: 265–93.

Agamben, G. 1995. *Homo Sacer: Sovereign Power and Bare Life*. Stanford, CA: Stanford University Press.

———. 2005. *State of Exception*. Chicago: University of Chicago Press.

Aikau, H. K. and H. K. Aikau. 2015. Following the Alaloa Kīapa of our ancestors: A trans-Indigenous futurity without the state (United States or otherwise). *American Quarterly* 67(3): 653–61.

Álvarez, L., and B. Coolsaet. 2020. Decolonizing environmental justice studies: A Latin American perspective. *Capitalism, Nature, Society* 31(2): 50–69.

Amnesty International. 2017. Situación actual de la comunidad indígena Yakye Axa. http://amnesty.org.py/situacion-actual-de-la-comunidad-indigena-yakye-axa/.

Anand, N., A. Gupta, and H. Appel. 2018. *The Promise of Infrastructure*. Durham, NC: Duke University Press.

Anaya, S. J., and C. Grossman. 2002. The case of *Awas Tingni v. Nicaragua*: A new step in the international law of Indigenous peoples. *Arizona Journal of International Comparative Law* 19(1): 1–15.

Anglican Church. 1979. Paraguayan Chaco Indian Colony: Project presented by the Anglican Church in Paraguay, November 1977. Asunción, Paraguay.

Anthias, P. 2014. The elusive promise of territory: An ethnographic case study of Indigenous land titling in the Bolivian Chaco. PhD dissertation, University of Cambridge.

———. 2018. *Limits to Decolonization: Indigeneity, Territory, and Hydrocarbon Politics in the Bolivian Chaco*. Ithaca, NY: Cornell University Press.

———. 2019. Ambivalent cartographies: Exploring the legacies of indigenous land titling through participatory mapping. *Critique of Anthropology* 39(2): 222–42.

Antkowiak, T.M. 2014. A dark side of virtue: The Inter-American Court and reparations for indigenous peoples. *Duke Journal of Comparative and International Law* 25(1): 1–80.

Asad, T. 2000. What do human rights do? An anthropological enquiry. *Theory & Event* 4(4). https://muse.jhu.edu/article/32601.

Asdal, K., T. Druglitrø, and S. Hinchliffe. 2017. *Humans, Animals and Biopolitics: The More-Than-Human Condition*. London: Routledge.

Asher, K. 2009. *Black and Green: Afro-Colombians, Development, and Nature in the Pacific Lowlands*. Durham, NC: Duke University Press.

Asociación Rural del Paraguay (ARP). n.d. La ganadería en el Paraguay: Historia, evolución y perspectivas. Presentation. https://www.arp.org.py/images/files/HISTORIA%20DE%20LA%20GANADAERIA%20PARAGUAYA%20PRESENTACION(1).pdf.

Auyero, J. 2012. *Patients of the State: The Politics of Waiting in Argentina*. Durham, NC: Duke University Press.

Auyero, J., and D.A. Swistun. 2009. *Flamable: Environmental Suffering in an Argentine Shantytown*. Oxford: Oxford University Press.

Ávila, C., and A. Portillo. 2018. Con las vacas hasta el cuello (pero con el estómago vacío). *Biodiversidad: Susteno y Culturas* 95(2): 17–21. http://www.biodiversidadla.org/Revista/95.

Ayala-Amarilla, Ó. 2014. Los derechos de los pueblos indígenas en tiempos de una impronta empresarial para el estado. In *Derechos Humanos en Paraguay 2014*, ed. E. Gauto Bozzano, S. Cáceres, and L. Battilana, 65–77. Asunción: Coordinadora del Derechos Humanos de Paraguay.

Barrios-Cáceres, M.J. 2018. Resulta imperativo revertir el patrón de muerte y amedrentamiento como respuesta a las reivindicaciones territoriales: Derechos de los pueblos indígenas. In *Derechos humanos en Paraguay 2018*, ed. Ó. Ayala Amarilla, R. Corvalán, and R. González, 53–66. Asunción: Coordinadora del Derechos Humanos de Paraguay.

Barros, C.J., A. Campos, and J. Griffin. 2018. Forced labor in Paraguay: The darkness at the bottom of the global supply chain. *The Guardian*, September 18, https://www.the-guardian.com/environment/2018/sep/18/forced-labour-in-paraguay-the-darkness-at-the-bottom-of-the-global-supply-chain.

Baumann, M., I. Gasparri, A. Buchadas, J. Oeser, P. Meyfroidt, C. Levers, A. Romero-Muñoz, Y.P. de Waroux, D. Müller, and T. Kuemmerle. 2022. Forest metrics for a process-based understanding of deforestation dynamics. *Environmental Research Letters* 17: 095010.

Beltran, G.A. 1991. *Regiones de refugio: El desarrollo de la comunidad y el proceso dominical en mestizoamérica*. Veracruz, Mexico: Universidad Veracruzana.

Benhabib, S. 2002. *The Claims of Culture: Equality and Diversity in the Global Era*. Princeton, NJ: Princeton University Press.

Berger, M., and C.C. Sineiro. 2012. *Environmental justice* in Latin America. Environmental Justice 5(2): 63–64.

Bessire, L. 2014. *Behold the Black Caiman: A Chronicle of Ayoreo Life*. Chicago: University of Chicago Press.

Bhandar, B. 2018. *The Colonial Lives of Property: Law, Land, and Racial Regimes of Ownership*. Durham, NC: Duke University Press.

Bhoola, U. 2017. Report of the Special Rapporteur on contemporary forms of slavery, including its causes and consequences on her mission to Paraguay. United Nations Human Rights Council, https://digitallibrary.un.org/record/1639596?ln=en.

Biermann, C., and R. M. Anderson. 2017. Conservation, biopolitics, and the governance of life and death. *Geography Compass* 11(10). https://doi.org/10.1111/gec3.12329.

Biermann, C., and B. Mansfield. 2014. Biodiversity, purity, and death: Conservation biology as biopolitics. *Environment and Planning D: Society and Space* 32(2): 257–73.

Blaser, M. 2010. *Storytelling Globalization from the Chaco and Beyond.* Durham, NC: Duke University Press.

Blaser, M., H. A. Feit, and G. McRae. 2004. *In the Way of Development: Indigenous Peoples, Life Projects, and Globalization.* London: Zed Books.

Bledsoe, A. 2019. Afro-Brazilian resistance to extractivism in the Bay of Aratu. *Annals of the American Association of Geographers* 109(2): 492–501.

Blomley, N. 2013. Performing property: Making the world. *Canadian Journal of Law and Jurisprudence* 26(1): 23–48.

Bobrow-Strain, A. 2007. *Intimate Enemies: Landowners, Power, and Violence in Chiapas.* Durham, NC: Duke University Press.

Bogado, M., R. Portillo, and R. Villagra. 2016. Alquiler de tierras y territorios indígenas en el Paraguay. *Cadernos do LEPAARQ (UFPEL)* 13(26): 106–23.

Bonifacio, V. 2013. Building up the collective: A critical assessment of the relationship between indigenous organizations and the international cooperation in the Paraguayan Chaco. *Social Anthropology* 21(4): 510–22.

———. 2017. *Del trabajo ajeno y vacas ariscas Puerto Casado: Genealogías (1886–2000).* Asunción: CEADUC.

Borras, S. M., J. C. Franco, S. Gómez, C. Kay, and M. Spoor. 2012. Land grabbing in Latin America and the Caribbean. *Journal of Peasant Studies* 39(3–4): 845–72.

Borras, S. M., J. C. Franco, S. R. Isakson, L. Levidow, and P. Vervest. 2016. The rise of flex crops and commodities: Implications for research. *Journal of Peasant Studies* 43(1): 93–115.

Braverman, I. 2016. *Animals, Biopolitics, Law: Lively Legalities.* London: Routledge.

Brown, L. A., and S. Strega. 2015. *Research as Resistance: Revisiting Critical, Indigenous, and Anti-Oppressive Approaches.* 2nd ed. Toronto: Canadian Scholars' Press.

Bryan, J. 2009. Where would we be without them? Knowledge, space and power in Indigenous politics. *Futures* 41(1): 24–32.

———. 2011. Walking the line: Participatory mapping, indigenous rights, and neoliberalism. *Geoforum* 42(1): 40–50.

———. 2012. Rethinking territory: Making sense of Latin America's territorial turn. *Geography Compass* 6(4): 215–26.

———. 2019. For Nicaragua's Indigenous communities, land rights in name only. *NACLA Report on the Americas* 51(1): 55–64.

Bryan, J., and D. Woods. 2015. *Weaponizing Maps: Indigenous Peoples and Counterinsurgency in the Americas.* New York: Guilford.

Bullard, R. D. 1990. *Dumping in Dixie: Race, Class, and Environmental Quality.* New York: Routledge.

———. 1993. Race and environmental justice in the United States. *Yale Journal of International Law* 18: 319–35.

———. 2020. From civil rights to Black Lives Matter. In *Lessons in Environmental Justice: From Civil Rights to Black Lives Matter and Idle No More*, ed. M. Mascarenhas, 2–18. Los Angeles: Sage.

Büscher, B., and R. Fletcher. 2020. *The Conservation Revolution: Radical Ideas for Saving Nature beyond the Anthropocene*. London: Verso.

Byrd, J. 2011. *Transit of Empire: Indigenous Critiques of Colonialism*. Minneapolis: University of Minnesota Press.

Byrd, J. A., A. Goldstein, J. Melamed, and C. Reddy. 2018. Predatory value: Economies of dispossession and disturbed relationalities. *Social Text 135* 36(2): 1–18.

Campbell, J. M. 2015. *Conjuring Property: Speculation and Environmental Futures in the Brazilian Amazon*. Seattle: University of Washington Press.

Canova, P. 2015. Los Ayoreo en las colonias mennonitas: Un análisis de un enclave agro-industrial en el Chaco Paraguayo. In *Capitalismo en las selvas: Enclaves e indígenas durante los siglos 19 y 20*, ed. F. Bossert, L. Cordoba, and L. Richard. San Pedro de Atacama, Chile: Ediciones del Desierto.

———. 2020. *Frontier Intimacies: Ayoreo Women and the Sexual Economy of the Paraguayan Chaco*. Austin: University of Texas Press.

Capek, S. M. 1993. The "environmental justice" frame: A conceptual discussion and an application. *Social Problems* 40(1): 5–24.

Cárdenas, R. 2012. Green multiculturalism: Articulations of ethnic and environmental politics in a Colombian "black community." *Journal of Peasant Studies* 39(2): 309–33.

Caretta, M. A., S. Zaragocín, B. Turley, and K. T. Orelleana. 2020. Women's organizing against extractivism: Toward a decolonial multi-sited analysis. *Human Geography* 13(1): 49–59.

Carruthers, D. 2008. *Environmental Justice in Latin America: Problems, Promise, and Practice*. Cambridge, MA: MIT Press.

Casanova, P. G. 1965. Internal colonialism and national development. *Studies in Comparative International Development* 1: 27–37.

Casey, T. T. 2020. Not in our lands: A Canadian comparative case study of Indigenous resistance strategies to natural resources development in British Colombia. In *Indigenous Environmental Justice*, ed. K. Jarratt-Snider and M. O. Nielsen, 160–78. Tucson: University of Arizona Press.

Castellón, I. I. 2021. Cancer alley and the fight against environmental racism. *Villanova Environmental Law Journal* 15: 15–43.

Chaco Sin Fronteras. 2019. "Pueblo Enxhet denuncia abandono por parte del estado." http://www.chacosinfronteras.com/2019/02/20/pueblo-enxhet-denuncia-abandono-por-parte-del-estado/.

Chacón, J. M. 2015. Producing legal liminality. *Denver University Law Review* 92(4): 709–67.

Chakrabarty, D. 2007. History and the politics of recognition. In *Manifestos for History*, ed. K. Jenkins, S. Morgan, and A. Munslow, 77–87. New York: Routledge.

Chapin, M., A. Lamb, and B. Threlkeld. 2005. Mapping indigenous lands. *Annual Review of Anthropology* 34(1): 619–38.

Chase-Sardi, M. 1972. The present situation of the Indians in Paraguay. In *The Situation of the Indian in South America*, ed. W. Dostal, 173–217. Geneva: World Council of Churches.

Chase-Sardi, M., A. Brun, and M. A. Enciso. 1990. *Situación sociocultural, económica, jurídico-política actual de las comunidades indígenas en el Paraguay*. Asunción: Centro Interdisciplinario de Derecho Social y Economía Política de la Universidad Católica.

Chase-Sardi, M., and A. Colombres. 1975. *Por la liberación del indígena: Compilación del Proyecto Marandú documentos y testimonios*. Buenos Aires: Editores del Sol.

Chávez, J. R. 2011. Aliens in their native lands: The persistence of internal colonial theory. *Journal of World History* 22(4): 785–809.

Chesterton, B. M. 2013. *The Grandchildren of Solano López: Frontier and Nation in Paraguay, 1904–1936*. Albuquerque: University of New Mexico Press.

Commission for Racial Justice. 1987. Toxic wastes and race in the United States: A national report on the racial and socio-economic characteristics of communities with hazardous waste sites. Commission for Racial Justice, United Church of Christ, New York.

Coolsaet, B. 2020. *Environmental Justice: Key Issues*. London: Routledge.

Coombes, B., J. T. Johnson, and R. Howitt. 2012. Indigenous geographies I: Mere resource conflicts? The complexities in Indigenous land and environmental claims. *Progress in Human Geography* 36(6): 810–21.

Coordinadora de Derechos Humanos del Paraguay. 2013. Situación de los derechos a la tierra y al territorio de los pueblos indígenas en el Paraguay. Asunción, Paraguay. http://www.tierraviva.org.py/archivo_biblioteca/situacion-de-los-derechos-a-la-tierra-y-al-territorio-de-los-pueblos-indigenas-en-paraguay/.

Córdoba, L., F. Bossert, and N. Richard. 2015. *Capitalismo en las selvas: Enclaves industrials en el Chaco y Amazonía indígenas (1850–1950)*. San Pedro de Atacama: Ediciones del Desierto.

Corntassel, J. 2012. Re-envisioning resurgence: Indigenous pathways to decolonization and sustainable self-determination. *Decolonization: Indigeneity, Education & Society* 1(1): 86–101.

Correia, J. E. 2018a. Adjudication and its aftereffects in three Inter-American Court cases brought before Paraguay: Indigenous land rights. *Erasmus Law Review* 11(1): 43–56.

———. 2018b. Indigenous rights at a crossroads: Territorial struggles, the Inter-American Court of Human Rights, and legal geographies of liminality. *Geoforum* 97: 73–83.

———. 2019a. Arrested infrastructure: Roadwork, rights, racialized geographies. *Roadsides* 2: 14–24.

———. 2019b. Soy states: Resource politics, violent environments and soybean territorialization in Paraguay. *Journal of Peasant Studies* 46(2): 316–36.

———. 2019c. Unsettling territory: Indigenous mobilizations, the territorial turn, and the limits of land rights in the Paraguay-Brazil borderlands. *Journal of Latin American Geography* 18(1): 11–37.

———. 2021a. All the land was stolen: Investigating the aporia of justice through countertopographies of Indigenous land rights and settler colonialism across the Americas. In *The Handbook of Space, Place, and Law*, ed. R. Bartel and J. Carter, 38–48. London: Edward Elgar.

———. 2021b. Infrastructures of settler colonialism: Geographies of violence, Indigenous labor, and marginal resistance in Paraguay's Chaco. In *Reimagining the Gran Chaco: Contemporary Perspectives on Identities, Politics and the Environment in Argentina,*

Bolivia and Paraguay, ed. S. Hirsch, P. Canova, and M. Biocca, 166–85. Gainesville: University Press of Florida.

———. 2022. Between flood and drought: Environmental racism, settler waterscapes, and Indigenous water justice in South America's Chaco. *Annals of the American Association of Geographers* 112(7): 1890–1910.

Corte Suprema de Justicia. 2003. *Digesto normativo sobre pueblos indígenas en el Paraguay: Historia de la legislación 1811–2003.* Asunción: Corte Suprema de Justicia, División de Investigación, Legislación y Publicaciones.

Costa, W. 2019. Past weighs heavy as Paraguay struggles with ghosts of dictatorship. *The Guardian*, December 10. https://www.theguardian.com/world/2019/dec/10/paraguay -dictator-alfredo-stroessner-dictatorship.

Coulthard, G. 2007. Subjects of empire: Indigenous peoples and the "politics of recognition" in Canada. *Contemporary Political Theory* (6): 437–60.

———. 2014. *Red Skin, White Masks: Rejecting the Colonial Politics of Recognition.* Minneapolis: University of Minnesota Press.

Cruz-Rodríquez, E. 2017. Justicia ambiental, justicia ecológica y diálogo intercultural. *Elementos* 105: 9–16.

Cusicanqui, S. R. 2010. The notion of "rights" and the paradoxes of postcolonial modernity: Indigenous peoples and women in Bolivia. *Qui Parle* 18(2): 29–54.

Daigle, M., and M. M. Ramírez. 2018. Decolonial geographies. In *Keywords in Radical Geography: Antipode at 50,* ed. T. Jazeel et al., 78–84. London: Wiley-Blackwell.

Daniels, M. 1916. *Makers of South America.* New York: Missionary Education Movement of the United States and Canada.

De la Cadena, M. 2000. *Indigenous Mestizos: The Politics of Race and Culture in Cuzco, Peru, 1919–1991.* Durham, NC: Duke University Press.

De Leeuw, S., and S. Hunt. 2018. Unsettling decolonizing geographies. *Geography Compass.* https://doi.org/10.1111/gec3.12376.

Deloria, V., Jr. 1988. *Custer Died for Your Sins.* Rev. ed. Norman: University of Oklahoma Press.

Derrida, J. [1992] 2002. Force of law: The "mystical foundation of authority." In *Jacques Derrida: Acts of Religion,* ed. D. Cornell, M. Rosenfeld, and D. Gray, 3–67. New York: Routledge.

Dhillon, J. 2018. Introduction: Indigenous resurgence, decolonization, and movements for environmental justice. *Environment and Society: Advances in Research* 9(1): 1–5.

Dirección General de Estadística, Ecuestas y Censos (DEEGC). 2012. Pueblos indígenas en el Paraguay: Resultados finales de población y viviendas 2012. https://www.ine.gov .py/Publicaciones/Biblioteca/indigena2012/Pueblos%20indigenas%20en%20el%20 Paraguay%20Resultados%20Finales%20de%20Poblacion%20y%20Viviendas%202012.pdf.

———. 2018. Paraguay: Proyecciones de población nacional, áreas urbana y rural, por sexo y edad, 2018. https://www.ine.gov.py/Publicaciones/Biblioteca/proyeccion%20nacional /Paraguay_Triptico_2019.pdf.

EFE. 2019. La izquierda paraguaya pide investigar al banco del expresidente Horacio Cartes. https://www.efe.com/efe/america/economia/la-izquierda-paraguaya-pide-investigar -al-banco-del-expresidente-horacio-cartes/20000011–3981761.

Eide, A. 2009. The Indigenous peoples, the working group of Indigenous populations and the adoption of the UN Declaration on the Rights of Indigenous Peoples. In *Making the*

Declaration Work, ed. C. Charters and R. Stavenhagen, 32–47. Copenhagen: International Work Group for Indigenous Affairs.

Engle, K. 2010. *The Elusive Promise of Indigenous Development: Rights, Culture, Strategy.* Durham, NC: Duke University Press.

Englert, S. 2020. Settlers, workers, and the logic of accumulation by dispossession. *Antipode* 52(6): 1647–66.

Escobar, A. 2008. *Territories of Difference: Place, Movements, Life, Redes.* Durham, NC: Duke University Press.

ESCR-Net. 2016. Case of the Sawhoyamaxa Indigenous community v. Paraguay. https://www.escr-net.org/caselaw/2013/case-sawhoyamaxa-Indigenous-community-v-paraguay.

Estes, N. 2019. *Our History Is the Future: Standing Rock versus the Dakota Access Pipeline and the Long Tradition of Indigenous Resistance.* London: Verso.

Every, E. F. 1915. *The Anglican Church in South America.* London: Society for Promoting Christian Knowledge. https://archive.org/details/anglicanchurchinooeveruoft.

Ezquerro-Cañete, A. 2016. Poisoned, dispossessed and excluded: A critique of the neoliberal soy regime in Paraguay. *Journal of Agrarian Change* 16(4): 702–10.

———. 2020. The agrarian question of extractive capital: Political economy, rural change, and peasant struggle in 21st Century Paraguay. PhD dissertation, Saint Mary's University.

Fanon, F. [1952] 2008. *Black Skin, White Masks.* New York: Grove Press.

———. [1963] 2004. *The Wretched of the Earth.* New York: Grove Press.

Farcau, B. W. 1996. *The Chaco War: Bolivia and Paraguay, 1932–1935.* Westport, CT: Praeger.

Farmer, P. 1996. On suffering and structural violence: A view from below. *Daedalus* 125(1): 261–83.

Foucault, M. 2000. "Governmentality." In *Power*, ed. J. D. Faubion, 201–22. New York: New Press.

———. [2004] 2007. *Security, Territory, Population: Lectures at the Collége de France 1977–1978.* Trans. Graham Burchell. New York: Picador Palgrave.

Friesen, M. W. 2016. *Nuevo hogar en el inhóspito Chaco.* Asunción: Departamento de Historia Loma Plata—Colonia Menno.

Galemba, R. B. 2013. Illegality and invisibility at margins and borders. *PoLAR: Political and Legal Anthropology Review* 36(2): 274–85.

Galeana, F. 2020. Legitimating the state and the social movement: Clientelism, brokerage, and collective land rights in Honduras. *Journal of Latin American Geography* 19(4): 11–42.

Galeano, E. 1971. *Las veinas abiertas de América Latina.* Madrid: Siglo XXI.

Galeano, L. A. 2012. Paraguay and the expansion of Brazilian and Argentinean agribusiness frontiers. *Canadian Journal of Development Studies* 33(4): 458–70.

Galtung, J. 1969. Violence, peace, and peace research. *Journal of Peace Research* 6(3): 167–91.

Garavito, C. R., and C. Kauffman. 2015. De las órdenes a la práctica: Análisis y estrategias para el cumplimiento de las decisions del sistema interamericano de derechos humanos. In *Desafíos del sistema interamericano de derechos humanos: Nuevos tiempos, viejos retos*, ed. M. Rojas, 267–318. Bogotá: Colección Dejusticia.

Garay Caballero, H. 2015. Plazas de Asunción: Antes y despúes de las rejas. *ABC Color*, April 21. https://www.abc.com.py/nacionales/antes-y-despues-de-las-rejas-1358798.html.

Gergan, M. D., and T. McCreary. 2022. Disrupting infrastructures of colonial hydro-modernity: Lepcha and Dakelh struggles against temporal and territorial displacements. *Annals of the American Association of Geographers* 112(3): 789–98.

Gibbings, J. 2016. "The shadow of slavery": Historical time, labor, and citizenship in nineteenth-century Alta Verapaz, Guatemala. *Hispanic American Historical Review* 96(1): 73–107.

Gilbert, J. 2016. *Indigenous Peoples' Land Rights under International Law*. Leiden: Brill Nijhoff.

Gilio-Whitaker, D. 2019. *As Long as the Grass Grows: The Indigenous Fight for Environmental Justice from Colonization to Standing Rock*. Boston: Beacon.

Gilmore, R. W. 2007. *Golden Gulag: Prisons, Surplus, Crisis, and Opposition In Globalizing California*. Berkeley: University of California Press.

———. 2011. What is to be done? *American Quarterly* 63(2): 245–65.

Glauser, M., and R. Villagra-Carrón. 2021. Procesos de despojo y re-territorialización contemporáneos de los Pueblos Ava Guaraní, Mbya Guaraní y los Paĩ Tavyterã de la región. *Revista de Estudios & Pesquisas sobre as Américas* 14(3): 103–40.

Global Witness. n.d. Land and environmental defenders: Annual report archive. https://www.globalwitness.org/en/campaigns/environmental-activists/land-and-environmental-defenders-annual-report-archive/.

Gonzales, T., and M. González. 2015. Introduction: Indigenous peoples and autonomy in Latin America. *Latin American and Caribbean Ethnic Studies* 10(1): 1–9.

Gordillo, G. 2004. *Landscape of Devils: Tensions of Place and Memory in the Argentinean Chaco*. Durham, NC: Duke University Press.

———. 2011. Longing for elsewhere: Guaraní reterritorializations. *Comparative Studies in Society and History* 53(4): 855–81.

———. 2014. *Rubble: The Afterlife of Destruction*. Durham, NC: Duke University Press.

Gordillo, G., and S. Hirsch. 2003. Indigenous struggles and contested identities in Argentina: Histories of invisibilization and reemergence. *Journal of Latin American Anthropology* 8(3): 4–30.

———. 2010. La presencia ausente: Invisibilizaciones, políticas estatales y emergencías indígenas en la Argentina. In *Movílizaciones indígenas e identidades en disputa en la Argentina*, ed. G. Gordillo and S. Hirsch, 15–38. Buenos Aires: La Crujía.

Graham, L. M., and S. Wiessner. 2011. Indigenous sovereignty, culture, and international human rights law. *South Atlantic Quarterly* 110(2): 403–27.

Grandin, G. 2006. *Empire's Workshop: Latin America, the United States, and the Rise of the New Imperialism*. New York: Owl Books.

———. 2011. *The Last Colonial Massacre: Latin America in the Cold War*. Chicago: University of Chicago Press.

Grossman, C. 2001. *Awas Tingni v. Nicaragua*: A landmark case for the Inter-American System. *Human Rights Brief* 8(3): 2–4, 8.

Grubb, W. B. 1911. *An Unknown People in an Unknown Land: An Account of the Life and Customs of the Lengua Indians of the Paraguayan Chaco, with Adventures and Experiences Met with during Twenty Years' Pioneering and Exploration amongst Them*. Ed. H. T. M. Jones. London: Seeley, Service & Co.

———. 1914. *A Church in the Wilds: The Remarkable Story of the Establishment of the South American Mission amongst the Hitherto Savage and Intractable Natives of the Paraguayan Chaco*. Ed. H. T. M. Jones. London: Seeley, Service & Co.

Guerrero, A. 1991. *La semantica de la dominación: El concertaje de indios.* Quito, Ecuador: Libri Mundi.

Guevara, M. A., and M. Rehnfeldt. 2013. Bank owned by Paraguay's leading presidential candidate linked to tax haven. International Consortium of Investigative Journalists. https://www.icij.org/investigations/offshore/bank-owned-paraguays-leading-presi dential-candidate-linked-tax-haven/.

Gupta, A. 2012. *Red Tape: Bureaucracy, Structural Violence, and Poverty in India.* Durham, NC: Duke University Press.

Gustafson, B. 2009. *New Languages of the State: Indigenous Resurgence and the Politics Of Knowledge in Bolivia.* Durham, NC: Duke University Press.

———. 2020. *Bolivia in the Age of Gas.* Durham, NC: Duke University Press.

Haglund, L., and R. Stryker. 2015. Making sense of the multiple and complex pathways by which human rights are realized. In *Closing the Rights Gap: From Human Rights to Social Transformation,* ed. L. Haglund and R. Stryker, 28–62. Oakland: University of California Press.

Hale, C. R. 2004. Rethinking indigenous politics in the era of the "indio permitido." *NACLA Report on the Americas* 38(2): 16–21.

———. 2005. Neoliberal multiculturalism: The remaking of cultural rights and racial dominance in Central America. *PoLAR: Political and Legal Anthropology Review* 28(1): 10–28.

———. 2006. *Más que un indio (more than an indian): Racial ambivalence and neoliberal multiculturalism in Guatemala.* Santa Fe, NM: School of American Research Press.

———. 2011. Resistencia para que? Territory, autonomy and neoliberal entanglements in the "empty spaces" of Central America. *Economy and Society* 40(2): 184–210.

———. 2020. Using and refusing the law: Indigenous struggles and legal strategies after neoliberalism. *American Anthropologist* 122: 618–31.

Hall, S. 1986. The problem of ideology: Marxism without guarantees. *Journal of Communication Inquiry* 10(2): 28–44.

———. [1992] 2019. The West and the rest: Discourse and power. In *Essential Essays,* vol. 2: *Identity and Diaspora,* ed. D. Morley, 141–84. Durham, NC: Duke University Press.

Harder-Horst, R. D. 2010. *The Stroessner Regime and Indigenous Resistance in Paraguay.* Gainesville: University Press of Florida.

Harjo, L. 2019. *Spiral to the Stars: Mvskoke Tools of Futurity.* Tucson: University of Arizona Press.

Harvey, D. 1990. *The Condition of Post-Modernity: An Enquiry into the Origins of Cultural Change.* Cambridge: Blackwell.

Hetherington, K. 2011. *Guerrilla Auditors: The Politics of Transparency in Neoliberal Paraguay.* Durham, NC: Duke University Press.

———. 2014. Waiting for the surveyor: Development promises and the temporality of infrastructure. *Journal of Latin American and Caribbean Anthropology* 19(2): 195–211.

———. 2018. Peasants, experts, clients, and soybeans: The fixing of Paraguay's civil service. *Current Anthropology* 59(18): 171–81.

———. 2020. *The Government of Beans: Regulating Life in the Age of Monocrops.* Durham, NC: Duke University Press.

Hillebrecht, C. 2012. The domestic mechanisms of compliance with international human rights law: Case studies from the Inter-American Human Rights System. *Human Rights Quarterly* 32(4): 959–85.

Holloway, L., C. Bear, and K. Wilkinson. 2014. Re-capturing bovine life: Robot-cow relationships, freedom and control in dairy farming. *Journal of Rural Studies* 33: 131–40.

Huang, C., et al. 2007. Rapid loss of Paraguay's Atlantic Forest and the status of protected areas—a Landsat assessment. *Remote Sensing of Environment* 106(4): 460–66.

Hunt, R. J. 1933. *The Livingstone of South America: The Life and Adventures of W. Barbrooke Grubb among the Wild Tribes of the Gran Chaco in Paraguay, Bolivia, Argentina, the Falkland Islands, and Tierra del Fuego.* London: Seely Service & Co.

Ibars, M. M. 2004. *Karú rekó: Antropología culinaria paraguaya.* Asunción: Servilibro.

Inter-American Commission on Human Rights (IACHR). 2007. Report 55/07 Petition 987–04 Admissibility Kelyenmagategma indigenous community members of the Enxet-Lengua people and its members. Paraguay, July 24. http://cidh.org/annualrep/2007eng/Paraguay987.04eng.htm.

Inter-American Court of Human Rights. 2005. Case of the Yakye Axa Indigenous Community v. Paraguay: Judgment of June 17, 2005 (Merits, Reparations, and Costs). http://www.corteidh.or.cr/docs/casos/articulos/seriec_125_ing.pdf.

———. 2006. Case of the Sawhoyamaxa Indigenous Community v. Paraguay: Judgment of March 29, 2006 (Merits, Reparations, and Costs). http://www.corteidh.or.cr/docs/casos/articulos/seriec_146_ing.pdf.

———. 2010. Case of the Xákmok Kásek Indigenous Community v. Paraguay: Judgment of August 24, 2010 (Merits, Reparations, and Costs). http://www.corteidh.or.cr/docs/casos/articulos/seriec_214_ing.pdf.

———. 2017. Resolución de la Corte Interamericana de Derechos Humanos de 30 de Agosto de 2017: Casos de las comunidades indígenas Yakye Axa, Sawhoyamaxa, y Xákmok Kásek vs. Paraguay—Supervisión de cumplimiento de sentencias. http://www.corteidh.or.cr/docs/supervisiones/3casosparaguayos_30_08_17.pdf.

International Justice Resource Center. 2014. Preventing and remedying human rights violations through the international framework advocacy before the Inter-American System: A manual for attorneys and advocates. http://ijrcenter.org/wp-content/uploads/2014/03/Manual-Advocacy-before-the-Inter-American-System-2014.pdf.

International Work Group for Indigenous Affairs (IWGIA). 1971. Declaration of Barbados. https://www.iwgia.org/en/resources/publications/305-books/2644-declaration-of-barbados.html.

Jackson, J. E. 2020. *Managing multiculturalism: Indigeneity and the struggle for rights in Colombia.* Stanford: Stanford University Press.

Jackson, J. E., and K. B. Warren. 2012. Indigenous movements in Latin America, 1992–2004: Controversies, ironies, new directions. *Annual Review of Anthropology* (34): 549–73.

Jarratt-Snider, K., and M. O. Nielsen. 2020. *Indigenous Environmental Justice.* Tucson: University of Arizona Press.

Kalisch, H., and E. Unruh. 2018. *¡No llores! La historia enlhet de la guerra del Chaco.* Asunción & Ya'alve-Saanga: Museo del Barro, Nengvaanemkeskama Nempayvaam Enlhet, and ServiLibro.

Kidd, S. W. 1992. A case-study amongst the Enxet of the Paraguayan Chaco. MA thesis, Durham University.

———. 1995. Land, politics and benevolent shamanism: The Enxet Indians in a democratic Paraguay. *Journal of Latin American Studies* 27(1): 43–75.

———. 1997. Paraguay: The working conditions of the Enxet indigenous people of the Chaco. In *Enslaved Peoples in the 1990s: Indigenous Peoples, Debt Bondage and Human Rights*, 153–81. Copenhagen: Anti-Slavery International and International Working Group on Indigenous Affairs.

———. 2021. *Love and Its Entanglements among the Enxet of Paraguay: Social and Kinship Relations within a Market Economy*. Lanham, MD: Rowman & Littlefield.

King, T. L. 2020. *The Black Shoals: Offshore Formations of Black and Native Studies*. Durham, NC: Duke University Press.

Kleinpenning, J. M. G. 2003. *Rural Paraguay 1870–1963: A Geography of Progress, Plunder and Poverty*. Madrid: Iberoamericana/Vervuert.

Kovach, M. 2010. Conversational method in indigenous research. *First Peoples Chile Family Health Review* 5(1): 40–48.

———. 2021. *Indigenous Methodologies: Characteristics, Conversations, and Contexts*. 2nd ed. Toronto: University of Toronto Press.

Kuehn, R. R. 2000. A taxonomy of environmental justice. *Environmental Law Reporter* 30: 10681–10703.

LaDuke, W. 1999. *All our Relations: Native Struggles for Land and Life*. Boston: South End Press.

Lambert, P. 1996. *The Regime of Alfredo Stroessner*. Westport, CT: Greenwood Press.

Larkin, B. 2013. The politics and poetics of infrastructure. *Annual Review of Anthropology* (42): 327–43.

Larsen, S. C., and J. T. Johnson. 2017. *Being Together in Place: Indigenous Coexistence in a More Than Human World*. Minneapolis: University of Minnesota Press.

Latinobarometro. 2018. "Religión." Database. https://www.latinobarometro.org/latOnline .jsp.

Lazala, Y. 2020. Spatiality, temporality and ontology: Constraints for the restitution of Indigenous peoples' territorial rights in Colombia. *Alternatus* 7(1): 47–61.

Leake, A. P. 1998. Subsistence and land-use amongst resettled indigenous people in the Paraguayan Chaco: A participatory approach. PhD dissertation, University of Hertfordshire.

Leguizamón, A. 2020. *Seeds of Power: Environmental Injustice and Genetically Modified Soybeans in Argentina*. Durham, NC: Duke University Press.

Lennox, C., and D. Short. 2016. Introduction to *Handbook of Indigenous Peoples' Rights*, ed. C. Lennox and D. Short, 1–11. London: Routledge.

Li, T. M. 2000. Articulating indigenous identity in Indonesia: Resource politics and the tribal slot. *Comparative Studies in Society and History* 42(1): 149–79.

———. 2007. *The Will to Improve: Governmentality, Development, and the Practice of Politics*. Durham, NC: Duke University Press.

———. 2010. To make live or let die? Rural dispossession and the protection of surplus populations. *Antipode* 41(s1): 66–93.

———. 2014. What is land? Assembling a resource for global investment. *Transactions of the Institute of British Geographers* 39(4): 589–602.

———. 2017. Rendering land investible: Five notes on time. *Geoforum* 82: 276–78.

Liboiron, M. 2021. *Pollution Is Colonialism*. Durham, NC: Duke University Press.

Locke, J. [1698] 1963. *Two Treatises of Government*. Cambridge: Cambridge University Press.

Loperena, C. 2016. Radicalize multiculturalism? Garifuna activism and the double-bind of participation in postcoup Honduras. *Journal of Latin American and Caribbean Anthropology* 21: 517–38.

Lorimer, J., and C. Driessen. 2013. Bovine biopolitics and the promise of monsters in the rewilding of Heck cattle. *Geoforum* 48: 249–59.

Louis, R. P. 2007. Can you hear us now? Voices from the margin: Using Indigenous methodologies in geographic research. Aboriginal Policy Research Consortium International. Paper 175. http://ir.lib.uwo.ca/aprci/175.

Lovera, M., and I. Franceschelli. 2019. De un toro y siete vacas a una oligarquía y 15 millones de vacas. Global Forest Coalition and Heñoi. https://globalforestcoalition.org/wp-content/uploads/2019/11/Paraguay-case-study-ES.

Lu, F., G. Valdivia, and N. L. Silva. 2017. *Oil, Revolution, and Indigenous Citizenship in the Ecuadorian Amazon*. New York: Palgrave Macmillan.

Lund, C. 2016. Rule and rupture: State formation through the production of property and citizenship. *Development and Change* 47(6): 1199–1228.

Lyons, B. J. 2006. *Remembering the Hacienda: Religion, Authority, and Social Change in Highland Ecuador*. Austin: University of Texas Press.

Mallon, F. E. 2005. *Courage Tastes of Blood: The Mapuche Community of Nicolás Ailío and the Chilean State, 1906–2001*. Durham, NC: Duke University Press.

Martin, A., and J. P. Spinetto. 2016. Can Paraguay escape decades of despotism, ineptitude, and corruption? *Bloomberg*, March 22. https://www.bloomberg.com/features/2016-paraguay-president-horacio-cartes/.

Martínez-Alier, J. 1997. Justiçia ambiental (local e global). *A Trabe de Ouro: Publicación Galega de Pensamento Crítico* 31: 73–86.

———. 2008. Conflictos ecológicos y justicia ambiental. *Papeles* 103: 11–27.

Martínez-Alier, J., L. Tember, D. Del Bene, and A. Scheidel. 2016. Is there a global environmental justice movement? *Journal of Peasant Studies* 43(3): 731–55.

Martínez-Novo, C. 2005. *Who Defines Indigenous? Identities, Development, Intellectuals, and the State in Northern Mexico*. New Brunswick, NJ: Rutgers University Press.

———. 2018. Ventriloquism, racism and the politics of decoloniality in Ecuador. *Cultural Studies* 32(3) 389–413.

———. 2021. *Undoing Multiculturalism: Resource Extraction and Indigenous Rights in Ecuador*. Princeton, NJ: Princeton University Press.

Martínez-Novo, C., and P. Shlossberg. 2018. Introduction: Lasting and resurgent racism after recognition in Latin America. *Cultural Studies* 32(3): 349–63.

Marx, K. [1867] 1976. *Capital Volume 1: A Critique of Political Economy*. Trans. B. Fowkes. New York: Penguin Classics.

Massachusetts Institute of Technology (MIT). n.d. Observatory of economic complexity. https://atlas.media.mit.edu/en/profile/country/pry/.

Mbembe, J. 2003. Necropolitics. Trans. L. Meintjes. *Public Culture* 15(1): 11–40.

———. 2019. *Necropolitics*. Durham, NC: Duke University Press.

McGregor, D. 2018. Reconciliation and environmental justice. *Journal of Global Ethics* 14(2): 222–31.

McGregor, D., S. Whitaker, and M. Sritharan. 2020. Indigenous environmental justice and sustainability. *Current Opinion in Environmental Sustainability* 43: 35–40.

McGurty, E. M. 2010. Warren County, NJ, and the emergence of the environmental justice movement: Unlikely coalitions and shared meanings in local collective action. *Society and Natural Resources* 13(4): 373–87.

McKittrick, K. 2011. On plantations, prisons, and a black sense of place. *Social & Cultural Geography* 12(8): 947–63.

———. 2013. Plantation futures. *Small Axe* 17(42): 1–15.

McSherry, J. P. 2005. *Predatory States: Operation Condor and Covert War in Latin America.* New York: Rowman & Littlefield.

Medina, L. K. 2016. The production of Indigenous land rights: Judicial decisions across national, regional, and global scales. *Political and Legal Anthropology Review* 39: 139–53.

Melamed, J. 2015. Racial capitalism. *Critical Ethnic Studies* 1(1): 76–85.

Menjívar, C. 2006. Liminal legality: Salvadoran and Guatemalan immigrants' lives in the United States. *American Journal of Sociology* 11(4): 999–1037.

Menton, M., C. Larrea, and J. Martinez-Alier et al. 2020. Environmental justice and the SGDs: From synergies to gaps and contradictions. *Sustainability Science.* https://doi .org/10.1007/s11625-020-00789-8.

Mezzadra, S., and B. Neilson. 2019. *The Politics of Operations: Excavating Contemporary Capitalism.* Durham, NC: Duke University Press.

Middeldorp, N., and P. Le Billon. 2019. Deadly environmental governance: Authoritarianism, eco-populism, and the repression of environmental and land defenders. *Annals of the American Association of Geographers* 109: 324–37.

Ministerio de Agricultura y Ganadería. 2019. Serie histórica: Cantidad de cabezas de ganado vacuno por departamento. http://www.mag.gov.py/datos/index-serie-vacuno .html#listado#arriba.

Mohai, P., D. Pellow, and J. T. Roberts. 2009. Environmental justice. *Annual Review of Environmental Resources* 34: 405–30.

Mollett, S. 2013. Mapping deception: The politics of mapping Miskito and Garifuna space in Honduras. *Annals of the American Association of Geographers* 103(5): 1227–41.

———. 2016. The power to plunder: Rethinking land grabbing in Latin America. *Antipode* 48(2): 412–32.

———. 2018. The Río Plátano Biosphere Reserve: A postcolonial feminist political ecological reading of violence and territorial struggles in Honduras. In *Land Rights, Biodiversity Conservation, and Justice: Rethinking Parks and People,* ed. S. Mollett and T. Kepe, 184–205. London: Routledge.

Moore, D. 2005. *Suffering for Territory: Race, Place, and Power in Zimbabwe.* Durham, NC: Duke University Press.

Moreton-Robinson, A. 2015. *The White Possessive: Property, Power, and Indigenous Sovereignty.* Durham, NC: Duke University Press.

Morgensen, S. L. 2009. Un-settling settler desires. In *Reflections and Resources for Deconstructing Colonial Mentality,* ed. Unsettling Minnesota Collective, 157–58. https://unsett lingminnesota.org/.

———. 2011. The biopolitics of settler colonialism: Right here, right now. *Settler Colonial Studies* 1(1): 52–76.

Muehlmann, S. 2009. How do real Indians fish? Neoliberal multiculturalism and contested indigeneities in the Colorado Delta. *American Anthropologist* 111 (4): 468–79.

————. 2013. *Where the River Ends: Contested Indigeneity in the Mexican Colorado River Delta*. Durham, NC: Duke University Press.

Münzel, M. 1973. *The Aché Indians: Genocide in Paraguay*. International Working Group on Indigenous Affairs Document No. 17. Copenhagen: International Working Group for Indigenous Affairs.

Murdock, E. G. 2020. A history of environmental justice: Foundations, narratives, and perspectives. In *Environmental Justice Key Issues*, ed. B. Coolsaet, 6–17. London: Routledge.

Nagel, B. 1999. Unleashing the fury: The cultural discourse of rural violence and land rights in Paraguay. *Comparative Studies in Society and History* 41 (1): 148–81.

Nally, D. 2010. The biopolitics of food provisioning. *Transactions of the Institute of British Geographies* 36(1): 37–53.

National Service for Animal Quality and Health (SENACSA). 2020a. Categorías de bovinos en existencia según tenedores de ganado por estrato. Año 2020. Report. https://www.senacsa.gov.py/application/files/1216/0009/0656/Avances_Estadistica_2020–04.pdf.

————. 2020b. Tenedores de ganado, establecimientos y población bovina por departamento: 1er periodo—Año 2020. Report. https://www.senacsa.gov.py/application/files/2816/0009/0653/Avances_Estadistica_2020–01.pdf.

Nelson, P. J., and E. Doresy. 2018. Who practices rights-based development? A progress report on the work at the nexus of human rights and development. *World Development* 104: 97–107.

Nemser, D. 2017. *Infrastructures of Race: Concentration and Biopolitics in Colonial Mexico*. Austin: University of Texas Press.

Newell, P., S. Srivastava, L. O. Naess, G. A. Torres Contreras, and R. Price. 2021. Toward transformative climate justice: An emerging research agenda. *WIRES Climate Change*. DOI: https://doi.org/10.1002/woc.733.

Ng'weno, B. 2007. *Turf Wars: Territory and Citizenship in the Contemporary State*. Stanford, CA: Stanford University Press.

Nichols, R. 2020. *Theft Is Property! Dispossession and Critical Theory*. Durham, NC: Duke University Press.

Nickson, R. A. 1988. Tyranny and longevity: Stroessner's Paraguay. *Third World Quarterly* 10(1): 237–59.

Niezen, R. 2003. *The Origins of Indigenism: Human Rights and the Politics of Identity*. Oakland: University of California Press.

Nixon, R. 2011. *Slow Violence and the Environmentalism of the Poor*. Cambridge, MA: Harvard University Press.

Offen, K. H. 2003. The territorial turn: Making black territories in Pacific Colombia. *Journal of Latin American Geography* 2: 43–73.

Oliva, P. 2011. El privilegio de ser vaca. https://paioliva.blogspot.com/2011/10/el-privilegio-de-ser-vaca.html.

Olive, A., and A. Rabe. 2016. Indigenous environmental justice: Comparing the United States and Canada's legal frameworks for endangered species conservation. *American Review of Canadian Studies* 46(4): 496–512.

Open Society Justice Initiative. 2017. Strategic litigation impacts on indigenous land rights. Report. Open Society Foundations, New York.

Organization of American States (OAS). 2017. Resolución de la Corte Interamericana de Derechos Humanos de 30 de Agosto de 2017. Casos de las comunidades indígenas Yakye Axa, Sawhoyamaxa, y Xákmok Kásek vs. Paraguay. Supervisión de cumplimento de sentencias. http://www.corteidh.or.cr/docs/supervisiones/3casosparaguayos_30_08 _17.pdf.

Palau, M., A. Wehrle, E. Díaz-Peña, G. Ortega, I. Franceschelli., J. Villalba Digalo, and L. Rojas Villagra, et al. 2015. Con la soja al cuello. Report. Base Investigaciones Sociales, Asunción.

Paschel, T. S. 2016. *Becoming Black Political Subjects: Movements and Ethno-Racial Rights in Colombia and Brazil.* Princeton, NJ: Princeton University Press.

Pasternak, S. 2014. Jurisdiction and settler colonialism: Where do laws meet? *Canadian Journal of Law and Society* 29(2): 145–61.

———. 2020. Assimilation and partition: How settler colonialism and racial capitalism co-produce the borders of Indigenous economies. *South Atlantic Quarterly* 119(2): 301–24.

Pellow, D. 2016. Toward a critical environmental justice studies: Black Lives Matter as an environmental justice challenge. *Du Bois Review* 13 (2): 221–36.

———. 2017. *What Is Critical Environmental Justice?* Cambridge: Polity.

Peloso, V. C. 1999. *Peasants on Plantations: Subaltern Strategies of Labor and Resistance in the Pisco Valley, Peru.* Durham, NC: Duke University Press.

Perreault, T. 2012. Dispossession by accumulation? Mining, water and the nature of enclosure on the Bolivian Altiplano. *Antipode* 45(5): 1050–69.

———. 2015. Performing participation: Mining, power, and the limits of public consultation in Bolivia. *Journal of Latin American and Caribbean Anthropology* 20(3): 433–51.

Postero, N. 2007. *Now We Are Citizens: Indigenous Politics in Postmulticultural Bolivia.* Stanford, CA: Stanford University Press.

———. 2017. *The Indigenous State: Race, Politics, and Performance in Plurinational Bolivia.* Oakland: University of California Press.

Povinelli, E. 1998. The state of shame: Australian multiculturalism and the crisis of indigenous citizenship. *Critical Inquiry* 24(2): 575–610.

———. 2002. *The Cunning of Recognition: Indigenous Alterities and the Making of Australian Multiculturalism.* Durham, NC: Duke University Press.

———. 2011. *Economies of Abandonment: Social Belonging and Endurance in Late Liberalism.* Durham, NC: Duke University Press.

Powell, D. R. 2007. *"... y entonces llegó un inglés ... ": Historia de la iglesia anglicana en el Chaco paraguayo (volumen conmemorativo de los cien años del templo de Makxawáya).* Asunción: Servilibro.

Pratt, G. 2005. Abandoned women and spaces of the exception. *Antipode* 37: 1052–78.

Pratt, G., and S. Hanson. 2007. Geography and the construction of difference. *Gender, Place, & Culture: A Journal of Feminist Geography* 1(1): 5–29.

Pride, A. 1932. Forty years: A retrospect. *South American Missionary Magazine* 66: 75.

The principles of environmental justice. 1991. https://www.ejnet.org/ej/principles.pdf.

Pugliese, J. 2020. *Biopolitics of the More-Than-Human: Forensic Ecologies of Violence.* Durham, NC: Duke University Press.

Pulido, L. 2006. *Black, Brown, and Left: Radical Activism in Los Angeles.* Berkeley: University of California Press.

———. 2017. Geographies of race and ethnicity II: Environmental racism, racial capitalism and state-sanctioned violence. *Progress in Human Geography* 41(4): 524–33.

Pulido, L., and J. De Lara. 2018. Reimagining "justice" in environmental justice: Radical ecologies, decolonial thought, and the Black Radical tradition. *Environment and Planning E: Nature and Space* 1(1–2): 76–98.

Quiroga, L., and Ó. Ayala-Amarilla. 2014. *Violencia e impunidad hacia el pueblo Paî Tavyterã-Kaiowa: Aproximacicón de derechos humanos en la frontera paraguayos-brasileña.* Asunción: Tierraviva.

Radcliffe, S. A. 1996. Gendered nations: Nostalgia, development and territory in Ecuador. *Gender, Place & Culture* 3(1): 5–22.

———. 2010. Re-mapping the nation: Cartography, geographical knowledge and Ecuadorean multiculturalism. *Journal of Latin American Studies* 42(2): 293–323.

———. 2015. *Dilemmas of Difference: Indigenous Women and the Limits of Postcolonial Development Policy.* Durham, NC: Duke University Press.

Rahder, M. 2020. *An Ecology of Knowledges: Fear, Love, and Technoscience in Guatemalan Forest Conservation.* Durham: Duke University Press.

Ramos, A. 1998. *Indigenism: Ethnic Politics in Brazil.* Madison: University of Wisconsin Press.

Ranganathan, M. 2017. Environment as freedom: A decolonial reimagining. Social Science Research Council. https://items.ssrc.org/just-environments/the-environment-as-freedom-a-decolonial-reimagining/.

Rappaport, J. 2005. *Intercultural Utopias: Public Intellectuals, Cultural Experimentation, and Ethnic Pluralism in Colombia.* Durham, NC: Duke University Press.

Ratzlaff, G. 1999. *La ruta transchaco: Proyecto y ejecución.* Asunción: Litocolor SRL.

Razack, S. H. 2020. Settler colonialism, policing, and racial terror: The police shooting of Loreal Tsingine. *Feminist Legal Studies.* https://doi.org/10.1007/s10691-020-09426-2.

Reed, R., and J. Renshaw. 2012. The Aché and Guaraní: Thirty years after Maybury-Lewis and Howe's report on genocide in Paraguay. *Tipití: Journal of the Society for the Anthropology of Lowland South America* 10(1): 1–18.

Renshaw, J. 2002. *The Indians of the Paraguayan Chaco: Identity and Economy.* Omaha: University of Nebraska Press.

Restrepo, E. 2018. Talks and disputes of racism in Colombia after multiculturalism. *Cultural Studies* 32(3): 460–76.

Reyes, A., and M. Kaufman. 2011. Sovereignty, indigeneity, territory: New practices of decolonization. *South Atlantic Quarterly* 110(2): 505–25.

Richard, N. 2008. *Mala guerra: Los indígenas en la Guerra del Chaco (1932–1935).* Asunción: Servilibro.

Rifkin, M. 2013. Settler common sense. *Settler Colonial Studies* 3(3–4): 322–40.

———. 2019. *Fictions of Land and Flesh: Blackness, Indigeneity, Speculation.* Durham, NC: Duke University Press.

Risling Baldy, C. 2018. *We Are Dancing for You: Native Feminisms and the Revitalization of Women's Coming-of-Age Ceremonies.* Seattle: University of Washington Press.

Rodríguez, I. 2020. Latin American decolonial environmental justice. In *Environmental Justice: Key Issues,* ed. B. Coolsaet, 74–90. London: Routledge EarthScan.

Rodríguez, J. C. 2001. Una ecuación irresuelta: Paraguay-Mercosur. In *Los rostros del Merocsur: El difícil camino de lo comerical a lo societal,* ed. G. De Sierra, 361–71. Buenos Aires: CLASCO.

Roldán Ortega, R. 2004. Models for recognizing indigenous land rights in Latin America. World Bank Environment Department. Accessed November 10, 2019. http://sitere sources.worldbank.org/BOLIVIA/Resources/Roque_Roldan.pdf.

Rosenberg, G. N. 2016. A race suicide among the hogs: The biopolitics of pork in the United States, 1865–1930. *American Quarterly* 68(1): 49–73.

Ryburn, M. 2018. *Uncertain Citizenship: Everyday Practices of Bolivian Migrants in Chile.* Oakland: University of California Press.

Saldaña-Portillo, M. J. 2016. *Indian Given: Racial Geographies across Mexico and the United States.* Durham, NC: Duke University Press.

Sanderson, J. 1944. The call from changing Paraguay. *South American Missionary Society Magazine* 858(78): 56–57.

Sassen, S. 2006. *Territory, Authority, Rights: From Medieval to Global Assemblages.* Princeton, NJ: Princeton University Press.

Schlosberg, D., and D. Carruthers. 2010. Indigenous struggles, environmental justice, and community capabilities. *Global Environmental Politics* 10(4): 12–35.

Scott, J. C. 1987. *Weapons of the Weak: Everyday Forms of Peasant Resistance.* New Haven, CT: Yale University Press.

———. 1999. *Seeing Like a State: How Certain Schemes to Improve the Human Condition Have Failed.* New Haven, CT: Yale University Press.

Shaw, W. S., R. D. K. Herman, and G. R. Dobbs. 2008. Encountering indigeneity: Re-imagining and decolonizing geography. *Geograpfiska Annaler Series B Human Geography* 88(3): 267–76.

Shukin, N. 2009. *Animal Capital: Rendering Life in Biopolitical Times.* Minneapolis: University of Minnesota Press.

Sieder, R. 2002. *Multiculturalism in Latin America: Indigenous Rights, Diversity and Democracy.* New York: Palgrave Macmillan.

SIMORE. n.d. Sistema de monitoreo de recomendaciones en derechos humanos. Ministerio de Relaciones Exteriores y Ministerio de Justicia. https://www.mre.gov.py/SimorePlus /Home/Page?idTipo=1.

Simpson, A. 2014. *Mohawk Interruptus: Political Life across the Borders of Settler States.* Durham, NC: Duke University Press.

———. 2016. Whither settler colonialism? *Settler Colonial Studies.* http://dx.doi.org/10.1080 /2201473X.2015.1124427.

Simpson, L. B. 2014. Land as pedagogy: Nishnaabeg intelligence and rebellious transformation. *Decolonization: Indigeneity, Education & Society* 3(3): 1–25.

———. 2017. *As We Have Always Done: Indigenous Freedom through Radical Resistance.* Minneapolis: University of Michigan Press.

Sletto, B. 2009. Indigenous cartographies. *Cultural Geographies* 16(2): 147–52.

———. 2016. Indigenous mobilities, territorialization, and dispossession in the Sierra de Perijá, Venezuela: Rescuing lands and meanings in Hábitat Indígena Yukpa, Toromo-Tütari. *Geoforum* 74: 117–27.

Sletto, B., J. Bryan, A. Wagner, and C. Hale. 2020. *Radical Cartographies: Participatory Mapmaking from Latin America.* Austin: University of Texas Press.

Smith, S., and P. Vasudevan. 2017. Race, biopolitics, and the future: Introduction to the special issue. *Environment and Planning D: Society and Space* 35(2): 210–21.

Sousa-Santos, B. D. 2007. *Another Knowledge Is Possible: Beyond Northern Epistemologies.* London: Verso.

Speed, S. 2017. Structures of settler capitalism in Latin America. *American Quarterly* 69(4): 783–90.

Spivak, G. C. 1998. Can the subaltern speak? In *Marxism and the Interpretation of Culture*, ed. C. Nelson and L. Grossberg, 271–313. Basingstoke: Macmillan Education.

Srinivasan, K. 2017. Conservation biopolitics and the sustainability episteme. *Environment and Planning A: Economy and Space* 49(7): 1458–76.

Stocks, A. 2005. Too much for too few: Problems of Indigenous land rights in Latin America. *Annual Review of Anthropology* 34: 85–104.

Stone, M. 1998. Map or be mapped. *Whole Earth* 94: 54.

Strong, R. 2007. *Anglicanism and the British Empire.* Oxford: Oxford University Press.

Sultana, F. 2020. Political ecology 1: From margins to center. *Progress in Human Geography.* https://doi.org/10.1177%2F0309132520936751.

Sundberg, J. 2008. Placing race in environmental justice research in Latin America. *Society and Natural Resources* 21(7): 569–82.

———. 2015. Ethics, entanglement, and political ecology. In *The Routledge Handbook of Political Ecology*, ed. T. Perreault, G. Bridge, and J. McCarthy, 117–26. London: Routledge.

Sze, J. 2020. *Environmental Justice in a Moment of Danger.* Oakland: University of California Press.

Tauli-Corpuz, V. 2015. Report of the Special Rapporteur on the rights of indigenous peoples, Victoria Tauli-Corpuz. http://unsr.vtaulicorpuz.org/wp-content/uploads/2014/06/images_docs_country_2015-paraguay-a-hrc-30–41-add-1-en.pdf.

Taylor, C. 1991. The politics of recognition. In *New Contexts of Canadian Criticism*, ed. A. Heble, D. P. Pennee, and J. R. Struthers, 98–131. Toronto: Broadview Press.

Tierraviva. 2014. Sawhoyamaxa: Historia de la lucha de una comunidad. http://www.tierraviva.org.py/wp-content/uploads/2015/05/Revista-Tierraviva-web.pdf.

———. n.d. Xapop, tierra: La esperanza de los Enxet. Report. Asunción: Tierraviva a los Pueblos Indígenas del Chaco.

Trouillot, M. R. 2003. *Global Transformations.* New York: Palgrave Macmillan.

Tuck, E., M. McKenzie, and K. McCoy. 2014. Land education: Indigenous, post-colonial, and decolonizing perspectives on place and environmental education research. *Environmental Education Research* 20(1): 1–23.

Tuck, E., and W. Yang. 2012. Decolonization is not a metaphor. *Decolonization: Indigeneity, Education and Society* 1(1): 1–40.

Tuhiwai-Smith, L. 2012. *Decolonizing Methodologies: Research and Indigneous Peoples.* 2nd ed. London: Zed Books.

Turner, V. 1969. Liminality and communitas. *Ritual Process: Structure and Anti-Structure* 94(113): 125–30.

Ulloa, A. 2016. Justicia climática y mujeres indígenas en América Latina. *LASAForum* 47(4): 12–16.

———. 2017. Perspectives of environmental justice from Indigenous peoples of Latin America: A relational indigenous environmental justice. *Environmental Justice* 10(6): 175–80.

UltimaHora. 2014. Cartes a empresarios brasileños: "usen y abusen" del Paraguay. https://www.ultimahora.com/cartes-empresarios-brasilenos-usen-y-abusen-paraguay-n767800.html.

———. 2019. Presidente intenta levanter imagen ante presión social. https://www.ultima hora.com/presidente-intenta-levantar-imagen-presion-social-n2828255.html.

United States Department of Agriculture. 2021. Livestock and Products Annual Report. Paraguay. Washington DC: US Department of Agriculture Foreign Agricultural Service. https://www.fas.usda.gov/data/paraguay-livestock-and-products-annual-6.

Vale, P., H. Gibbs, R. Vale, M. Christie, E. Florence, J. Munger, and D. Sabini. 2019. The expansion of intensive beef farming in the Brazilian Amazon. *Global Environmental Change* 57. https://doi.org/10.1016/j.gloenvcha.2019.05.006.

Van Cott, D. L. 2005. Building inclusive democracies: Indigenous peoples and ethnic minorities in Latin America. *Democratization* 12(5): 820–37.

Vázquez, F. 2010. *Geografía humana del Chaco paraguayo: Transformaciones territoriales y desarrollo regional.* Asunción: ADEPO.

Velásquez-Runk, J. 2012. Indigenous land and environmental conflicts in Panama: Neoliberal multiculturalism, changing legislation, and human rights. *Journal of Latin American Geography* 11(2): 21–47.

Villagra-Carrón, R. 2010. *The Two Shamans and the Owner of the Cattle: Alterity, Storytelling, and Shamanism amongst the Agaité of the Paraguayan Chaco.* Asunción: Centro de Estudios Antropológicos de la Universidad Católica.

———. 2014. *Meike makka valayo: No habían paraguayos. Reflexiones etnográficas en torno a las angaité del Chaco.* Asunción: AGR Servicios Gráficos.

Voyles, T. B. 2015. *Wastelanding: Legacies of Uranium Mining in Navajo Country.* Minneapolis: University of Minnesota Press.

Westra, L. 2008. *Environmental Justice and the Rights of Indigenous Peoples: International and Domestic Legal Perspectives.* London: Routledge.

Wainwright, J. 2008. *Decolonizing Development: Colonial Power and the Maya.* London: Blackwell.

Wainwright, J., and J. Bryan. 2009. Cartography, territory, property: Postcolonial reflections on indigenous counter-mapping in Nicaragua and Belize. *Cultural Geographies* 16: 153–78.

Walker, G. 2012. *Environmental Justice: Concepts, Evidence, and Politics.* London: Routledge.

Watts, M. J. [1983] 2013. *Silent Violence: Food, Famine, and Peasantry in Northern Nigeria.* Athens: University of Georgia Press.

Whyte, K. P. 2016. Indigenous experience, environmental justice and settler colonialism. In *Nature and Experience: Phenomenology and the Environment,* ed. B. E. Bannon, 157–74. London: Rowman & Littlefield.

———. 2018. Settler colonialism, ecology, and environmental injustice. *Environment and Society: Advances in Research* 9: 125–44.

———. 2020. Too late for indigenous climate justice: Ecological and relational tipping points. *WIREs Climate Change* 11:e603.

Wolf, E. R., and S. W. Mintz. 1957. Haciendas and plantations in Middle America and the Antilles. *Social and Economic Studies* 6(3): 380–412.

Wolfe, P. 1999. *Settler Colonialism and the Transformation of Anthropology: The Politics and Poetics of an Ethnographic Event.* London: Cassell.

———. 2006. Settler colonialism and the elimination of the native. *Journal of Genocide Research* 8(4): 387–409.

———. 2016. *Traces of History: Elementary Structures of Race.* London: Verso.

Wolford, W. 2007. Land reform in the time of neoliberalism: A many-splendored thing. *Antipode* 39(3): 550–70.

———. 2020. The Plantationocene: A Lusotropical contribution to theory. *Annals of the American Association of Geographers* 111(6): 1622–39.

Ybarra, M. 2018. *Green Wars: Conservation and Development in the Maya Forest*. Oakland: University of California Press.

Yeh, E. T., and J. Bryan. 2015. Indigeneity. In *The Routledge Handbook of Political Ecology*, ed. T. Perreault, G. Bridge, and J. McCarthy, 531–44. London: Routledge.

Zaragocín, S. 2019. Gendered geographies of elimination: Decolonial feminist geographies in Latin American settler contexts. *Antipode* 51(1): 373–92.

INDEX

Many names are found in the index by first name only at the request of the interlocutor.

9 780520 393103